AF893437

Egalitarian Envy

Egalitarian Envy

The Political Foundations of Social Justice

Gonzalo Fernández de la Mora

Translation by Antonio T. de Nicolás

Paragon House Publishers
New York

First English translation published by

Paragon House Publishers
90 Fifth Avenue
New York, New York 10011

Copyright © 1987 by Paragon House Publishers

All rights reserved. No part of this book may be reproduced, in any form, without written permission from the publisher unless by a reviewer who wishes to quote brief passages.

Originally published in the Spanish language under the title *La envidia igualitaria* (Barcelona: Planeta, 1984).

Library of Congress Cataloging-in-Publication Data

Fernández de la Mora, Gonzalo.
Egalitarian envy.

Translation of: La envidia igualitaria.
Bibliography:
Includes index.
1. Equality. 2. Envy. I. Title.
JC575.F4713 1987 320'.01'1 86-30510
ISBN 0-913729-70-1

Contents

Introduction

"The direction and rhythm of human progress do not depend on the masses, even when they add up to hundreds of millions; they depend on superior minorities."

"The quality of a society depends on its capacity to produce eminent personalities."

"Demagogues appeal to envy because its universality makes potential victims of all the people and because the invincible inequality of our own personal capabilities and of the irremediable limitation of many social goods makes it inevitable that the majority will feel inferior to certain minorities."

Strong statements. And there are many more that strike the same note in this book. Gonzalo Fernández de la Mora's *Egalitarian Envy* pulls no punches. It is unembarrasedly elitist. It brooks no liberalistic sentimentality. It swims against the tide.

Covering ground already broken by Nietzsche and Max Scheler, de la Mora argues that *envy*, both individual and group envy, is a personal vice that has been made into a political virtue, a pernicious yet all too human emotion which over the years has slowly, imperceptibly, become politicized, woven into the innermost tissue of Western governmental systems under the high-sounding rubric of "egalitarianism."

Hiding behind such sacred terms as human rights and distributive justice, de la Mora argues, politicians and intellectuals alike have perpetrated a gargantuan ruse on humankind: they have convinced us that mass homogeneity is more essential for the betterment of society than is individual initiative, and they have adorned this dubious assumption with assurances that by leveling all distinctions between human beings, collective peace and unity will result as a matter of course, just as water runs downhill or the cart follows the ox.

De la Mora (1924-) is one of Europe's most distinguished political philosophers. His *Twilight of Ideologies*, published more than fifteen years ago, is currently in its ninth printing. He has enjoyed a distinguished career as Director of the Diplomatic School in Madrid, has acted as Minister of Works, and has served as an editor of *Razon Española*, a distinguished and avowedly traditional Spanish journal.

Bringing his vast learning and uncanny analytical acumen to the perennial problem of the individual versus the state, in *Egalitarian Envy* the author argues that political systems that champion across-the-board egalitarianism among citizens, acting regardless of their merit or ability, and which recognize no individual distinctions between people according to intelligence, capability, experience, and affinity are, in fact, producing a society dedicated to *sameness* rather than *equality*. Because people are so different, de la Mora argues, true social equality, the kind championed, for instance, by the Marxists, is simply not achievable in this most imperfect of worlds. What such states produce instead, he claims, is an ersatz equality, one based on the envy of the incompetent for the competent, of the weak for the strong, of the ungifted many for the gifted few.

Envy, in this regard, wearing the mask of "righteous indignation," becomes the fuel to fire the so-called egalitarian process. While de la Mora does not deny the spiritual dignity of each individual he insists that the need to "equalify" all of society leads inevitably to the politics of expropriation, and that "egalitarianism is the opiate of the envious, and demagogues are its distributors who intend its massive consumption." Moreover, organized envy, which usually takes the form of radical politics, insidiously suggests that "those in positions of superiority are evil exploiters, and those who feel their position is inferior are innocently exploited. This corollary sounds like heavenly music to the envious person who sees his own pain as required for the happiness of others and his resentment therefore as fully justified. Those who appear to be the best are really the worst." Finally, people come to believe that this supposed equality is not only politically justified but ethically essential. Thus, egalitarianism becomes "a moral imperative that does not require proof, but fulfillment, like an 'ought' that is evident to every conscience."

Envy, claims de la Mora, is one of the great unspoken human taboos. Everyone indulges in it; few admit to it. All the more ironic then that when envy is assimilated into political ideology it ceases to be considered contemptible and becomes instead the very fulcrum of human justice. After all, reasons the envious citizen, does not every man, woman, and child in this society, including myself, have the God-given right to feel jealous of its leaders, and this *simply because these leaders have power and I do not?* No matter whether the members of the governing elite are wiser or more skillful than myself. What of it? Are not all men created equal? Is it not an affront to these sacred principles of liberty to raise one man higher than the next? Do not *I* deserve to be given my turn?

Tracing the historical relationship between envy and politics in the sacred scriptures, then through the Greeks, Romans, medieval scholastics, up to Schopenhauer, Nietzsche and Unamuno, de la Mora makes the interesting observation that the most capable individuals in society, and hence the most envied, protect themselves against the animosity of the masses by courtesy, by pretended suffering, and by concealing their own good fortune. Yet such dissimulation, he claims, is socially harmful. Only by learning to *admire excellence* rather than to disguise it are we inspired to do our best; emulation of talent and virtue is the highest road to social stability. Indeed, the author maintains that we must learn to take pleasure in the mere existence of the individualistic and competitive spirit if we are to move ahead. He then proceeds to make the bold statement that the self-respecting are too proud to feel envy, and too careful of their own dignity to wallow in self-contempt. One example that comes to mind is the American South of the recent past, in which many people refused to accept welfare assistance.

Nor does the church escape the author's eagle eye. In recent times, de la Mora points out, Christian authority has happily sponsored egalitarian envy while ignoring scriptural texts that command its opposite: the necessity of individual effort, and the sinfulness of envy. Christians believe that "Christ died for all." Yes. But nowhere does Christ's divine mission claim that social ranks must be leveled as part of the redemptive process, that all men and women regardless of aptitude or character shall "get their turn," or that all people on earth must be provided with identical material provisions. To the contrary, Christian teaching has always been clearly aware that "many are called, few chosen," and that it is folly to "throw pearls before swine."

Egalitarian Envy concludes with a prolonged and brilliant argument relating to what de la Mora titles the "necessity of inequality." While he pays some respect to the ideal of equality of opportunity, he argues simultaneously that to achieve such equality, men and women must be made equal before they compete, which is an impossible objective and an excuse for total regimentation. Recent attempts in the United States at non-discriminatory hiring, he points out, have led to deficient workmanship, decreased efficiency, and general chaos. Even equality before the law, he argues, is often based on high-sounding statutes that apply the same rules to all individuals no matter how circumstances may differ, even while *de facto* egalitarian legal methods end up punishing the innocent, freeing the guilty, and leaving everyone in despair. And since ideological egalitarianism inevitably requires some form of economic or social coercion to make citizens conform to a standard of sameness—what persons of quality and intelligence, after all, will voluntarily allow themselves to be held down by the "mean average" of the masses?—physical force must be used by the "fathers" and "comrades" in charge, to implement this unnatural reductionism. Such violence is then rationalized by high-sounding slogans, then finally institutionalized. "There is no equality," the author writes, "without coercion." One is reminded of the motto adopted by the ruling elite of pigs in Orwell's *Animal Farm:* "All animals are equal" the sign in front of the communal (and Communistic) barnyard proclaims. "But some are more equal than others.'"

The rest of de la Mora's appeal is to the spirit of freedom, for inequality is "the inseparable companion of freedom and nature." What de la Mora stresses most of all is *a meritocracy*, the system of rule based on ability, not on sentimental notions of "liberty, equality, and fraternity." Rather than creating barriers between people, he argues, all members of society would be united in a single and purposeful drive towards excellence, if they could but learn to promote creative emulation as the standard collective aspiration.

In closing, it should be said that de la Mora's book comes as a welcome corrective to a long line of writings on political philosophy starting with Rousseau's *Discourse on the Origins and Foundations of Inequality Among Men*, running through Tocqueville's *Democracy in America*, and ending with such works as John Rawl's *A Theory of Justice*. The compulsion to establish equality has given birth to the rural democratic ideal of Thomas Jefferson, yes; but on the darker side, it has also contributed to the reigns of terror unleashed by successive revolutions, from 18th century France to 20th century Russia. The passion for equality has, in fact, been the central political preoccupation of our time, not just for Marxists but for a line of thinkers that can be traced back to the radical salons of the French Enlightenment. Indeed, the association of the origins of property with the crime of theft did not begin with Marx nor even with 19th century anarchism. That association was already present in Rousseau's theories and in other 18th century visionaries who sought to reconstruct social bonds on the basis of their private dreams.

Egalitarian Envy is a brave and brilliant contribution to contemporary political theory by one of the seminal thinkers of our era, a work that confronts the most serious problems of modern political theory and challenges assumptions that are rarely examined by leaders in the free world. One may hope that this work will prove useful in helping shift the balance *away* from the pluralistic policies and easy, knee-jerk solutions of our time, and towards those societal ideals that stress merit and creative emulation as the highest social good. As in his previous work, de la Mora steadfastly insists that in a world of modern politics and modern lies, we must learn to search directly into the roots of human motivation for the sources of political strife—even if this search reveals truths that contradict everything we have so far been led to believe, and so blindly to follow.

M. E. Bradford
The University of Dallas

A. THE HISTORICAL PROBLEM

The existence of envy is acknowledged in all historical periods and in all cultures. Is envy an innate predisposition or is it an acquired habit? Is envy an exclusive inclination of humans or do they share it with other species? And why is such a universal feeling one of the least acknowledged? Envy is raised by whatever is considered a source of happiness. Are some people's values more envied than others? And do these preferences vary with social usage? What is closer, due to intellectual vocation or physical proximity, is envied more than what is distant. What circumstances increase such a feeling? Envy is painful to the one who feels it, and also to the one against whom it is directed. Does it, however, fulfill a social function? These are some of the many questions that such a unique passion raises.

It would not be proper to tackle these questions, either ethically or logically, without first considering, even if only in a general overview, the efforts undertaken in the past to clarify this matter psychologically and morally. The doctrinal and literary sources are abundant; it is not a question of exhausting them but rather of evoking the most significant ones with respect and rigor. This fast journey through some of the peaks of wisdom, unfortunately not travelled by anyone until now, will reveal aspects of the problem, contribute solutions and will avoid that something which is no longer acceptable but which so often happens: the discovery of the moon. Finally, when our task is thinking, we must carry the tradition with us as a condition for enriching it.

I. The Greeks

1. The Pre-Socratics

From the origins of our culture, the Greeks were aware of envy as a universal feeling, so basic and common that all of us have to face it. Periander (627–585 B.C.), the famous tyrant of Corinth and one of the Seven Sages of Greece, already warned: "Hide your misfortunes so that those who hate (*ἐχθρός*) do not rejoice."[1] This is the defense against the constant companion of envy: the joy at the misfortune of others. It is not enough to hide happiness, the same must be done with misery; neither may be shared with others. The first answer by the fathers of the Greek spirit to the constant siege by the ever-present envy is to build a wall around the personal and familiar intimacy.

Thales of Miletus (624 B.C.), founder of the first school of Greek philosophy and also one of the Seven Sages used to say: "Better to be envied than pitied (*οἰκτρός*)."[2] This sentence is not to be interpreted in the active sense that it is a lesser evil to envy than to feel compassion, but rather in the passive sense, for to inspire envy means that we own goods conducive to happiness, while if we inspire compassion it is a sign that something is lacking in us or that we are afflicted by something. This sentence is not a definition, but a recommendation for the happy life.

Pindar (522–470 B.C.), the greatest Greek lyric poet of his period and an aristocrat, complains "that the human spirit allows itself to be easily seduced by envy,"[3] and points out the proportionality of this passion with quality, "the higher the fortune the more it excites to envy,"[4] and that the higher fortune is that of intelligence: "on the works of intelligence [*λόγος*] the envious [*φθονερός*] feed, for the envious do not attack evil, but the good."[5] He was talking out of his own experience, for the mediocre poets, unable to erode his poetic greatness, accused him of being friendlier to the tyrant Hieron I of Syracuse than to his own countrymen of Thebes.[6] He proposes as the best defense against envy to flee: "One can avoid the attacks of envy if one lives in isolation, far from the destructive pride."[7] This solution, like the one suggested by Periander, is one of resignation.

Gorgias (485–380 B.C.) of Leontini in Sicily, the most celebrated sophist and orator, accomplished stylist and dialectician, provides this fundamental formula for a happy life: "That I may dare to say what I want and that I may wish to say what I ought avoiding thus divine vengeance [*νέμεσις*] and human envy [*φθόνος*]."[8] He is not afraid of tyrants and oligarches, but of the envious; his vital and dominant preoccupation is to avoid them and hide from them. Such a creative and independent spirit claims, above all, one single freedom, to escape the anguishing social siege of envy. This feeling of envy appears to the superior man as the most alienating.

The sophist Hippias of Elis, a teacher and an ambassador, names "two types of envy [*φθόνος*]: the just one [*δίκαιος*], or the envy towards undeserving people when they receive honors, and the unjust one [*ἄδικος*], of those who envy good people."[9] This is the first formulation, though mistaken in its terminology, that Aristotle later on will establish as the proper definition of indignation and envy. Hippias points out also the self punishing character of envy: "The envious is afflicted not only by his own sufferings, but by the joys of others."[10]

The disciples of Hippasus, the mathematician who discovered incommensurability, asked him for his own rule of conduct. He answered with this pessimistic recipe: "Do nothing that others might envy [*nihil quidem mihi invidetur*]."[11] We may imagine this intellectual, who eventually headed the Pythagorean school, watching out for the reactions of others and being permanently paralysed by the fear of the envy of others. Is this an appeal to solitude, secrecy, or inactivity? This fear of being envied might explain why the ancient sages, obsessed with remaining in hiding, have left us so little about their lives.

2. The Writers of the Fifth Century

According to Herodotus (484–406 B.C.), the Father of History, "envy appears in men from the very beginning [*ἀρχῆθεν*]."[12]

Aesop, a contemporary of Herodotus and the best spinner or collector of fables of his time, dedicates three fables to envy. In one of them he points out that in the same manner that bees, when they attack, lose their sting, so "the envious suffer in themselves."[13] In another he underlines the subjective character of envy: "The powerful and the rich are surrounded by dangers [*κίνδυνος*]," and thus their position is not desirable.[14] In the last and the most pessimistic fable, he advised "not to compete with the best on account of envy [*κρείττων*]."[15] The first observation becomes a common place in the literature on the subject; the second is less frequent, and the third one, though for different reasons, becomes one of the central themes of the stoics.

Callimachus, born in Cyrene in about 310 B.C., was a learned critic and poet and connected with the Alexandrian Library as an industrious bibliographer. In trying to describe the power of somebody's voice he let out this metaphor: "It was stronger than envy."[16] The above three men of letters give evidence of the universal power of envy.

This biographical silence in front of others that are susceptible and vigilant may be understood, but, could not envy enter within and produce the temptation of envy? Not even great men can escape this inclination of the species and for this reason the genial Democritus (460–370 B.C.) did not hesitate to advise: "Discard from your life envy and jealousy [ζῆλος] . . . not paying much attention to the envied."[17] This advice was the closing line of one of the clearest and longest fragments by the author. It was also the advice of Cyrene: "The wise man will not envy."[18]

Why is not to envy such a capital rule? The Pythagorian Philolaus (fourth century B.C.) discovered, while praising numbers, that envy belonged to the region of the "unlimited [ἄπειρος], of the stupid [ἀνόητος] and of the irrational [ἄλογος]"[19] These are three epithets of an unsurpassable harshness. The unlimited was for the Greeks the chaotic and unharmonic. Aristotle dedicated to this theme the admirable Book III of the *Physic*, and for him the unlimited is a potency, always unfinished and always defective. And this is what envy is in so far as it is insatiable. The irrational was the opposite of the *logos*, the most noble reality of the universe according to the Greek mind. For this reason Gorgias called the envious person "the worse [κάκιστος]."[20]

The main and most pragmatic reason for condemning envy is the negative character of such a feeling. Democritus wrote: "The envious tortures himself as if he were his own enemy."[21] This same idea is repeated by Isocrates (436–338 B.C.) and its echo reaches us today: "Envy is a great evil for whomever suffers it."[22] The vice of envy carries with it the punishment of an immanent justice; it is a form of self-punishment, an affliction inflicted by the one suffering it—hence the stupidity and irrationality of the envious.

This passion, however, creates not only intimate and bilateral tensions but also collective ones. Euripides pointed out around 421 B.C. that "the poor, inclined to envy, are deceived by the speeches of perverse leaders,"[23] namely the demagogues, while Herodotus has established a relation between "the party spirit and envy."[24] It was Democritus, however, who first formulated this thesis as a sociological one: "Envy is the cause of political division [στάσις]."[25] This sentence expresses the conclusion the ancient philosopher reached after travelling through Greece, Persia, India, Ethiopia, and Egypt; after having lived through the occupation of his native Abdera at the hands of the Persians, as a result of what a poet called "the fatal divisions of the Greeks"; and after having witnessed the fights between factions and cities, the fratricidal Peloponnesian and Ionian Wars, the fall of Athens, the destruction of its walls, and the defeat of Cronion that turned the beautiful Heraclea into an enemy camp. Democritus saw that the division rising out of envy is "bad for both parties . . . ; only through harmony may great things be achieved."[26] This is, in sum, a theory of the State and of History in relation to a passion: the more the envy the less the progress and peace.

Antisthenes (453–384 B.C.), founder of the Cynic School of Philosophy at Athens, a pupil and friend of Socrates, and an ascetic, made popular a metaphor that with variations has had secular fortune: "As oxide eats up iron so is the envious devoured by this passion."[27] This is an acknowledgement of the self-devouring and introspectively negative character of envy, its total lack of vital sense.

The Greeks, particularly the older and more pious, saw in envy not only an affection connatural to the human species, but also an almost transcendental property of intelligent existence and thus they extended its reach to the gods: even the immortals felt envy. They became obsessed not as much with the heavenly jealousies of the gods among themselves but with the envies the gods felt towards humans; the former were distant mythology but the latter carried out immediate unhappiness.

Homer, at the end of one of his key passages in the *Odyssey*, speaks through the nymph Calypso these surprising words: "You gods are cruel and more inclined to envy than the rest."[28] And in another passage: "Zeus grew angry [*νεμεσάω*] when Ajax fought a superior hero."[29] Such anthropomorphism becomes a vital element of Greek religion and ethics until illuminism rationalizes ancient theology. Speaking to an athlete winner at the LXIX Olympiad Homer wishes that "the envy of the gods does not destroy his happiness."[30] This is a vow that the winning poet turns into a desperate prayer in a lyric moment: "Let no envious god disturb the sweet rest I wish to live in."[31]

The somber Sophocles (497–406 B.C.), respectful of the gods, prefers to speak of the *nemesis* or indignation they feel, for though this feeling implies a certain vengeance, its aim is to bring justice. Thus he wishes that the heroes "escape the indignation of the gods."[32] There is, however, a text that is essential to understand that here the author was dealing in euphemisms for he believed in the passionate condition of the gods. When Aegisthus contemplates the dead body of his lover Clytemnestra the poet brings in his most powerful and dramatic sound: "I have before my eyes a spectacle that would not have been possible but for the envy of the gods [*φθόνος*]; but if this word provokes them to anger [*νέμεσις*], I will take it back."[33]

Euripides (485–407 B.C.) distinguishes, too, between the indignation of the gods,[34] which may have a justification of more or less justice, and envy. When Heracles, the semidivine hero, rescues from death the beautiful Alcestis, he surrenders her to her husband with these words: "And now may not the envy of the gods fall upon him."[35] Here he recalls the ultimate human guarantee against the danger of the divine.

Herodotus, born later than Euripides and surviving him by a few years, is more orthodox than the playwright and, carried by his didactic and moralistic style, tries to convince: "I know for certain that the gods are envious [φθονερός]," [36] and so is fortune.[37] But the gods are envious to punish the sin of pride, of rebellion against the order of the world: "The vengeance of heaven fell upon Croesus as punishment of his pride of believing that he was the happiest of men."[38] Men need to recognize their insignificance, in the same manner that the gods need to establish their pre-eminence. This is Herodotus' doctrine: "Zeus will not allow for anyone to compete with him trying to reach higher: only Zeus is great by nature and he wants to be seen like this."[39] As humans try to become divine it proceeds to the gods to feel envy to restore the lost order, according to the historian Herodotus. This is not a personal and arbitrary passion but a normal and objective dynamism. Envy, then, is not a weakness of the gods, but their strength and power in action. This subtle exegesis, the most logical within the confines of orthodoxy, sheds light on the doubts so many shared when attributing envy to the gods, either as indignation reflecting justice or as the passion of envy.

The traditional Greek lives oppressed by the envy of his fellow citizens and fearful of the gods, who also envy. They see man as the animal who thinks and also envies and the gods as powers jealous of themselves and of humans. Slowly, however, philosophical criticism dissolves the mythical past and the people are becoming more and more distant from those who condemned Socrates as an impious man. This allows the sarcastic and iconoclastic Aristophanes to pour irony on the envy of the gods. In the last of his comedies staged around 388 B.C. he says through the mouth of the blind Pluto: "Zeus has done this to me out of his envy [φθόνος] towards humans . . . , he is particularly envious these days of those with property."[40] Here Zeus is a vulgar being, sad at the prosperity of others and aiming at cancelling it. This total and gross anthropomorphism, very distant from the shy counsel of Sophocles and shared by Herodotus, aims at belittling the gods, but it makes cosmic presence of envy, enthroned as the main passion of humans and gods.

3. Socrates, Plato and Aristotle

If the testimony of Xenophon is to be believed, Socrates (470–399 B.C.) dealt with envy thematically and defined it as "a painful [λύπη] feeling produced not by the misadventures of our friends, nor the prosperity of our enemies, but by the happiness of our friends."[41] This surprising confinement of envy to the sphere of friendship caused, as remembered by Xenophon, astonishment among the listeners and this led Socrates to explain that this happens only to a few people. Which people? This is how Socrates explained: Envy "is not the vice of wise men, [φρόνιμος] but of stupid ones."[42] But this analysis is not satisfactory. It is not true that only friends are envied, and it does not help to accuse the envious of stupidity. There are other Socratic texts that are not easy to reconcile with the previous one and that complicate the issue: "There are those that cultivate virtue and that envy one another."[43] Thus, it is not only the stupid that envy. And also: "Friends eliminate envy either by offering their own goods to their friends, or because they consider their friends' goods as theirs."[44] This opinion contradicts the first statement. Is Socrates being ironical, slippery, paradoxical, or is Xenophon suffering from loss of memory, being asystematic and light? Most probably both. The Socratic contribution to the clarification of envy is not very solid. It is, perhaps, Aeschylus (525–456 B.C.) who comes closer to the truth with his poem: "There are few men who by nature [συγγενές] do not envy the happy friend."[45] This is not a case where envy is restricted to friends, but of admitting that friends are also envied. Envy remained for the life of Socrates a concept, but at the end of this life it became its co-protagonist. At the end of his legal proceedings the philosopher exclaimed: "If I am to be condemned, let the responsibility of this act not go to Meletus or Anytus; calumnies and envy condemn me."[46] The fatal chorus of the Socratic tragedy was formed by the envious.

Plato (427–347 B.C.) is evasive, ambiguous, and even contradictory when mentioning the gods of Olympus, perhaps out of fear of being accused of impiety. His theodicy is mixed with mythology; but his idea of the *demiurgus* places him near a rational monotheism. Plato's concept of the divine has lost many of its anthropomorphic and legendary features that degraded it. Consequently, passions become the monopoly of humans. God is "free from envy,"[47] and "envy is outside the circle of the gods."[48] This is the theoretical conclusion of a jealous and vengeful *nemesis* that had been the obsession of the classical Greek mind.

Plato understands "envy [φθόνος] as pleasure [ἡδονή] at the misfortune of others":[49] that is, "to rejoice [ἥδομαι] at the suffering of others";[50] but this confuses envy proper, or sadness at the happiness of others, with the joy at the misfortune of others, or what the Germans call *Schadenfreude*. Nonetheless, Plato admonishes that envy "is a sad companion for the person with whom it lives"[51] for it causes "a pain in the soul [λύπη ψυχῆς]";[52] but this observation does not allow him to distinguish between two different feelings, one pleasurable the other painful, and thus he concludes that envy is "a mixture of pain and joy."[53]

Plato, however, insists that envy is not a sporadic event, but a general one; it is not a private happening but a social one: "When our city reached its glory, it suffered the destiny that men inflict on whatever is well achieved, first jealousy and then envy."[54] Plato accepts that what is successfully achieved [εὖ πράττω] awakes rivalry and then envy. This is the reason why ordinary men, like those in the Assembly, envied sages like Socrates and Euthyphro[55] and, in general, they envied "'the best [ἄριστος]."[56]

Is all that is valuable, independently of its affinity, envied? Plato argues that "envy occurs among similars [ὁμοιότης] and also dissension and hostility, while friendship takes place between what is most different."[57] Aristotle will pick up this idea, probably earlier than both, and turn it into a topic; but it is ambiguous and wrong in part. In order to envy one must desire what the other has, and through that desire both become equal, and there is no need to share a social similarity. On the other hand, it is not true that friendship is based more on differences than on affinities.

Is envy an innate passion or an acquired habit? Plato presupposes a primitive, golden period when men lived "in a society without riches or poverty . . . , where there is no abuse, no injustice, no jealousy, no envy."[58] But this situation is totally imaginary and historically untrue; what is important, however, is not its degree of verisimilitude but the fact that it implies that envy is not instinctual, but the result of feelings due to the social environment. This is the thesis that will more or less be repeated by Rousseau in a generalized way.

Plato puts down this passion, for "envy does not grow in those who are good [ἀγαθός]."[59] Plato thought envy could be avoided but he also thought it was improbable, for "if the intellect is busy in the contemplation of essences [τἀόντα] there is no room for envy."[60] This is clearly an elitist interpretation: the masses are the active subject of envy; the superior minorities are the passive subject.

Plato proceeds beyond a description of envy and gives moral evaluation: "To feel oneself overpowered by envy, whether or not it causes damage [βλάβη] to others, is . . . unjust [ἀδικία]."[61] Justice [δικαιοσύνη] for Plato consists in each one attending to his own business and not to that of others,[62] namely, finding one's social place. This is an unegalitarian ethic, for each citizen's function depends on the class to which he belongs. Others had pointed out earlier the centripetal power of envy, its self-punishing power, but Plato was the first to single out its centrifugal character as it goes against the division of labor and the hierarchization of the state, namely, a well-ordered society. He writes: "Let us compete with nonenvious [ἀφθόνως] virtue, for thus the city is made stronger, while envy makes it weaker.[63]

Envy is not only antisocial, it is also antinoetic: "Prudence [φρόνησις] and intelligence [γοῦς] shed light on a question when it is discussed without envy dictating the questions or the answers."[64] Plato is the first to separate envy from ethics and make it an epistemological question. Though this remark is a casual one, it points out the confusing and prejudicial character of envy.

It is difficult to catch the envious for he finds refuge in the sanctuary of his conscience. Plato complained that Socrates was forced to fight the envious people accusing him "as if he were fighting shadows."[65] How is it possible to defend oneself against such a subtle and pervasive aggression? Homer, Hesiod, and many others, "fearful of envy, covered their art with a veil."[66] Plato, experienced as he was "in the calumnies of the envious,"[67] had reached the conclusion that "political power breeds envy."[68] Though less overtly than his predecessors, Plato recommended avoiding the ever-present and invisible envious. The philosopher should aim for the contrary, wisdom. The Platonic ideal was formulated by the mouth of Protagoras, when Plato was still young: "Among my merits I count being the less envious of humans."[69]

Plato discarded divine jealousy and thus he took an important step in humanizing and rationalizing envy. His main contribution was to point out that envy leads to injustice on account of its egalitarian pretense that dehierarchizes, devalues, hides merit, and is antisocial. Plato took envy out of mythology and out of individual happiness and turned it into a political question, as Democritus had already pointed out.

Thus we arrive at the most clear and almost superhuman mind of the tradition. Aristotle (384–322 B.C.) distinguishes three types of properties of the soul: faculties, habits and passions [ἐπιθυμία]; among passions we find envy.[70] In other contexts he considers envy as an affection [πάθος] of the soul[71] which, for this reason, is felt and expressed through the body.[72]

Envy, according to Aristotle, is "pain at the good of others"[73] and "joy at the misery of others,"[74] since both feelings are related and rise out of an identical attitude of the spirit. But Aristotle goes further than his predecessors, and using a moral criterion he faces squarely the difference between envy and indignation. Envy is felt towards a deserved good, while indignation only towards those who do not deserve [ἀνάξιος] the goods they receive: "The indignant person feels anger at the prosperity of those who do not deserve it, and the envious at that of everyone,"[75] or in different terms, "indignation is felt at the well-being of evil persons, while envy at the happiness of the good ones."[76] Indignation is based on a sense of distributive justice, "for it is evil what happens against those who merit rewards."[77] It is, therefore, "a noble [χρηστός]" feeling, which may be attributed to the gods without belittling them. This analysis is found in the *Rhetoric*. But in the *Eudemian Ethics* we find a text that might appear contradictory: "Indignation is the middle ground [μεσότης] between envy and malice."[78] If both these feelings are evil, how can the one between them be good? Aristotle is the one who said: "Virtue is in the middle,"[79] but not as an equidistant point, but rather as a synthesis of the positive elements of both extremes.

What gives rise to envy? According to Aristotle, "practically everything that assures happiness wakes up envy,"[80] namely, the real in so far as good. What others have earned is not the only cause of envy, but also "what comes out of luck [τύχη]."[81] Thus he closes the speculation that goods acquired by luck are not to be envied or the cause of envy. What may be envied is, in sum, numberless. Who are the envious? In general, "the lovers of glory [φιλόδοξοι],"[82] namely, those with ambitions and in the degree of those ambitions, a qualification that includes almost the whole of humanity.

Plato had already pointed out, quoting Hesiod, that "out of a general necessity, envy, fights and hostility are common among the equal."[83] Aristotle developed this idea further by asserting that "envy is felt against those who are or appear as our equals."[84] This word "equal" is not to be understood in its literal and full sense, but in its partial and metaphorical meaning of "proximity of time, place, fame, birth"[85] and "habits."[86] It is obvious one can only envy what one knows and we know best what is nearer; it is also possible to know something of what is distant, the more so the more developed are the means of communication. It is also possible to develop real or imaginary envies, precise or confused, individually or in groups. The classical observation that envy made a habitual similitude between envious and envied was more likely to occur in the ancient, traditional societies rather than in the developed societies of our time. The Marxist practice of class struggle is an example of collective envy towards what is distant and even presupposed.

The Aristotelian evaluation of envy is negative not only because he conceives it as "painful"[87] for the one bearing it, but also because he considers it "bad in itself,"[88] and "evil [φαῦλος] and of evil people."[89] This is quite hard for someone as measured as Aristotle. For this reason "to fear envy is not cowardice."[90] Aristotelian objectivity avoids in dealing with envy, confessions, or the advice of wisdom, as it was common among his predecessors. Aristotle represents a new type of intellectual, that of the modern scientist as opposed to the classical spiritual director.

4. China, Fascination, The Evil Eye

The East, in the fourth century B.C., faced the transcendental question twenty centuries before Rousseau tried to actualize in the West the question of the natural goodness or evil of man and before Kant tried to intervene as mediator.[91]

Mentius is the herald of the idealist thesis, the most lucid disciple of the systematic, obscure, and ambiguous Confucius. This is the sentence, one of the most famous of Chinese literature: "The tendency of human nature towards the good is like the tendency of water to run downwards."[92] Though it is not possible to interpret Oriental metaphors literally, this analogy of the natural inclination of human nature towards the good as within a gravitational field was understood by his contemporaries as a radical anthropological optimism. Within this context it is not possible for human psychic tendencies to have a negative connotation: "Natural passions impregnate and give life to the body;"[93] they are the generating power of human dynamism.

Mentius's arch enemy is Hsün, a truly implacable critic. The conclusion of his rigorous and numberless arguments, that in many ways already anticipate the *Summa* of St. Thomas, is always the same: "The nature of humans is evil, and the good it shows is artificial."[94] Consequently, passion and also envy are innate: "Men are born with envy and hate."[95] The art of a happy life consists in mastering the passions: "Human nature, that is evil, must submit to the teachings of the sages and of the law."[96]

The arguments of Hsün against Mentius are about one of the most radical problems of philosophy and are common to cultures as different as the East and the West, and from such distant periods as the classic and the modern. The problem of envy, carried to a deep analysis, leads necessarily to the important question of the origin of evil. Is human nature perverse, good, or simply "fallen" as Empedocles maintained?[97]

Riding between classicism and hellenism we come across the fascinating sortilege. From very old times the Greeks believed that the envious, despite the secret character of their passion, could harm those they envied. How? Through an intangible and mysterious act. Thus, a relation was established between the psychological and the magical. The name *βασκανία*, that initially meant fascination or evil eye, eventually meant also envy. Semantics confirm this narrow relation. According to Democritus, "The envious emit, not always intentionally, certain forms [εἴδωλον] charged with perversity and the evil eye."[98] We find Socrates in the *Phaedo*, when talking about the immortality of the soul, adding, "Do not speak so loud, dear Cebes, so that the evil eye [βασκανία] does not derail your argument."[99] Socrates saw it as dangerous that reasoning could be heard, "wrongly seen," and, therefore, wrongly concluded by some envious person from outside his circle. Aristotle also mentions rue [πήγανον] as a remedy against the evil eye.[100] The Greeks, as much as other people, the more so the more primitive they were, believed that envy had evil powers, a conviction that became an oppressive superstition. The Romans inherited this spirit.

The Latin word for envy, *invidere*, is derived from *videre*, to see. Thus the passion became joined to the evil eye. The literary testimonies are many. Thus, the poet Catullus (84–55 B.C.) was concerned that "some miserable creature would throw the evil eye"[101] upon him and his lover Lesbia. Virgil (70–19 B.C.) puts these verses on the lips of a young shepherd: "I ignore what evil eye [*fascinatio*] has landed on my tender sheep that has left them thin to the bones."[102] Pliny the Elder (24–79 A.D.), a great naturalist, spent a great deal of time gathering cures against the evil eye: "the polished kernel of a date,"[103] "the roots of grass,"[104] "the frontal skin of the hyena,"[105] and, above all, the phallus, the symbol of "Fascinus, guardian of children and emperors, adored by vestals of the Roman religion and hanging from the chariots of the winners,—the physician that protects from envy [*medicus invidiae*]."[106] The phallic amulet became popular all through the West.

Persius (34–62 A.D.), the most stoic and most difficult of the Latin poets, writes about a matron who cast counter spells against "devouring [*urantes*] eyes" with the phallic sign of "her indecent finger moist with shining saliva."[107]

Plutarch (46–121 A.D.) dedicated one of his dialogues in the *Symposiaca*, with no irony and perhaps too much severity, to the evil eye. He takes advantage of the dialogue form to give both sides of the issue, the damning and the beneficial. One of the speakers sustains, trying to be empirical and rational, that living bodies emit certain emanations [ἀπορροή] and that "in all probability the most active of those emanations passes through the eye . . . and has a marvellous [θαυμαστός] power."[108] It is Plutarch who revives the extravagant episode about Eutelidus, who upon looking at himself in the mirror of the river "cast an evil eye upon himself."[109] Modern anthropology has gathered enough evidence of how this Greco-Latin belief in the evil eye has perdured around the Mediterranean and even on the other side of the oceans. Envy was thus made responsible for the malevolent incantation known as the evil eye.

5. Epicureans and Stoics

Epicurus (341–270 B.C.), founder of the Epicurean school of philosophy, was one of the most prominent men of Greece. He was wrongly interpreted by the populace and his practical morality was, to a great extent, parallel and, in cases, ahead of the Stoic. Epicurus believed that the harm that comes to us is the result of "hate, envy, or scorn, but the sages overcome it through reasoning [λογισμός]."[110] This context clarifies that we are not dealing here with active envy, inconceivable to the philosopher, but rather with the defense against the envious through reflection. Somewhere else Epicurus unveils his reasons: "We must not envy anyone: the good people because it would not be just [ἄξιος], and the bad people because the greater their luck the more damage will come to them."[111] The second argument seems to imply that there is joy in the misery of others, just the contrary of envy; thus, it is contradictory and of little value. The Epicurean development of that thesis does not constitute a proof but becomes, rather, a postulate of doubtful truth: "It is better to be right [εὐλόγιστος] and be miserable than fortunate and wrong [ἀλόγιστος]."[112] The Epicurean doctrine on envy, though very marginal in its ethics, is full of dogmatic *aprioris* and lacks realism.

Chrysippus of Soli (280–207 B.C.) wrote that envy is "a passion"[113] that he defined as "pain at the good in others,"[114] and it "belongs to whomever wishes to lower others so that he may climb."[115] Envy, as a passion, is "irrational [ἄλογος]"[116] and is based "on a distorted [διάστροφος] judgement."[117] Chrysippus establishes, though in a negative vein, a relation between the passions and reason and his naturalist interpretation of reason leads him to affirm, as his master Cleanthes had done before him, that the passions "are against nature [παρά φύσιν],"[118]—a very problematic thesis.

II. THE LATINS

1. Cicero

Cicero (106–43 B.C.) was a great Roman orator and statesman, though not a great jurist. Philosophy owes him the romanization of many Greek terms, the summary of works lost, but not much more. His thought lacked originality and rigor and followed the diffused pattern of his political life: at times he sided with the people, at others with the Senate; at times with Pompey, at others with Caesar and finally with Antony; he sided with Platonism, also Aristotelianism, and though more inclined towards the Stoics and Epicureans, on many occasions he followed the skeptics and probabilists. He provides, however, a very interesting testimony on envy, for he develops extensively the problem of its utility.

He changed the term *invidia* to *invidentia*[119] and defined it as "sadness caused at the happiness of others, even when no damage is caused by it."[120] As did the Greeks, he distinguishes it from *nemesis* or indignation.[121] So far he is in complete accord with the Stoics; but Cicero goes further and asks if there is a temperamental predisposition in humans or are the passions voluntary accidents alien to nature. He took the second alternative: "There is a certain predisposition in some towards certain illnesses," and this also applies to the passions [*perturbatio*]. A man is called envious because he is inclined to envy, not because he falls into it all the time. This proclivity needs to be understood as a morbid predisposition [*proclivitas ad aegrotandum*] the same way the body is inclined to certain illnesses.[123] The fact that he did not consider envy immanent in human nature did not let him consider it lightly; on the contrary, he considered it "the most common and universal [*perpetuus*] vice."[124] Cicero believes that "the sicknesses of the soul are more difficult to cure than any vices,"[125] but, nevertheless, "they are curable."[126]

Cicero makes the Aristotelians say, as he interprets them freely, that "desire [*libido*] and passion [*cupiditas*] are extremely useful gifts of nature."[127] He names in this context anger, sadness, and emulation, but not envy. Cicero disagrees with the Peripatetics and believes that "all passions are born from error and we must pull them out and remove them rather than fix them or prune them."[128] He states: "Since envy produces sadness and a certain joy in the pleasure at the misery of others it must be suppressed denouncing its brutality [*feritas*] and its monstrosity [*inmanitas*]."[129] Against those who think that passions may be moderated and guided, Cicero affirms that passions are like inclined planes and that once the passions are installed in them "it is impossible to stop them."[130] Hence Cicero's radical opposition to passions, in particular envy, "out of place in the wise man [*non cadit invidere in sapientem*]."[131]

As it happens in most of Cicero's writing what is important are not his personal conclusions but the information he brings in and, in this case, the reconstruction of what is given and what is acquired in envy and on its efficacy and damage.

2. Horace and Ovid

Horace (65–8 B.C.), who turned poet out of poverty, has given us the perfection of his form and, after love—a passion he sung in all its forms,—envy is the passion which moved him most. He reflected on it in a personal manner, without erudition, even when he was inclined towards the Stoics. He defined the envious as someone who "dries up [*macresco*] looking at the good of others."[132] Is this a rare happening? No, for "it is necessary not to live on this earth to overcome envy."[133] In a letter addressed to his protector, Augustus, he reminds him that Hercules learned that on this earth" only death overcomes envy."[134] Envy, then, is an ineradicable feeling connatural to the human species and the eyes play the main role [*ex oculis invidere*].[135] The effects of envy are painful to those undergoing it: "Not even the Tyrants of Sicily invented a greater torture."[136] Horace complained that the praises bestowed on the archaic poets were hiding "envious hate against ourselves,"[137] namely, against the poets of the Augustan period. In pain, he confessed to Melpomene, the muse of tragedy: "Rome, the princess of cities, has placed me in the chorus of the poets, and already envy is tearing me apart with its fangs."[138] If we were to remove envy and the experiences connected with it from the most lyric of the Roman poets his vision of the world would become maimed and we would lose understanding of this period at its highest moment.

The prolific Ovid (43 B.C.–A.D. 17), who could hardly say anything unless it was said in verse, did not have a moral scheme. His torrential imagination and his capacity for expression allowed him to write classical mythology in one of the largest Latin poems, *The Metamorphoses*. In this poem, inhabited by hundreds of greater and lesser gods, he described Envy with an overpowering plasticity. Here is a summary of thirty dactylic hexameters, some of them of extraordinary beauty: "The residence of Envy, spattered with black pus, is at the end of a pit, empty of sun, where the air does not reach, sad, flooded by an inert cold, lacking fire and covered with fog. The heroic Minerva, who seeds fear in battle, as soon as she reached there stopped at the door, for she was forbidden to enter; she tapped it with the tip of her spear and it opened. She saw Envy inside devouring the flesh of vipers, the food of her vices, and she cast her eyes aside. Envy rose slowly from the ground as she let the half-eaten bodies of the snakes fall off of her, and moved forward with dying steps. As soon as she saw the goddess Minerva, dressed with her weapons and so beautiful, she cried with mourning gestures. Her face was pale, her whole body appeared emaciated, her gaze was always to the side, the teeth of pale oxide; her breasts flowered bile, her tongue was dripping poison, and smiled only at the sight of pain. She never slept, she always lay awake with multiple cares, and suffered deeply at the successes of men. She devoured and devoured herself . . . She took a staff all covered with thorns, she covered herself with a black cloud, and wherever she crossed she smashed the flowering fields, burned the grass and lowered the high peaks. Her breath contaminated nations, cities and homes."[139]

Ovid's Envy is the most repulsive figure of Greco-Latin mythology and his verses are the most damning poetic sentence on any passion. For the Romans to see themselves in this mirror must have been, against the gallant intentions of the poet, one of the best spiritual exercises available.

3. Seneca, Dion, and Plutarch

Seneca (A.D. 5–65) is one of the most admirable figures of the classical period and a supreme master of moral self-discipline. He has left us the most moving and extensive testimony of stoicism. He is the director of consciences who uses intimate advice to provide us with a personal confession. Against what is envy directed? Against "riches,"[140] and for this reason "the less the success, the less the envy."[141] In the end he addresses the quality of envy: "Envy is a pernicious dart directed at the best."[142] Seneca follows his masters in believing that men are born without passions: "They are our fault, and not nature's";[143] but he acknowledges that this is an immemorial characteristic and not restricted to any particular period.[144] Which is the situation that most easily brings out envy? "The unhappy time of leisure when one wishes to destroy everything for he feels unable to succeed."[145] This is an insight of deep consequences.

Seneca advises against the capital vices: "Three things must be avoided . . . hate, envy and scorn."[146] But with wise temperance he advises "not to look for scorn to avoid envy."[147] Seneca thus agrees with the pre-Socratics: "You will avoid envy if you avoid being seen, do not boast of your riches, and are happy in private [*in sinu*]."[148] The constant fear "of the bellicose [*inimicissima*] envy"[149] ends up almost in solitariness: "Speak little with others and plenty with yourself."[150]

Seneca does not take passion to be innate: "Nature does not predispose us to any vices, it has gendered us pure [*integer*] and free." Our vices are not born with us, they overcome us [*supervenire*], they are inflicted on us [*ingestus*].[151] This agreement between the Stoic and Mentius is a testimony to their similarities.

The Stoics took it for granted that the wise man, master of his soul, could not envy, and they became concerned only with the negative aspect of the question: how to avoid the thrusts of the envy of others. Thus they gave testimony of the fact that most humans envy.

Dion Chrysostom of Prusa in Bithynia (A.D. 40–112), eloquent orator and a friend of Trajan, wrote eighty speeches; the most extensive is called *On Envy* and is written in the form of a dialogue. This is a long commentary to the verse of Hesiod, already mentioned by Aristotle: "The potter abhors [κοτέω] the potter, and the carpenter the carpenter."[152] Dion reduces envy to "the desire that others do not have our jobs."[153] This is his reasoning: "One envies others [φθονερός] if he receives fewer benefits from his work because there are too many carrying it out."[154] The law of supply and demand dictates that the greater the competition the less the value; on the other hand, exclusivity has all the advantages of a monopoly. Dion, on glancing at different occupations, comes to the conclusion that this situation does not take place in all jobs, for some accept plurality, like medicine and those "more serious [σπουδαιότερος]"[155] professions. Professional competition may incite to feeling pain at the good of others and, therefore, bring in envy; but the feeling of envy cannot be reduced to unassimilated professional rivalries. Dion's reductionism mutilates.

According to Dion "envy is a corruption [διαφθείρω] of the soul."[156] This "sickness [νόσημα]" is particularly grave and needs to be treated with the "most fervent caution." This metaphor has a rigorous translation: the remedy against envy is to "purify [καθαρεύω] the mind [διάνοια] with reason [λόγος].[157] This text is one of the clearest from the Greeks to establish the irrational character of envy and its possible cure through reason.

These people should be without envy: "The noble [γενναῖος] and generous [μεγαλόφρων],"[158] and the sensible [φρόνιμος] and wise [σοφός],"[159] the prudent [σώφρων] and moderate [κεκολασμένος]."[160] This superior man is not dominated by material goods, nor the "applause of the crowds."[161] This elitism of Dion is absolute: "He will not pay attention to the opinions of the crowd, nor will seek admiration by any means, nor will consider their praise important, valuable or even good."[162] This is the hellenic ideal of Dion intermixed with Stoicism, providing a model that is the opposite of envy and whose objective is to promote social "harmony [ὁμόνοια]."[163]

Dion underlies two important notes about envy—its illogic and antisocial character—even if he had had antecedents in this respect.

Plutarch (A.D. 46–121) had the fortune of living during the most luminous days of Trajan and Adrian. We find in his large and uneven work a sober and vigorous essay *On Envy and Hate*. His method is, to contrast them, as he did with the lives of the famous. Envy is a passion [πάθος][164] that takes place only among humans, contrary to hate, which happens also among irrational creatures. Envy "breeds in the soul more deeply than any other passion and thus it contaminates the body too."[165] This is a feeling that does not take place on account of some particular object or action, but "by anything that shines [λαμπρός],"[166] and in particular by the prosperity of others. Plutarch brings here an obvious fact, but original in his day: it is not necessary that it be a real prosperity, it needs only to appear [δοκέω] so to the envious,[167] and this explains that people may envy a real, as well as a nonexisting reality, either fancied or imagined.

According to Plutarch "no one may be justly envious,"[168] for what is held just would be unjust to remove even by thought, since "being lucky [εὐτυχιά] is not unjust."[169] Two very original observations are added regarding the modesty and ingratitude of the envious: "No one claims to be envious"[170] but on the contrary envy is always "masked and hidden" with excuses in the face of the feeling at the fortune of others. The writer ends with this magnificent sentence: "Among the disorders of the soul, envy is the only one no one confesses to [ἀπόρρητος]."[171] We are dealing with the most hidden of vices, one we do not dare to unveil to an intimate friend, one that the subject does not even wish to acknowledge to himself.

The other observation is that, unlike hate, envy neither diminishes nor ends even when one knows what one envies is just, or that it does not harm the envious, or benefits him. On the contrary, those three circumstances torture the envious for "if he receives favor from the fortunate he suffers even more, and envies him for his attention and power to do so."[172] The envious is, by nature, evil, insatiable and ungrateful. Envy can not be stopped from the outside for it is moved by an inner mechanism that causes it to grow under any positive pretext. It is a cancerous passion and, thus, it extends and spreads to other areas.

The short treatise of Plutarch, though cold and limited, will weigh on the classics and more so on the Fathers of the Church who will overcome it without even quoting it.

The almost anonymous Diogenes Laertius (A.D. 200–250) called envy "omnivorous [πάντα διεσθίων],"[173] a radical qualification that surprisingly has not been repeated. This epithet may be interpreted actively and passively: envy is able to consume anyone, and it may be excited by any type of good.

III. Sacred Scripture

1. The Old Testament

Envy appears as a fact in the Old Testament. It is the envy of the Philistines against Isaac,[174] of Rachel against Leah,[175] of his brothers against Joseph,[176] of Israel against Moses and Aaron[177] and of Ephraim against Judah.[178] The doctrinal explanation of envy appears only in Deuteronomy, and not even in the later books written under the influences of cultures other than Judaism. In the Book of Proverbs there are eight collections of sentences belonging to different periods, some of Egyptian influence; the version we have had not been put together till the fourth century A.D. Ecclesiastes, composed around 200 B.C., is the work of various, noncontemporary authors and keeps a structure similar to the classical one. Finally the Book of Wisdom, that the Protestant and Orthodox churches have eliminated from the biblical canon, was composed in Greek by a Jewish disciple of the neo-Platonic Philo in the first century B.C. This work is clearly within the coordinates of Hellenic philosophy. In sum, the texts from these books reflect genuine, Hebrew thought only tangentially.

The tight union between envy and the human species is clearly accepted in the Old Testament for it is said that the difference between the living and the dead is that in the dead there is no love, nor hate, nor envy.[179] There is another verse stating a similar conclusion from the point of view of the passive subject: "All work and whatever men do that is good moves other men to envy,"[180] namely, all that is valuable is envied. There are two definitive notes on envy which also point out its self-destructive character—"it is the caries of bones,"[181] and its overwhelming reach—"anger is cruel, wrath is furious, but, who will be able to contain envy?"[182] Finally, as a deduction on the temptation of Paradise, envy is proclaimed the origin of all evil: "Because of the envy of the devil death entered the world."[183]

The similarities between these texts and the Greek ones are evident, though the Biblical ones are more naive, more poetic, and less analytic. The point is that from the oldest to the more modern books the authors of the Old Testament bear witness, too, to the powerful presence of envy among people.

2. Paul of Tarsus

Paul of Tarsus, (A.D. 6–67) the father of the new theology, denounced several times the dangers of envy, in all probability because he was obsessed by its incommensurable extension. Writing to the Corinthians he says : "For whereas there is among you envying [ζῆλος], and strife, and divisions, are you not carnal and walk as men?"[184] This text seems to imply the general envious condition of humans, an interpretation confirmed in his epistle to Titus: "For we ourselves also were sometimes . . . living in malice and envy [φθόνος] . . . But after that the kindness and love of God our Saviour appeared . . . and saved us."[185] It was necessary that God intervene so that the proclivity of mortals towards envy could be conquered. Paul went even to the extreme of warning those that "preached Christ out of envy,"[186] intimating thus that faith was not sufficient to conquer the inclinations of fallen nature.

IV. The Fathers of the Church

1. Clement, Justin, and Tertullian

Clement is one of the first Fathers, he was the third to succeed Peter and he is known as Clement of Rome. Around the year 96 he wrote a letter to the Corinthians and the first six chapters are dedicated to "the unjust and impious envy [ζῆλος] through which death entered the world."[187] He reminds his audience that because of envy [φθόνος] Cain killed his brother Abel, Jacob had to take flight, Joseph was sent into slavery, Moses had to leave his people, Aaron was set aside, Dathan and Abiron were condemned, Saul and David were at war; envy was the cause of the persecution of the Apostles, the sufferings of St. Peter, of the many martyrs under Nero; in sum, the root of the most important happenings to humans. He proposes Christian virtues against the powers of envy: obedience, humility, peace, and above all, that "everyone should occupy their own place [τάγμα]."[188] The conclusion of Clement, Bishop of Rome, is that every citizen should develop his own proper level and his own proper function within the hierarchical society, a combination of ethics and politics.

Justin (A.D. 165), a Palestinian trained in Stoic philosophy and a convert to Christianity, was the most eminent apologist of the second century. He defended Christians and taught philosophy at Rome until he was decapitated during the reign of Marcus Aurelius. To the long list of historical misfortunes caused by envy and brought out by Clement, Justin added "Jesus . . . who had to be envied [φθονούμενος], unrecognized and crucified,"[189] repeating the Gospel's text: "For he [Pilate] knew that for envy they had delivered him."[190] Envy is thus presented as the reason for the supreme crime and, indirectly, as the basis of redemption. Envy is, therefore, a fundamental passion that is to be avoided. Justin thus advises, "Wash your souls of ire, avarice, envy and hate, and your body will stay clean [καθαρός]."[191]

Tertullian (A.D. c. 221) is one of the most energetic writers of primitive Christianity. A Roman jurist and orator, he converted to Christianity towards the end of the second century and a short time later he broke away from ecclesiastical discipline to join the Montanists and form his own sect within it. He was yet within formal orthodoxy when he wrote his treatise *On Spectacles*, where he proscribed attendance to pagan games. Among the reasons for doing so he adduced one that was a clear defense of the joy at the misfortune of others in the other world: "But there are other spectacles, like the one of the day of the last judgment . . . There I will rejoice and be happy at the sight of so many great monarchs of whom it was said they had made it to heaven, to see them crying in deep darkness next to Jupiter and those who believed in him . . . And seeing also how some wise philosophers blush in front of their disciples, who are also damned, and to whom they thought that the souls do not exist and that they join their bodies."[192] This serious text, as Nietzsche already pointed out,[193] is written with a resentful desire for vengeance, and it is impossible to defend in its tone and doctrine.

2. Cyprian and Basil

Cyprian (A.D. 258), Bishop of Carthage, was a brilliant teacher of Rhetoric until his conversion, which came late in his life; he wrote a dozen treatises and eighty-one epistles and was decapitated during the persecution by Valerian. He became the most powerful Western authority for over a century and a half until the arrival and establishment of Augustine of Hippo. He is the author of the first thematic Christian treatise dedicated to envy, written around the year 256, towards the end of his life. *De zelo et lavore*, as he titled his work, is a monograph that is noetically dense, originally constructed, and written in a pompous and affected Latin.

To envy, according to Cyprian, is "to suffer at the joy of others,"[194] and he calls this passion "a great evil,"[195] and "a contagious plague,"[196] "a viper's infection,"[197] "moth of the soul and the rottenness of thought."[198] When Cyprian reconstructs the Old Testament history of envy he adds to the details of Clement and Justin the rebellion of Lucifer, "guilty of evil envy against God."[199] Cyprian believes that cosmic evil[200] originates in the feeling of envy, "root of evil in all of us."[201] Envy is the source of hostility, avarice, ambition, pride, cruelty, perfidy, discord, etc.[202]

Cyprian is particularly cautious and detailed in the description of the characteristics of envy. It is, first, "the executioner of the soul;"[203] suffering it is "very damaging,"[204] for it is "unlimited and permanent"[205] and increases in proportion to the "success of the envied."[206] Envy, besides, is "a hidden vice . . . we carry closed within";[207] "the envious never declare their envy."[208] Finally, envy is a vice that appears "widely [*late*],"[209] as shown by the fact that Cyprian addresses a normal reader who, repeating the Pauline text, addresses himself: "You, who were possessed by envy"[210] and who supposedly the Gospels had cured. In sum, envy is self-punishing, unending, inconfessable, universal and its antidote is Christianity. Thus Cyprian proposes as a remedy the new virtues: "simplicity of mind,"[211] "humility,"[212] "fraternity,"[213] "love,"[214] and "charity."[215] His last advice is "to rejoice and be happy at the fact that others are better,"[216] namely, to do the contrary of envy, for to feel envy "is not proper for a disciple of Christ."[217]

Cyprian continues the legacy of the Greco-Roman and Christian traditions on the matter and goes farther than his predecessors when he maximizes the immorality of envy: the origin of all evil without any admixture of goodness. This radicalization is not primarily axiological, but rather historical and psychological; it is not normative, but empirical. The thesis comes down to the fact that evil is born of envy and the rest of the vices originate in it.

Basil of Caesarea (A.D. 330–379) was a great admirer of Greek culture and taught rhetoric in his own town after his studies at Constantinople and Athens. He soon gave up rhetoric to dedicate himself to theology and preaching. He was an active religious reformer. His writings are written in a clear and brilliant Greek. Among his famous homilies the eleventh one is *On Envy*, given around the year 370. He takes the common definition of envy as "pain at the joy of others' success [εὐπραγία]"[218] and "joy at their tears."[219] His qualifications of envy are harsh: "the most fatal vice,"[220] "the corruption of life,"[221] "the impurity of nature,"[222] "a viper's doctrine,"[223] and "an event contrary to reason [ἀλογότατος],"[224] "contradictory of God."[225] It is evident that in the last two expressions the Stoics are at work.

Basil insists more than his predecessors on the imminent punishment of this passion: "Even if it does not harm others, it is a primary and main evil in the one suffering it";[226] "As oxide eats up iron, so envy eats up the soul,"[227] and "The more passionate is envy, the more the pain it carries."[228] Basil examines the question if envy may be placated or annulled through favors and comes to the conclusion that contrary to what happens with other hostile feelings that are diminished through attentions "the envious [βάσκανος] become more so with favors," "for the suffering that is caused by the power of their benefactor is greater than the gratitude they feel."[229] This is a reaction that, according to the author, not even the dogs or the lions share with humans.

Another classical theme touched by Basil is the secrecy of envy. "The pain of this sickness is that the envious is not able to diagnose it."[230] Why? On account of an invincible shame," he is ashamed [ἐρυθριάω] of making public his misfortune."[231] There are also several Greek precedents as to the question of envy becoming more prominent among those who are near or those distant. "We are trapped by envy through familiarity [οἰκειότης]."[232] And he adds: "The Scythian does not envy the Egyptian, but those of his own nation, and from among those, he does not envy strangers but those he deals with, in particular the neighbors and those of the same job."[233] He concludes with this image, so representative of his style: "Just as the weevil is the accompanying sickness of wheat, so envy is the weakness of human [φιλία] relations."[234]

Basil is even more innovative when he denounces the logical character of envy as it inflicts moral damage to the soul deprived of its ability to judge correctly: "Find the criterion of truth [ἀληθείας κριτήριον] about things."[235] Envy misses what is great and good and focuses only on "what is rotten [σαπρός]." When judging others envy turns all positive values into negative and "all kinds of virtues receive the name of vice."[236] It is not, then, a temporary clouding of the mind, as happens with anger, but a total collapse of practical judgment that ends up negating all concrete value.

Basil is the first Christian moralist to take up the problem of the evil eye: "There are those who believe that the envious project harm just with their eyes."[237] He rejects this belief as "an old wives' tale."[238] But his interest points out the extension of such popular belief, enclosed in the etymology of the verb "*invidere*."

Are there any remedies against envy? Basil recommends the two paths already traveled: the isolation of the Stoics and the virtues of Christianity. We must place ourselves "out of the reach of the darts of envy,"[239] even avoiding "all vital relations [κατά τόυ βίου κοινονία] with the envious."[240] It is not, then, isolation proper, as it is the avoidance of communication with envy. This is a physical, negative solution. There is, besides, the moral treatment, and this consists in thinking that the goods of this world "do not bring us happiness,"[241] and that the goods of others, if properly administered, bring us also benefits,[242] the theological knowledge of a few brings goods to the rest of us.[243] Here, Basil, is obviously preaching *pro domo sua*. There is, besides, a reason of justice: whoever uses riches, power, and health well must be "honored and loved."[244] This last advice is the effort of transforming the passion of envy into the will "to acquire virtue."[245]

The eleventh homily by Basil, known as The Great, is, from the point of view of style, the peak of Greek writing on envy, and the same may be said from its conceptual point of view, even though it lacks a systematic structure. It is more dense and precise than the studies by Plutarch, Justin and Cyprian. It is a highlight of the ancient world on the theme of envy.

3. Jerome, Augustine, Chrysostom and Chrysologus

St. Jerome (A.D. 347–420) was born in Dalmatia and studied humanities at Rome. He translated and interpreted the Scriptures, but his popularity, especially during the Middle Ages, is based on his *Letters*. In one of them he writes that "even in the Apostles and the angels envy may slip in [*subrepere*];"[246] but this explanation does not seem to make envy connatural with intelligence; it appears that envy is an imperfection of all that is contingent, for he gives only one theological reason: "Only in God there is no sin."[247] Jerome repeats the known temptation of Eve, the death of Abel, etc., and insists that "envy chases always after virtue,"[248] namely, all behavior that has value. We cannot accept his thesis that "justice implies envy [*ipsa iustitia habet in se livorem*],"[249] for justice implies indignation at the undeserved good, and this is a very different question. The texts of St. Jerome on envy are only tangential and more dogmatic than rational.

Augustine (A.D. 354–430) deals with envy in the same tangential manner. For him, "he who lives well does not envy anyone,"[250] and to live in this manner is like living in Paradise where "there are many mansions, but not a single one for envy."[251] Augustine defines envy as "hate at the happiness of others,"[252] because we only envy "on account of what we want to appear to be or want to be,"[253] thus in the end "envy equals pride."[254] It is in this sense that, for Augustine, "envy is the root of the sin of the bad angels,"[255] and its ugly head rears even in children.[256]

John Crysostom (A.D. 354–407), the most classic of the Greek Fathers, wrote six hundred homilies to comment on the Scriptures, particularly the New Testament. He tackled the theme of envy in the fortieth homily commenting on St. Matthew, in the thirty-seventh on St. John, and in the seventh on the *Epistle to the Romans*. These are writings full of maturity and written after the year 390.

The "envious" enjoys the sufferings of others . . . and considers as his own joys the misfortunes of others."[257] This is a polemic statement. He agrees that "this sin appears now indifferent and no one pays attention to it."[258] Even then, Chrysostom holds that "no other vice [*κακία*] is comparable to it,"[249] for it is "the most evil [*ἐναγέστερος*],"[260] "most perverse [*πονηρότερος*][261], "most abominable [*μιαρότερος*] of all passions."[262] His verification rests in dogmatic testimonies: Lucifer's rebellion, Cain's fratricide. He adds an ethical argument: "The fornicator may excuse himself with the pretext of instinct; the thief with that of poverty, the criminal with that of ire . . . ; but the envious has no excuse, except his enormous malice."[263] There is no excuse for envy. He also affirms and reasons out that envy is worse than war, among other motives because it is carried out in secret and knows no peace.[264] He brings in the end a sociopolitical argument: other vices damage the subject or a few determined victims, but "envy subverts the Church and causes the whole universe [*οἰκουμένη ἅπασα*] to shake."[265] This last consideration, based as it was on his episcopal and palatial experience, appears for the first time in Western writings: this is envy in its universal and basic role as an adversary of hierarchical social order.

He pointed out, with less emphasis than his predecessors, that the envious "attempts against his own health,"[266] "pierces himself with his own sword,"[267] and "hates his benefactor."[268] His treatment against this vice is "to flee this pestilence,"[269] "remove all envy and place charity in the soul."[270]

Chrysostom was implacable against envy and not because, as Cyprian had said, envy was the origin and source of so many vices, but because envy is the highest evil in itself. He repeated this position that became more solid and virulent as the years went by. Was he speaking of the envy of the bishops and of the Empress Eudoxia that forced him out of the patriarchate of Constantinople and into exile? I suspect that both the man of politics and the confessor were speaking at once, out of a deep, extensive and objective knowledge of humans.

Peter Chrysologus (A.D. 450), archbishop of Ravena around 450, died three years after the fall of the Roman Empire. There are 175 sermons in the production that has reached us and the fourth is dedicated to envy. He goes over, as was customary, the historical crimes of this passion: original sin, Cain's fratricide, the crucifixion. He calls envy "an interior enemy,"[271] full of shame for "the envious lie and pretend always."[272] His novelty lies in the fact that he touches on the sociopolitical aspect of envy, when after calling envy "the poison of the centuries,"[273] he affirms that "because of envy the immensity of the world turned narrow for two brothers,"[274] Cain and Abel, which means that envy makes social life impossible; it is the social vice par excellence. The therapy for it is the Christian virtue of love, for "love joins people to God, while envy separates them."[275]

4. Caesareus, Isidore and Gregory

Around the second half of the sixth century, the archbishop of Arles, Caesareus, wrote 288 sermons and three letters. The second of these is a commentary to Cyprian's treatise on envy and the archbishop reflects on the difficulties that envy encounters for a cure. Why its chronic character? Because "the envious one frequently covers up his feeling, he does not confess it;"[276] that is, "he does not want to make it public [*patefactus*]."[277] The difficulty of cure lies in the fact that this vice always remains clandestine.

The Spanish Isidore, bishop of Seville, was an encyclopedic writer at a time when a Gothic kingdom had already become Christian. Writing at the beginning of the seventh century he dedicated a brief chapter of *The Sentences* to envy and insisted on the already known universality of its object: "There is no virtue that envy does not go after; the only thing that envy does not envy is misery."[278] All that is good, real, and owned by someone is envied. Isidore insists that the envious "overlook virtue and search [*perquo*] for vices,"[279] and adds that in this process of partial search and exchange the envious resort to "defamation,"[280] that is, the deformation of the envied. Does Isidore have in mind here the diatribes of the demagogues leading the masses against the already dead Senate of the Roman Empire? We have here a crucial sociopolitical facet of envy: the aspect of propaganda in the promotion of envy among the social classes.

Gregory I (A.D. 540–604) was the prefect of Rome; then, after his religious conversion, the Nuntio to Constantinople; and later, Pope in a Vatican that Byzantium conquered from the Barbarians. He left hundreds of letters, homilies on the Bible, a *Pastoral Rule*, and under the suggestion of Leander of Seville a

Commentary to the Book of Job, which happens to be one of the earliest written introductions to the direction of souls. His uneven works were much read by the medievals and dealt with envy which he describes in the person who in secret raises this question: "Where am I less than this or that one? Why am I not superior or equal to them?"[281] In this brief, but subtle and deep passage we find the problem of envy stated in sociological terms. Here it is suggested that envy hides a capital and silenced question: the envious motivation of egalitarianism.

V. The Medievals

1. John of Salisbury

John of Salisbury (1115–1180) appears from his letters to be a complex figure. He is more a moralist and man of the world than a man of letters and priest, even though his Ciceronean Latin is filled with classical quotes and he ended up being bishop at Chartres. His main work, *The Policraticus (The Statesman's Book)* is an intelligent and erudite mirror of princes. This is the earliest theory of the State in a medieval period that is not familiar with the *Politics* of Aristotle, written in a deep puritanical vein that is exemplified by its invectives against women. One of the chapters of the book is dedicated to envy.

In the prologue entitled *Entheticus,* written in verse, he defines the envious as he "who enjoys the misfortune of others and considers as his own misfortune the fortunes of others."[282] For this reason the envious wishes that "what is lacking in him be also lacking in the envied."[283] He credits philosophers with the following definition of envy: "the sadness that rises at the apparent prosperity of others."[284] He distinguishes envy from the legitimate sentiment of indignation "against the tyrant or the perverse . . . who succeed."[285]

Envy is a passion directed against those "who shine with the most illustrious merits"[286] and, in general, against "those we think are superior."[287] Citing Horace,[288] he writes that not even the tyrants of Sicily invented a greater torture, and affirms that there is nothing more miserable than envy for "it rejects happiness voluntarily."[289] The envious "destroys or lowers the goods of others, exaggerates or emphasizes their defects or invents them when these do not exist."[290] The favorite pastime of the envious is "to belittle [*detrahere*]," either frontally or indirectly, as when "he preaches praises of others and pretends their friendship; but in the end, he slips in some misinformation [*modicum*] that destroys the previous praises."[291]

Which is the solution against envy? The author opts for the Christian solution of charity; but he also makes a pitch for the Greco-Roman tradition: "gifts"[292] are not enough to appease envy; "a cautious humility or a very solid truth are far better."[293] If all else fails then there is no other solution than "to pretend or fall into misery,"[294] and this includes more than economic misery.

Does John of Salisbury refer to the wrong reasoning on which envy is founded when he mentions "truth"? I do not think so. His is a reference to the obvious superiority of the truth, that everybody may acknowledge. Though the author does not develop it, he points out a very important idea, the subjective character of envy: it is not necessary that the superiority of others be real; all that is needed is that the envious may judge it so [*putare*] or that it may appear [*apparire*] to him so. Thus it is possible to envy what is not objectively enviable. Also important is the author's suggestion of "false justice"[295] in relation to envy. This could be an intuitive premonition of the egalitarian pseudo-justice, systematically postulated by contemporary socialisms. Be that as it may, these are not more than fugitive suggestions in the writings of this author.

2. Thomas Aquinas

Thomas Aquinas (1225–1274) is no doubt the most powerful mind of the medieval period and dedicates to envy one of the *questiones* that happens to be the longest dedicated to the vices. He defines envy as "sadness at the good of others in so far as they are superior to our own [*in quantum alter excedit ipsum*]."[296] This important clarification allows him to distinguish envy from the other passions: jealousy [*zelus*] is sadness at the good of others, but not because they have it but because we lack it; indignation [*nemesis*] is sadness at the good of others in so far as they do not deserve it. A derivation of envy [*ex ea sequitur*] is "the joy at the misfortune of others."[297]

In trying to discover the subjective roots of envy Thomas Aquinas strives to find a rational explanation and comes to the conclusion that "the envious feels that the good of others is his own evil in so far as it diminishes his own glory and excellence."[298] The envious feels sadness because he believes the good in others is the cause of his own misery. This belief is not objectively true. This vice, then, springs from a false judgment, as the Stoics had already affirmed.

Thomas Aquinas follows Aristotle in that we "envy not those that are far from us, in time and state, but those near, whom we try to equal or excel."[299] When others "excel over us by too much we do not envy."[300] Aquinas is not particularly consistent with his line of thought when he affirms that the pusillanimous are the most envious, for to them any superiority of others appears "too great."[301]

Thomas' evaluation of envy is totally negative: "envy is bad always," it carries "a joint suffering" for the sufferer,[302] it is "a capital sin."[303] Thomas Aquinas, however, adds a moral distinction that has escaped the commentators: the distinction between the "motus" and the "vice." The first [*motus invidiae*] "in so far as it is a passion of sensuality is an imperfect human act where reason does not intervene, and therefore, it is not a mortal sin."[304] In this important text Aquinas admits the existence of a spontaneous, envious impulse rooted in sensuality and thus connatural and instinctive. This impulse is ethically neutral. Angels may be proud and envious only in spirit [*pure spiritualia peccata*].[305]

Under the influence of Avicenna[306] and the Commentators[307] Thomas Aquinas keeps alive and tries to explain rationally the "evil eye," that is, "the poisonous and harmful look"[308] that since antiquity is linked to envy. This is the surprising position of Thomas: The soul, through a most powerful effort of the imagination, changes the humors [*spiritus*] of the body which are connected to it. This mutation of the humors appears principally in the eyes, where the most subtle humors flow; thus the eyes contaminate the surrounding air."[309] This opinion, reminiscent of that of Plutarch, is a testimony to the extraordinary importance that the evil eye had for the medieval mind.

In the *Additions* to the *Summa*, which St. Thomas left uncorrected, we find a conclusion on envy which could be interpreted in the lines of Tertulian, as a defense of the joy at the misfortune of others." So that the happiness of those that are saved [*beatitudo sanctorum*] becomes deeper, and so that they may render thanks to God, they are granted a perfect intuition of the sufferings of those condemned."[310] Then Thomas adds his reasons that appear to be more logical than moral: "Nothing belonging to the perfection of their happiness may be removed from the saved; this is known better through a comparison of the contraries, for these become clearer when placed against one another."[311] The most metaphysically problematic point of this Thomist position lies in the way of knowing of the saved: do they know by dialectical contrast or through intuition? If the first is true then the fruition of God would demand a type of knowledge or contemplation similar to that of the fallen angel.

3. Raymond Lull

Raymond Lull (1232–1316) is as wide in scope and deep in thought in poetry as in philosophy and his motive is apologetic and edifying. Envy appears several times in his works with an ambiguity that ranges from a desire of what others have to sadness at the good of others: [envy] "is to wish the goods of others without merit to own them";[312] it is a desire against charity, without reason."[313]

According to Lull, "men are by nature envious on account of their sensitive capacity,"[314] and for this reason envy "has multiplied in this world."[315] Envy is "the great temptation."[316] It is, therefore, a psychological and moral fact of great proportions.

What is it we envy? Mainly, "the goods and honor of men."[317] Thus he advises "not to speak of riches to the envious."[318] Lull repeats the classical thesis that we envy "similar things in nature and family,"[319] a text that equals those of Aristotle.

He considers that "the same way love is a good, envy is an evil,"[320] "contrary to justice, grace and charity."[321] And he adds, that "vices multiply in men through envy,"[322] for envy carries "deceit and falsehood."[323] Lull is also aware of the self-punishing character of envy and describes it in detail: it causes "anxiety, sadness, anguish, sighs",[324] habitual companions of the envious who "knows no rest."[325] In sum, the envious is a wretched creature."[326]

Lull considers the social effects of envy as being negative because, on account of envy, "men become enemies and speak evil of one another."[327] For this reason he concludes that "envy and greed have destroyed and disorganized the whole world."[328]

But why is envy natural and at the same time negative and to be avoided? Lull does not even raise this vital and disquieting question in spite of its theological implications.

4. Dante

Dante Alighieri (1265–1321) was the greatest of the philosopher-poets, an excellent writer in erudite Latin, canonized by popular acclaim, and a man of deep religious spirit who defended the empire. These seeming paradoxes could be reconciled by his brilliant mind trained in Aristotle and Thomism. Dante writes that "pride, avarice and envy are the three sparks that ignite the heart."[329] Dante placed envy in the second circle of Purgatory. The walls of this place and the dress of the envious were of "a livid color,"[330] and the envious speak out their own vice: "I was happier with the pain of another than with my own happiness,"[331] my blood boiled with so much envy that if I ever saw a happy man I would have been seen turning livid."[332] Dante compares the envious to "dogs turned into wolves."[333] One of the damned speaks of Florence as "a city so filled with envy that it overflowed,"[334] an accusation that Dante repeats of his own neighbors,[335] who forced the poet to live in exile. Dante speaks of envy with tremendous harshness: "Whore with greedy eyes fixed on Caesar's home, common death, a vice of the whole court."[336] Dante places in the mouth of the envious the same sentence Cain dictated upon himself: "Whoever finds me will kill me."[337]

Dante makes his own the Platonic thesis that "envy exists where there is some equality."[338] He points out that a "certain comparison"[339] takes place and this leads to the cancellation of judgment[340] and defamation.[341] Dante was wounded in his own flesh by those who opposed his use of the vernacular, and he writes: "There is the equality of a common tongue among those sharing a common language, and since some are not as proficient as others in its use, there is envy. The envious does not argue against those who claim not to be able to write, but that which appears in the writing of their work."[342] Dante does not draw all the consequences of this personal experience; had he done so he could have affirmed that the envious denies the values he is unable to cultivate. This is a refined form of self-justification that subverts the world of objective values. For example, to envy an athlete turns into a disqualification of physical fortitude, and so on. This tacit lesson and his own hard, personal experience of being highly envied are the two most significant contributions of Dante to the theme of envy.

VI. The Renaissance

1. Luis Vives

Juan Luis Vives (1492–1540), the most important Spanish humanist of the period, dedicates to the passions the third and last book of his main philosophical work, *De Anima et Vita* (1538). This is the first systematic effort to work out an empirical, rather than a psychological, metaphysics of envy.

Vives feels like a pioneer and complains that the theme of the passions "has not been treated with sufficient effort by the followers of wisdom."[343] Vives works out a definition that is less ontological than functional: "The passions are movements of the soul, either in act or potency". . . .[344] "that make us lean towards the good and against evil."[345] Their origins are "in some natural impulses"[346] arising immediately from sensation, or from images, or from judgments. "Judgments are not necessary to awake a passion [*afflectum*]."[347] There is a reciprocal interaction between the intellective faculty and passions: judgments may determine the impulses of the soul, and these, in turn, may determine reason and, in some cases, cancel it. Vives, an intellectualist to the end, believes that "the purer and higher the judgment, the less and lighter are the passions it admits."[348]

The impulses of the passions are not evil in themselves, but the opposite, for they are necessary to human mobility: "they are stimuli to move the soul so that it does not lie dead [*penitus*],"[349] a thesis that anticipates by more than two centuries those of Helvetius and Holbach. Our affective dynamism, according to Vives, works with "stimuli and restraints,"[350] depending on the desire or aversion they bring. Vives, furthermore, points out the physical character of our emotional life: "The passions are joined [*adjuntus*], in part, to our animal flesh,"[351] and "they all acquire their strength from the constitution of the body."[352] It is obvious Vives develops a physiological realism absent from the earlier descriptions of the passions, and that his method is inductive.

Vives separates envy from desire and jealousy and also from indignation. He defines envy as "a shrinking of the soul at the good of others, where there is a certain bite [*morsus*] and pain, and thus, gives out sadness";[353] and "it hurts us without consideration to our use, but only because we consider evil that others may be happy."[354] Envy may also cause body alterations, like "turning pale, livid, thin, sunken eyes, and a grim appearance."[355]

Vives follows Aristotle literally, even citing Hesiod's verse, and asserts that "certain types of envy take place among people that are equal or similar,"[356] and are not about all that is valuable, but only "as the result of comparing certain types of goods."[357] Vives believes, as a result, that when there is a large distance between the motive and the subject envy diminishes. But, he goes further than Aristotle in affirming that there is a radical envy that "does not understand differences: it invades and destroys everything,"[358] even when there is no relation of similitude between the envied and the envious. Vives describes, ahead of the French Renaissance, the social masks of envy: "It twists [*deforquere*] to the worst sense whatever is good; it makes people believe that details are too cumbersome and that the most beautiful is repugnant; . . . [the envious] are never tamed nor accept excuses, and even become more angry with gifts."[359] Four hundred years later Schopenhauer would offer as his sensational discovery a similar description.

The damnation of envy proper, rather than indignation, or jealousy, is complete in Vives: "It is abject, servile . . . stupid and evil,"[360] as well as "most unjust."[361]

The recognition of the influence of Vives on Bacon, Descartes, Hume, and through Hume on the whole of modern philosophy is long overdue, as well as the recognition that Vives is the founder of experimental psychology and the first systematic theorist of the passions this side of the Renaissance.

2. Luis de Granada, Melchor Cano, Miguel Sabuco

Luis de Granada (1505–1588) dedicated to envy a deep and penetrating study in the second edition of his book *Guía de Pecadores* (Guide for Sinners). He defined envy as "thinking of the happiness of others: of those above because the envious sees it is impossible for him to equal them; of those below because they try to equal him; and of those that are equal because they compete with him."[362] It was obviously right for Granada to place the vice of envy on situations related to happiness; but the extrapolation is not accurate for no one envies an inferior's happiness, nor the hypothetical possibility that it might increase. Consequently, he affirmed the habitual correlation between envy and descending egalitarianism: "[The envious] is not as concerned with reaching the happiness of others . . . but rather in making everyone as miserable as himself."[363]

Granada sees envy as one of "the most damaging and most universal sins,"[364] it is "diabolical,"[365] acts in "silence,"[366] and is "a just vice . . . for it is its own punishment and dispenses justice with it."[367] The root of envy is pride, for pride "cannot suffer the superior nor the equal."[368]

Are there remedies against envy? Granada does not even mention the classical ones of taking flight and hiding. He mentions interreligious dependence: "You share in all the good works of your neighbor."[369] This is a proper recall of the Christian principle of the Communion of Saints. There is another form of therapy: it is possible that the good of others "is not good for you to have."[370] There is an earthly translation of those two theological principles: the fact of human solidarity and the subjective and circumstantial character of happiness.

Is there any objective reason why we should become sad because others enjoy a good we do not have? Luis de Granada suggests an argument based on economics: the envious believes that "if another enjoy[s] what he desires, he either takes it from him completely, or at least, diminishes what he gets."[371] The fact is that we envy goods that are not transferable, like beauty, intelligence or a good child.

Despite many unfounded generalities, Granada's analysis of envy has the great merit of making clear that envy is not based on sensations but on mental calculations.

Melchor Cano (1509–1560) was a theologian of the Counter-Reformation and wrote a beautiful book entitled *De la Victoria de si mismo* (Victory over Oneself, 1550) dealing with the passions. He presupposes a radical anthropological duality: "Since man is composed of flesh and spirit, as a means between two extremes, beasts and angels, it is necessary that he shares in the properties of both, that is, sensuality and reason."[372] Sensuality has two powers, concupiscence and anger, and two "corresponding inclinations, appetite for the pleasurable and disdain for the unpleasant."[373] These "natural and thin"[374] inclinations are innate and "their first movements bear no sin,"[375] for they are involuntary. Among these are "envy, that is, sadness at the prosperity of others,"[376] and "joy at their adversities."[377] Why does envy take place? According to Cano because "the envious feels that the goods of others diminish his own honor and excellence."[378] Consented envy is a vice "that causes pain and harm to whomever suffers it,"[379] for "whatever good is heard, seen or felt of others becomes toxic."[380] Cano considers envy "an abominable and miserable vice,"[381] that "destroys all the virtues of the soul."[382]

Cano, agreeing with St. Thomas, believes that "the sudden or almost sudden moves of envy are not sins, for they are not in our hand, or at least they are not mortal sins."[383] This is the important ethical consequence of the *motus invidiae* that is spontaneous and connatural, but not invincible. Traditional philosophy seems to agree that there is a natural impulse towards envy in the human species.

Miguel Sabuco (1535–1591) is a forerunner of modern biosociology. His book *Nueva Filosofia del Hombre* (A New Philosophy of Man, 1587) is a comparative study between affects and passions in the different living species. According to Sabuco, animals share with humans fear, sadness, courage, desire, love, hate, anger, shame, jealousy, and so forth. He brings out dramatic examples to clarify his claims such as the dolphin that died out of sadness for having caused the death of the child he used to play with. Sabuco defines envy as "sadness at the good of others."[384] He frames the important question of whether envy exists in all species and comes to the conclusion that "envy exists in man only."[385] He identifies envy as a vice that is exclusively human, and as such, a biological distinctiveness of *homo sapiens*.

3. Bacon

Francis Bacon (1561–1626) was a politician of agitated life and the father of modern empiricism. His moral outlook, more pragmatic than speculative, is contained in the *Essays* (1597), a book on which he worked for thirty years. The ninth chapter is dedicated to envy. According to Bacon, envy is, of all the passions, "the most obstinate and constant,"[386] and "it is born of the comparison of oneself with others; where there is no comparison there is no envy."[387] Under the influence of the classics Bacon believes that "in the envious attitude there is an ejaculation or irradiation of the eye,"[388] and that it is possible "to transfer to others this spell."[389]

Who are the most inclined to envy? The "inquisitives,"[390] "the deformed, the eunuchs, the old, the bastards"[391] and "those seeking glory."[392] And who are the envied? Those who were originally equal who became "outstanding,"[393] "though those whose honors are linked to great voyages, cares and dangers are less envied."[394] For this reason those who triumph complain of hardship not so much "because they feel it, but to dull the edge of envy."[395]

Envy does not "know a day's rest,"[396] "acts with subtlety in the dark,"[397] and "attacks the best things."[398] Private envy falls on particular persons, while "public" envy is directed towards "high public administrators and ministers."[399] When envy produces public discomfort it is "a sickness of the State, like an infection[400] . . . that causes the best actions to stink."[401] There is, however, a certain form of public envy that Bacon, led by his pragmatism and classicism, believes to hold some good—ostracism—for it "eclipses the men who become too big."[402]

We need to interpret the allusions that the persecuted Bacon makes of the tricks happy people use to inspire compassion instead of envy; as a pessimistic and valuable contribution to the theme of envy, that is, they replace a feeling of inferiority towards others with one (though untrue) of superiority. Bacon does not denounce egalitarianism as a direct consequence of envy, and limits his description to pointing out the ill feelings towards leaders and the collective way to counteract the extraordinary man,—exile or civil death. This late defense of ostracism is ambivalent: Was it a conviction, a concession, or the mental inertia of a very cultivated spirit that becomes nostalgic, as all good Renaissance men do for things Greek? I am inclined to think it is the last possibility.

VII. The Baroque

1. Quevedo and Nieremberg

Francisco de Quevedo (1580–1645) is one of the great Spanish writers of the Golden Age and one of the deepest in conceptual density. Between 1634 and 1636 he wrote a treatise, partly philosophical, partly asthetic, entitled *Virtud Militante contra las Cuatro Pestes del Mundo: envidia, ingratitud, soberbia, avaricia* (Militant Virtue against the Four Pests of the World: Envy, Ingratitude, Pride, Avarice). This treatise was published posthumously in 1651. His sources are St. Paul, Seneca, Plutarch, Peter Cyrsologus, Augustine, John Crysostom and St. Bonaventure; but Quevedo asserts in the Prologue that the main source is his own "experience," for he has suffered "as a sick man"[403] the passions he analyzes.

The primary aim of Quevedo is to state the universal character of envy: "It is the most ancient of all the vices . . . It poisons all ages."[404] Envy has a specific character: "Man is either envious or envied, and most are envied and envious . . . ; whoever does not want to be envied, he does not want to be a man."[405] Quevedo affirms, following a very subtle description of the inner conflicts among the faculties, that "the whole man is made up of envy,"[406] "we are a population of envies."[407] In sum, humans are not only "envied and envious, but a republic of envies, that are not only near, close to our persons, but form our person and are within."[408] Following the line started by Sabuco, Quevedo asks if humans share this passion with other species; his conclusion is that the dog is the only animal that suffers envy "contaminated" by man.[409]

Quevedo repeats the classical observation that envy "torments those that suffer it,"[410] and adds the known testimony from authority. He is original when he observes that we "envy the virtuous, not virtue,"[411] that is, not goods but whomever enjoys them. He brings as an example the fact that no one envies the treasures of the sea, but "the atom of gold" someone owns, even if he is a beggar. And what is the reason? He brings out two: The first is that inert realities "cannot suffer affliction at being envied,"[412] suggesting thus that the envious aims to hurt. The second reason is that we do not envy things, but happiness—"peace . . . , praise . . . , credit . . . , respect[413]—as found in others. Quevedo points out here something very important, namely, that envy is not the outcome of comparing objective patrimonies, but subjective situations, that is, our own happiness and that of others, real or imaginary.

Quevedo is meticulous in his descriptions of the maneuvers of dissimulation of the envious: "There is no envious person who confesses that he is one,"[414] his "evil is hypocritical,"[415] and masks it "with praises . . . interpretations . . . care . . . , judgment . . .."[416] Quevedo might go too far when he affirms that "we not only envy goods but also evils; not only honors, but also insults; not only prosperity, but also misery,"[417] for this could only be true in the case that the envious might think that such calamities would bring some comfort to the envied.

Quevedo suggests several remedies, but he proposes primarily, ahead of Nieremberg, moral sympathy: "Feel as happy with the fortune of others as with your own, as commiserative for the misfortune of others as for your own,"[418] and adds the argument that in this way one doubles the pleasure in the case of positive feelings. Would it be then that in the case of commiseration one doubles one's pain? Another remedy he proposes is stoicism: "The envy of the court must be avoided by fleeing,"[419] and "by not dealing with the envious."[420] But, how is the envious to be avoided if, according to Quevedo, we are all envious? The only total flight would be into solitude.

Quevedo's description of the theme of envy follows the classical line, though he enriches it with deep observations like the one affirming that the formal object of envy is the imagined subjectivity of another.

Juan Eusebio Nieremberg (1595–1658) wrote in Spanish and Latin, and was a humanist of deep knowledge and one of the most eminent writers of the Spanish Golden Age. Nieremberg defines envy in the familiar manner: "It is sadness at the good of others, and sorrow at the happiness of others."[421] What he offers, in fact, is a double characterization of envy, from the objective [the good] and the subjective [the happiness] point of view. He describes envy's self-punishing quality in less abstract terms than his predecessors: "Envy burns the heart, dries up the flesh, tires the understanding by not allowing men to live well or happy, for as termites born in the wood the first thing they eat is the wood where they are born, thus envy born in the heart the first thing it torments is the heart where it grows."[422]

Is there a reasonable justification of envy? Not really, for the envious "act as devils, they envy pretending that they do not care about the happiness of others, and try to bring everyone to share their misery."[423] From this point of view envy is not the outcome of selfishness, it is sheer evil. Nieremberg, however, admits a form of envy or envious ambition for which he allows a certain pretext. This is his reasoning: "Temporal goods become less in proportion to the numbers of those sharing them, thus tormenting the soul who desired them, for if another receives them, he either loses them completely or receives them in less quantity, thus it is impossible for this soul to stop feeling sad, for someone else has what she desires."[424] This argument restricts envy to the economic plane, that is, to that which is necessarily limited. If this reasoning, however, were linked to the idea of an arithmetic, distributive justice the conclusion would be an egalitarian slogan. Nieremberg is not unsympathetic to this position for he postulates a welfare of spiritual goods which goes further than Adam Smith would go two centuries later with his principle of sympathy as the foundation of ethics. Nieremberg proposes the following remedy against envy: "The good and the bad things that fall on your neighbors feel as if they fell on you rejoicing in the first and feeling sad in the second, weeping with those who weep, thinking that the same could happen to you; for we are all members of the same body, animated by the same spirit and we must rejoice and be sad as if what happens to one happened to the rest of us."[425] Nieremberg proposes a spiritual communism and an egalitarian psychologism that take to their last conclusions the charity of St. Paul. The theme of envy leads the great writer and thinker to remove the last roots of morality.

2. Descartes and Spinoza

Rene Descartes (1596–1650), a philosopher who at times was in a most unCartesian manner, obscure and imprecise, never developed an ethics but wrote a *Traite de Passions* (1649), which, though inserted between physiology and psychology, has moral implications. What are the passions? The "emotions of the soul . . . caused, maintained and reinforced by some movements of the humors."[426] These *esprits animaux* or humors[427] are, as much as the nerves and blood, corporal entities. This is his anatomical description: "The near cause of the passions is none other than the agitation with which the humors move the [pineal] gland placed at the center of the brain."[428] There are some reactions, like flight produced by the passion of fear, where the soul does not intervene.[429] Passions have, therefore, their seat and origin in the body, and basically they are physiological realities. Their principal effect is that they "incite and predispose the soul to desire those things for which the body has become ready: fear moves to escape and valor to fight."[430]

There are six generic or simple passions (admiration, love, hate, desire, joy and sadness) and an indefinite number of complex or more determined passions,[431] among these there is a species of sadness that is envy," sadness at the good happening to others"[432] and that gives the skin "a livid color."[433] Glory, according to Descartes, is what is envied most.[434] There is also a type of envy that is not a vice, and this is indignation; but the proper passion is "the most damaging to human happiness for those who suffer it afflict themselves and, besides, disturb, as much as they can, the happiness of others."[435]

How can passions be eliminated? Descartes, who in so many other instances shows the influence of the Stoics, rejects them here by not claiming the autonomy of reason and the will: "Passions may not be directly recalled or eliminated by some act of our will; but they may be indirectly controlled through the representation of those things that are habitually associated with the passions we wish to have and that are the opposite of those we wish to reject."[436] The actual method consists, therefore, in "separating within oneself those movements of the blood and of the humors and of the thoughts to which they are associated;"[437] and, as a last resort, "to distract oneself with other thoughts until time and rest calm the emotion."[438] These operations are easier for the stronger than the weaker souls[439] but even the latter may "acquire a complete dominion over their passions if they dedicate enough effort to tame and guide them."[440]

Descartes concludes his book affirming that "passions are by nature good and that all we must avoid is their abuse and wrong use,"[441] and that "men more moved by passion are more likely to enjoy the pleasures of life more."[442] It is not easy to articulate these ideas with the above schema. What is naturally good in envy and what possibilities of joy does it bring? Descartes falls here into contradiction and ambiguity. On the one hand, he assimilates the Stoic formulae against passional states—"the knowledge of truth,"[443] "being able to follow virtue exactly ... and the tranquility of the soul"[444]; but on the other hand, he proclaims the naturalness of passional instincts, their intrinsic neutrality and their positive possibilities. The Cartesian theory of envy has three elements that are hard to match: the classical one of self-discipline and serenity, the renaissance cult of vitality and the modern of pineal physiology. There appears in Descartes a deep chasm between the doctrine of the passion and their epistemology; Cartesian ethics are hardly visible and psychology is mediocre. Cartesian greatness lies in other philosophical areas.

Baruch Spinoza (1632–1677), a Dutch Jew of Spanish origin, tried to examine human conduct with mathematical techniques and an experimental method. He was more interested than other philosophers up to then in the study of feelings, and among them, envy "that is no other thing than hate, in so far as it may be considered as preparing man to enjoy the misery of others and, contrarily, to feel sad at their happiness."[445] The cause of envy, as with any other form of hate, is the idea of a fact external to the person,[446] and the most inclined to it are "the proud,"[447] and those "who appear as most insignificant and humble."[448]

Is envy, therefore, only a reaction, or is it an inclination? Envy is a predisposition. Spinoza repeats this statement again and again: "Men are by nature envious,"[449] men tend by nature towards envy,"[450] "men by nature are predisposed ... to envy;"[451] in sum, envy "is a property of human nature."[452] Spinoza is more radical than Thomas Aquinas when he establishes that the *motus* or the dynamics of envy is connatural to the human species. Education increases it, for "parents generally incite their children by appealing to the only resource they have: honor and envy."[453] If parents resort to envy, it is because children already have an innate predisposition that guarantees its efficacy.

This connaturality explains why "the majority of humans are envious,"[454] namely, "the majority envy one another and cannot stand each other."[455] This fact is perilously antisocial: "To the degree that humans are carried away by envy to oppose one another, or by some feeling of hate, they confront each other and are the more frightening for they have more power than any other individual in nature."[456] Envy is not, therefore, a positive feeling: "envy is evil."[457]

Spinoza advises us to live "according to the precepts of reason"[458] even if this is an "uncommon"[459] attitude. This adjustment of behavior to reason demands "that we govern ourselves, that we control our feelings."[460] This is an ethic very similar to the Stoics' though the moral discipline that Spinoza proposes is difficult to match with his metaphysical determinism. Spinoza's contribution is his assertion that envy is connatural; but is there any reason to believe that the human species is envious by nature? The question remains unanswered.

3. Flechier and Feijoo

Esprit Flechier (1632–1710) was an incisive and sententious historian who became the most authoritative moralist of his time. Among his many writings his *Sermon on Envy* is the most outstanding, written in a precise and seductive prose.

His definition of envy is different from the classics and, though incomplete, is deeper: "Envy is no more than the anxiety and impatience of a man who sees and acknowledges himself inferior to another."[461] Ahead of Nietzsche he discovers in this inferiority feeling an important connotation, "the affliction of impotence."[462] Hence, the envious is "always a coward."[463]

The primary aspect of envy is its extension. Envy causes "the majority of classes [to] be confused and the same with the human conditions"[464] because "it is universal."[465] Envy does not belong to one particular epoch, it is "as old as the world,"[466] "it was the first sin on this earth"[467]—an inclination shared by all from the beginning. This universal character of envy forces us to recognize it as a weakness that is "almost incorrigible."[468]

Flechier, in agreement with his predecessors, underlines the self-punishing character of this passion: the sufferer "carries in his heart the pain of his envy;[469] and he repeats this assertion with the symmetrical though apparently contradictory statement: "This is the only vice that may be called just . . . for it punishes with its own punishment whomever is affected by it."[470] He agrees with Aristotle when he affirms that "envy is never as cruel as among those who share the same profession,"[471] that is, it is more common among neighbors.

Flechier affirms that "there is no other sin that share[s] more in evil than envy."[472] Why is he so harsh? Because envy is the contrary of the most radical and supreme Christian virtue, charity or love in Christ. Envy is antisocial and antisolidarity; "it breaks the union, it distances from those who are most happy."[473] This, however, is no obstacle for the envious "to form unions of inequity; regardless of how divided they might be in everything else, some become united against a man from whom they only fear his merit."[474] These associations are formed with the highest degree of hypocrisy, that is, pretending to be moral "under the pretext of equality and decency [*bienseance*]."[475] It is with this analysis, with so many social consequences, that Flechier appears most original, sharp and prophetic at one century before the French Revolution. It is in this line that his corollary reads with such modern tones: "Secular civility seems to have been invented to veil envy."[476] This thesis has been verified with large lists of empirical instances by modern anthropology.

This elegant prelate has provided some of the most unexpected and insightful observations about envy to come out of that French century.

Benito Jeronimo Feijoo (1676–1764) was so successful with his writings that a legion of adversaries followed him everywhere, and the author called them envious. He found consolation in thinking that such "poison"[477] produces in the envious "a continuous torment in their hearts . . . and they deserve compassion." But the passive object also suffers as he sees himself "treacherously bitten by envy,"[478] not finding consolation in knowing that "it dies with the envied."[479] According to Feijoo, the worse part of envy is not "that envy burns like a furious passion,"[480] but that because it spreads libels its social implications are grave for "there are those who buy them [libels] and that applaud them."[481] Apparently the author thought the number of these is very large, which proves the extension of this vice, and that they are found mostly among intellectuals. Feijoo shared this experience with other men of letters.[482]

VIII. The Moderns

1. Hume and Smith

David Hume (1711-1776), the iconoclast of rational metaphysics and the father of modern empiricism, dedicates the extensive second book of his *A Treatise of Human Nature* (1738) to a detailed description of the passions. According to Hume, "each part of extension and every numerical unity awake an emotion as soon as they are conceived by the mind."[483] The sum of these effects constitutes an emotional whole [compound] that "accompanies every sensation and every image formed in fantasy."[484] These impressions derived from sensation are the passions. Hume's ethics are based on the principle that the stimuli of human action are not rational, but sentimental; we act searching for pleasure and to avoid pain. Hence, Hume's thesis, that he calls "extraordinary" and which is certainly one of his most polemical: "Reason is and must be the slave of the passions, and must not pretend to have any other function than to serve and obey them."[485] And he adds: "Properly speaking a passion is never irrational."[486] What in fact happens is that there are two types of passions, the violent and the mild, and these last are mistakenly taken for reason: "The so called fortitude of spirit is the predominance of mild over violent passions."[487] This is the most radical exaltation of the pathetic that the history of philosophy has recorded.

We call passions "direct" when they are the result of immediate pain or pleasure; thus, desire or fear. We call it "indirect" when other reflections intervene; thus, love and hate. Hume dedicates a whole section of this chapter to the joy at the misfortune of others [malice] and to envy, to show how they belong to the indirect passions and he gives us one of the most extreme and original interpretations on the subject.

Envy, according to Hume, is sadness at the joy of others and joy at the misery of others; it is "joy at the sufferings and miseries of others, even when they do not cause us offense or harm."[488] How are these passions generated? According to Hume "men judge objects not on account of their intrinsic merit and worth, but through comparison."[489] This thesis applies equally to intellectual and to sentimental operations: "Every object appears larger or smaller by comparison with others . . . hence the passion of envy and the joy at the misery of others."[490] Thus we have that "the misery of another gives us a more vivid idea of our happiness, and the happiness of others of our misery; the first produces joy, the second misery."[491] This is Hume's main thesis.

Hume maintains that these logical reactions are not specifically directed against our neighbor, for they happen not only facing others but also ourselves. There is joy at our own misery when we compare a past misfortune with a present joy, and we feel envy in the opposite case. This opinion is not true: we never feel happiness at having felt miserable, and the joy of past happiness is not envy, for we do not try to remove such experience; rather, it is a form of nostalgia.

Hume follows tradition when he affirms that only "proximity" produces such feelings, and justifies this assertion, saying: "A great disproportion interrupts communication, and either we are unable to compare with what is distant or it diminishes the effects of the comparison."[492] It is also necessary, Hume adds, that such comparison take place among objects "of the same species," for as he says "the poet is not competent to envy the philosopher."[493] Both these observations are truly problematic.

Hume does not condemn the passions systematically. They are good in the measure they are able to produce pleasure; and those that cause sadness should be overcome not by reason, but by other passionate impulses that produce pleasure. From this perspective and in so far as envy that produces pain is not commendable, it does not seem that the joy at the misery of others should be avoided. This subjective utilitarianism takes Hume to the other extreme of the position that a century later Schopenhauer will adopt. Pure descriptionism, in so far as it neutrally explains the passions, serves also to justify them.

Hume's analysis of envy is introspective and does not take into account the effects of envy on the envied nor the social consequences. It is a solipsistic, self-centered and doubtfully moral psychologism. Besides, it is not easy to ground ethics upon determinism, a basic presupposition of Hume, nor use a simple phenomenological analysis, as Hume does. Someone might say that Hume tries to show *how* envy is; but, can such a passion be described just following its effects on human sociability? Obviously not, since a moral dimension of individual conduct is how it affects the others. Hume uses a Robinsonian analysis of envy, which is not truly empirical, since it is conditioned by his more or less dogmatic systematic presuppositions of what he understands to be his system of philosophy.

Adam Smith (1723-1790), professor of ethics at Glasgow during eleven years, writes the summary of his teachings in *The Theory of Moral Sentiments* (1759). In 1766 he wrote *An Inquiry into the Nature and Causes of the Wealth of Nations*, a true canon of classical economics.

Adam Smith's psychology and ethics are grounded on the observation that "whatever passion is awakened in a person by an object, a similar emotion rises in the chest of an attentive observer when he thinks of that person's situation."[494] This fellow-feeling is sympathy and forms part of human nature: "men . . . [are] naturally sympathetic."[495] Communicating our passions produces pleasure, even if, "we derive more satisfaction from the sympathy of our friends towards our disagreeable passions than to the agreeable ones."[496] There are two relative exceptions to this general rule: hate and resentment, "the two unique passions whose manifestations do not dispose nor prepare to sympathize with them, as long as we are uninformed about the causes provoking them,"[497] but once we know the causes sympathy takes place.

Adam Smith, under the powerful influence of the Stoics, considers that "self-command is not only a great virtue, but all the virtues seem to take from it their main splendor,"[498] for only self-command will be able to stop the passions from "taking and inducing to the breaking of all the rules."[499]

The above theory serves Adam Smith as reference to explain the different feelings, good and evil, virtues, justice, utility; and, where does envy come in? He defines envy as "the passion that watches with evil disgust the superiority of those who are really entitled to the superiority they have."[500] He calls it a "hateful and detestable passion"[501] and he includes it among those that "separate man from man and tend to break the bonds of human society." It is surprising, however, that Adam Smith believes that "the masses never envy their superiors."[502] He considers envy a common passion for he uses the word "envied"[503] to refer to fortunate personal situations. He repeats often that sympathy with the joy and misery of others happens only "when there is no envy."[504] And he maintains that it is the envy of the poor towards the rich that demands the establishment of civil government as a guarantor of property.[505] On the other hand, Adam Smith shares the preoccupation and criterion of the Stoics and states that "prudence often advises [us] to carry our prosperity with moderation, and teach[es] us to avoid envy, that is due, more than on any other account, to success."[506] Adam Smith, then, does not deny, but on the contrary, affirms the powerful and omnipresent phenomenon of envy.

If humans, however, naturally sympathize with any feeling when they know the motives, why can we not sympathize with those that envy? The general theory exposed not only fails to explain this universal feeling, but finds in envy an objection of serious importance. If sympathy is a moral tuning with others, envy is the opposite, being out of tune. We cannot ground our moral and emotive lives on something that does not have a universal character.

Sympathy is to Adam Smith's moral theory what preestablished harmony and solidarity are to his science of economics. These notions imply an optimistic conception of the world, and it is envy precisely, with its extension and depth, which most induces to pessimism in human psychology. Adam Smith realizes this but is unable to explain it. Despite certain very perceptive and deep concrete descriptions of the passions, his theory of moral sentiment remains ethereal and naive.

The silence that liberal thinkers impose on envy starts with Adam Smith and is the result of a moral hypothesis that relies on the intrinsic goodness of humans, of a political hypothesis of a natural state of goodness, and of the economic hypothesis of a preestablished harmony.

2. Kant

Immanuel Kant (1724–1804), father of modern philosophy, distinguishes between "the noble emotions," passing obstacles of reflection, and "disguised passions,"[507] that are "cancer of pure practical reason,"[508] "impossible to conquer through reason."[509] There are innate and ardent passions, like sexuality, and there are others that are acquired and cold, like avarice.[510] Envy is "the inclination to contemplate with pain the good of others, even if it does not harm our own good."[511] Envy is a "passion"[512] whose "impulse [*Regung*] proceeds from human nature,"[513] and this places envy among the innate qualities. Envy is distinguished from plain dislike [*Missgunst*] in that "when it operates it tries to diminish the good of others."[514]

Kant follows the British empiricists pointing out that envy emerges in the comparison with others through value judgments: the envious believes "that the good of others shadows his own which is measured [not] by its own intrinsic worth, but only in comparison with that of others."[515] A proof of this is that we call "enviable [*beneidigungswürdig*]"[516] those situations we consider advantageous and superior. Kant considers envy to be truly "awful"[517] for "it tortures those who suffer it and aims at destroying the happiness of others, at least in desire, and this is contrary to the duty of humans towards themselves and towards others."[518]

Kant adds a list of the relatives of envy: "The horrible family of envy is made up of ingratitude [*Undankbarkeit*] and the joy at the misery of others [*Schadenfreude*],"[519] which he also calls "hostile and evil joy [*feindselige Freude*]."[520] This last one he also calls "horrible."[521] It is a general fact that "in the misery of our friends there is something that does not displease us completely."[522] This passion, as much as envy, is founded "in nature according to the laws of imagination and contrast."[523] The evil of such behavior is evident: "To rejoice and even desire the misery of others is a secret hate and just the opposite of the love for others, on which duty is based"; it is, besides, a feeling opposed to the principle of solidarity and sympathy [*Teilnehmung*].[524]

In a significant scholium that requires special exegesis, Kant returns to the problem of envy being a specific feature of humans. He answers: "From the objective point of view these vices are inhuman; but they are human from the subjective viewpoint, that is, as experiences that our species offers us."[525] This text does not contradict the previous ones if we interpret the objective as moral duty and the subjective as anthropological data. But this question becomes complex when, as a conclusion, Kant affirms that "though some men fall into these bestial vices, we are not authorized to attribute them to all humans as proper dispositions [*Anlage*] of the human species."[526]

How are such dispositions or capacities defined? According to Kant "the dispositions of any being consist in those essential parts that shape him and also in the forms according to which the said parts come together. Dispositions may be originary [*ursprünglich*] if they are necessary for such a being to exist, or accidental [*zufälling*] if one can be without them."[527] Originary dispositions, that distinguish man from the animals, are "the technical dispositions to manipulate things, the pragmatic ones to make use of other men, and the moral ones to act with freedom."[528]

Kant, apparently, does not believe that envy is an intrinsic property of humans, which, as Thomas Aquinas noted, is based on a movement or impulse [*motus* or *Regung*] of human nature. The ethical problem arises when such a natural motion breaks loose [*Ausbruch*].[529]

Kant's doctrine on envy is basically moral, and the method he uses is primarily deductive. His analysis leads to a damnation of envy without exceptions. His weak point is in relation to the connaturality of envy. On this point he takes an eclectic position similar to the traditional, scholastic position. His most significant contribution is the relative character of envy and the comparative structure of the judgment on which it is based. But this is not original and is less deeply and systematically formulated than it was by Hume.

3. Holbach and Staël

Paul Heinrich Holbach (1725–1789), a radical materialist for whom the classical distinctions of body-soul, passion-reason bear no sense, deals with envy in his own peculiar way. He affirms that "all the passions may be reduced to desiring some real or imaginary good, and fearing and avoiding some real or imaginary evil."[530] Consequently, "passions and desires are essential to men, inherent to his nature, inseparable from his existence and necessary for his conservation."[531] Holbach faces squarely the Stoic tradition which had influenced so deeply the previous moralists: "The man who is free of passions and desires, far from being perfect, as some philosophers have claimed, would be useless to himself and to others, and contrary to social life."[532] These passions, however, may not be developed freely; they have two limits: not to harm one's self or others. "The good man is not the one who does not know passion, but the one who has passions according to his permanent well-being, inseparable from the well-being of those who must contribute with him to achieve his own happiness."[533] An action is moral if it has any bearing on human happiness: "Virtue is the habit of contributing to the welfare of the social life, and vice is the habit of harming and destroying the good of society."[534]

A negative natural movement occurs when negative, vicious envy happens, but envy is positive when it generates virtuous emulation.[535] The envious is that person "who hates those with worthy advantages and qualities."[536] Envy is not an exceptional occurrence: "Envy and jealousy are natural passions in all men,"[537] for "every mortal who becomes outstanding on account of his talents, his merit, his happy luck, his credit or wealth, is the object of public envy."[538]

Holbach appropriates the old observation that "social life is a continuous torment for whomever is afflicted by this miserable passion,"[539] and adds that the only resource is solitude. In anticiption of Schopenhauer, Holbach points out that envy always appears in a hypocritical manner, pretending to have "virtuous feelings,"[540] or disguised under the "name of author of the public good."[541] In the first case hypercriticism and gossip are used; in the second we witness the birth of certain political ideologies. Holbach comes nearest to this penetrating and prophetic message of envy.

Which are the resources used by demagogic envy? They are: to clamor against the posts granted to men supposedly without any merit, to accuse the rich of not deserving their goods, to attribute the lowest motive to noble actions, to exalt the defects of the envied and so forth.[542] In sum, "the envious disguises himself with love for the public good when he wants to appease those that bother him."[543] (Holbach's texts resemble an advanced version of egalitarianism as it found its peak in Baboeuf and which found its way into the succeeding socialisms.) Hence, Holbach concludes, "envy is an unsociable quality,"[544] which, within its materialist empiricism, is equivalent to saying that it is intrinsically immoral. It is important to notice that the harshest and earliest damnation of the revolutionary ideology comes from an atheist, hedonist, and mechanist who is also an antitraditionalist.

Germana Necker, baroness de Staël (1766–1817), wrote, while living one of the crises of her amorous life, an insightful book *On the Influence of Passions in the Happiness of Individuals* (1796). Chapter six is dedicated to envy and shame. The author believes that to envy "is to feel inferior."[545] This inferiority need not be real but can be imaginary, for the envied is attributed "unknown advantages." This "terrible feeling" does not evaporate until the envious believes the envied "is inferior in fortune, talent and happiness." The final obsessive goal of the envious is egalitarianism at any cost: "He prefers the equality of hell to any of the hierarchies of heaven."[546] This strong sentence summarizes the experience of one of the most brilliant women of the modern world. The Baroness de Staël, direct witness of the French Revolution, of the Empire and the Restoration—perhaps one of the periods of history with the most lessons to learn—denounced the ultimate root of envy: the feeling of inferiority.

IX. The Contemporaries

1. Schopenhauer

Arthur Schopenhauer (1788–1860), famous for a pessimism that is more essential than existential, deals with envy in much more detail than any other human weakness. He starts from the fact that "envy is natural in man,"[547] since "it is a property man carries in him [*in sich*],"[548] and for this reason "no man is free from it."[549] How does envy arise? Through a comparison of what we have with what others have. Envy "is born of the inevitable [*unvermeidlich*] comparison between our own situation and that of others,"[550] and occurs when this results in an apparent inferiority. Schopenhauer takes for granted the "inevitability" of this comparison, and trying to go further he asks why the real or imagined inferiority causes sadness. His explanation agrees with his own conception of life. Envy does not occur on account of just any type of inferiority, but only if we discover an inferiority in happiness: the belief that the other person is happier. But why does the happiness of others cause sadness? Here we reach Schopenhauer's more basic and radical answer: "It is natural to taste as bitter our own scarcity when we contemplate other people's property and joy;"[551] "men are unable to bear witness to the happiness of another for in this they feel miserable."[552] Envy underlies unhappiness, which is for Schopenhauer the normal human condition. Envy is, therefore, a feeling that grounds the ultimate human existence.

If man is habitually unhappy, if it is inevitable for him to compare his level of happiness with that of others, if this comparison unveils for him other situations of happiness that are more intense than his own, and if this shows a permanent deficit in his own happiness, then envy is, through observation and deduction, an inevitable, universal feeling. If this is the case, is it possible for what is necessary to be ethically evil? Schopenhauer becomes indulgent towards the envious in his final sentencing: "Envy, though evil, is basically human, and thus it maybe excused."[553] This moral conclusion follows logically from the way the problem is stated.

It is also consequent with this argumentation in Schopenhauer's thesis that "the joy at the misery of others [*Schadenfreude*] is, to a large degree, the contrary of envy;"[554] and in another place he finds them "diametrically opposed."[555] Schopenhauer disagrees here with the general opinion that holds both sentiments to be equal. Schopenhauer's reasoning follows the line of the previous presentation: "To feel envy is human; to enjoy other people's misfortunes is diabolical . . . Selfishness may lead to crimes and misdeeds of all types, but the pains and damages it causes are not an end, they are only means and caused by accident. On the other hand, cruelty and the desire to cause evil have the suffering and the pain of others as their end; and when they are achieved they cause pleasure. This gives them a greater power of moral perversity. The rule of the highest selfishness is: Do not help anyone, and, if it is useful to you, do harm. The rule of wickedness is: Cause others as much harm as you can. The joy at the harm of others is, theoretically, cruelty; cruelty, in practice, is happiness at the misery of others."[556] There is no excuse for the *Schadenfreude*; its evil is absolute. What distinguishes it from envy is its moral quality.

Schopenhauer's sharp reasoning is enriched by phenomenological descriptions. Envy, as he had already pointed out, is "an affliction"[557] for the one who suffers it, but the philosopher notes that it does not develop in proportion to the superior quantity of the good envied, but in proportion to the type of quality envied. Here Schopenhauer surpasses his predecessors. There are qualities that are temporary, and when they disappear so does envy. But there are qualities that are essential and they remain: "Those who envy natural gifts or personal superiorities, like beauty in women and intelligence in men, have no consolation or hope, and have no other alternative left to them but to hate irreconcilably those who have them."[558] This envy "directed against personal qualities is the most insatiable and poisonous because the envious is left without hope; it is also the lowest type of envy for it hates what it ought to love and respect."[559]

Schopenhauer sides with Aristotle when he affirms that envy happens among equals. He cites "three types of aristocracies: of birth, of riches and of the spirit . . . Each aristocracy is surrounded by an army of envious people which is bitterly frustrated by all aristocracy and, when they are not afraid of them, they try to make sure they know that 'You are not better than we are' . . . On the other hand, those belonging to one type of aristocracy deal easily and without envy with the other two."[560] On this point Schopenhauer improperly extrapolates his own experience as a philosopher who envies neither the rich nor the noble; but he does not seem to be aware of such habitual facts as the envy of the *parvenu* towards the aristocrat and the envy of many intellectuals towards the powerful.

Schopenhauer deals with the tortuous and clandestine dialectics of envy. The envious "hides as carefully as the secret, lustful sinner and becomes the endless inventor of tricks and stratagems to hide and mask himself. Thus he is able to pretend to ignore the superiority of others which eats up his heart, as if he did not see them, nor hear them, nor were aware of them, nor had ever heard of them. He is a master simulator. On the other hand he tries with all his power to connive and thus prevent any form of superiority from appearing in any situation. And if they do, he casts on them obscurity, hypercriticism, sarcasm and calumny like the toad that spits poison from its hole. On the other hand he will praise endlessly insignificant men, mediocre people, and even the inferior in the same type of activities."[561] It is difficult to find a more relentless dissection of the tortuous and clandestine dialectics of the envious in all of literature.

Schopenhauer advises "not to provoke envy."[562] The envied must keep distance from the envious and, as far as possible, avoid all contact to neutralize the causes."[563] It is a reminder of the ivory tower of the best and the isolation of the most favored which the Greeks already pointed out. And if this fails, there is still the alternative of self-humiliation or even scorn: "Talent and genius must beg pardon of the world, for they are not always in a position to despise it with pride and courage."[564]

Envy is the most antisocial feeling we may have, for it leads to incommunicability and disunity: "Envy reinforces the walls between the other and the I, while sympathy and compassion makes them thin and transparent and in full maturity the distinction between the I and the non-I disappears."[565] Envy is the antisocial feeling par excellence. This is the anguishing conclusion the world of the envious reaches: "The more brilliant, the more lonely one is."[566]

The most problematic part of Schopenhauer's analysis of envy is the contrast he draws between envy and the joy at the misery of others, which he reaches through an axiological judgment and not through experience. The clearest part of his analysis is the unmasking of the machinations of the envious; and the most advanced is his denunciation of the radical unsociable character of envy.

2. Marx

Karl Marx (1818–1883), writing in his *Manuscripts of 1844* (first published in 1932), distinguishes between "that other underdeveloped communism" (p. 531) and his own form of communism, which he calls "developed communism." He calls the former "vulgar" while he calls his form "scientific." He then labels the first type of communism "envious."

Marx defines envy as "a disguised form of greed," but this is very imprecise, for it is rare for greed not to wear a disguise. He adds that envy is directed "towards every form of private property that appears more wealthy," but this is not true, for there are many who do not envy those who are richer, and therefore, not "every form of wealth" is envied. He concludes that the desire of the envious is "to reduce everything to a common level." This is a precise statement, which clarifies the relationship between communism and envy. But he also maintains that "only the 'vulgar' type of communism is the outcome of such envy and of the leveling of everyone on a minimum as a foundation." It is taken for granted that Marx's "developed communism" does not require a minimum as the basis for egalitarian private property, for it only allows public property.

The Marxist effort to free communism from envy is partly rhetorical and partly utopian. Marx acknowledges the envious character of all egalitarianisms and particularly of communism, even while caricaturing all other systems and idealizing his own. But Marx is not satisfied to simply blame envy on *other* forms of communism; he also tries to implicate advocates of free trade when he affirms that "envy and egalitarianism constitute in fact the essence of competition." This is not true, for the open market leads to emulation and establishes hierarchies, not egalitarianism.

Marx's position regarding envy is not speculative but political. He is aware of the accusations against his form of communism and is content to deny the charges or to apply them to others without any basis in observable fact.

(The quotes are from "Of Private Property and Communism," the third Fragment from the *Manuscripts of 1844*, translation by T. B. Bottomore included in the Appendix to E. Fromm, *Marx's Concept of Man*, 1961. Spanish trans. Mexico, 1962, pp. 133–134.)

3. Nietzsche

Friedrich Nietzsche (1844–1900) was moved all his life by an agonic animadversion to classical morality in its several versions, Aristotelian, Stoic and above all Christian. His critical effort was not compensated by the establishment of what he called the morals of the noble man, "the blond beast [*blonde Bestie*]."[567] Though trained in Greek philology, Nietzsche's style of thinking and writing was in line with the wisdom literature of China, Hinduism and Hebrew, rather than with the styles of the West. This explains his parabolic, aphoristic, diffuse, and sumptuous style. His brain, always boiling at very high pressure until it exploded, did not produce a rigorous system of thought, but only lightning. He lived obsessed with the New Testament, and many of his written pages tried to produce an antigospel, but this he was far from achieving. His most academic book, and in my opinion the most philosophically interesting, is *On the Genealogy of Morals* (1887). Its main theme is resentment that he relates, from the passive side, to frustration and impotence, and from the active side, to vengeance and envy.

According to Nietzsche, resentment is the state of the soul of "those who have been denied [*versagen*] the authentic reaction, that of action, and that they make up with an imaginary vengeance."[568] Resentment is not the consequence, therefore, of a prohibition, not even of a renunciation, but rather of the inability to act. Resentment is "the impotent *ohnmächtig*,"[569] with "an insatiable instinct"[570] that he satisfies with a mental operation. Nietzsche describes in detail the workings of this mental operation: "The true causes of resentment, vengeance and other related vices is found in the desire to distract [*betäuben*] a tormenting pain, that is hidden and that becomes less and less bearable, by means of a stronger emotion . . . , and in order to provoke it, the first and best excuse is to think that someone else is responsible that I feel so lousy."[571] This transfer of responsibility for one's own misery onto another transforms into evil people those who govern, the bosses, the father, the neighbor, or even society as a whole.

Resentment moves within a world of "subterranean and endless vengeance, insatiable in explanations against the happy people,"[572] who are taken as responsible for our own misery. Resentment equals envy, then, since "to see suffering causes happiness, and to inflict pain even more happiness."[573] But the supreme vengeance of the resentful will consist in convincing the happy ones "that it is a shame to feel happiness when there is so much misery."[574] The resentful inverts ethics: "The evil person according to the morals of resentment is the good person of the other morals";[575] which is the "world upside down [*verkehrte Welt*],"[576] a transvaloration or inversion of values [*Umwertung*]."[577]

Resentment is a mental operation to discharge on others the responsibility of our own failure, to sublimate impotence, and, in the last analysis, to build a table of values that makes of the happy and successful a criminal, and of the good person a bitter failure. These operations of machination falsify. The resentful deceives himself, for he is "neither sincere, nor naive, nor honest, nor straight with himself."[578] Besides being fallacious, these operations are subtle, and the habit of performing them develops the mental faculties. For this reason Nietzsche, referring to the Jews, went so far as to write that "a race of resentful people will in the end become necessarily more intelligent [*klug*] than any other noble race."[579] There are passions that are hereditary: "A certain twisted envy . . . proper of the plebeian crowd [*Pöbel-Typus*] must pass on to the son."[580] This last remark, which is to be expected from the greatest enemy of resentment, amounts to establishing a correlation at the sociobiological level between a resentful tradition and a high intellectual quotient within a genetic group. This is one of the many surprises Nietzsche dispenses.

Among those emotions most like resentment, [*verwandte*], envy is the most prominent, and much of what Nietzsche says about the former applies to the latter. He calls envy "bilious,"[581] "twisted,"[582] related to "bitchy sensuality"[583] and casting "an oblique gaze"[584] that produces "the evil eye [*Bösenblick*]."[585] Nietzsche insists in the self-punishing character of envy as a feeling that "causes people to go mad . . . asphyxiation,"[586] "destroys,"[587] and that "turns upon itself its own poisonous sting like the scorpion."[588]

The happiness of others causes envy, according to Nietzsche. "Those smoked, overheated, stale, livid and tormented souls, how can their envy [*Neid*] bear my happiness?"[589] We envy "whoever climbs high,"[590] "the great man,"[591] "the rich,"[592] and even the "non-envious."[593] Nietzsche agrees with the classics that "great favors [*Verbindlichkeit*] do not fill with gratitude those who receive them, but rather revengefulness, and when the small favor is not forgotten it becomes poison in the soul."[594]

Zarathustra, Nietzsche's ideal, addresses thus the solar deity: "Bless me, tranquil eye, for you may contemplate a happiness that is too great without envy."[595] This theodicy is in complete opposition to the mythology of Olympus. We need, therefore, to be "sufficiently great not to know either hate or envy."[596]

And this is his confession: "I prefer to be a saint in the desert than a whirlwind with thirst for vengeance."[597] At times Nietzsche takes solutions close to Seneca's though he often scorns the Stoics: "The tendency to let oneself be humiliated, robbed, deceived and destroyed could well be the modesty of a god among men."[598] We must, therefore, bear masks: "We present ourselves as being more simple than we are so that we may rest from our equals,"[599] and "we need to have permission from others to have talent."[600] An antidote against envy is love: "With it we frequently try to jump over envy."[601] This though lowers the ideals of love and this is consequent with the champion of the "will to power." The most innovative aspect of Nietzsche's thought on envy is his awareness of the link between envy and morality, particularly when envy becomes resentment producing thus an inversion of values. Thus a passion, originally secret and self-punishing, becomes a transforming agent in our conception of the world. This is the thesis that Scheler will develop even further than its originator.

4. Freud

Sigmund Freud (1856–1939) is nearer to metaphysics than to natural science for his hypothetical, abstract models on the structure and function of the human psyche are his most dominant preoccupations. Psychoanalysis, like Marxism, has become almost a religion.

"After long hesitations and doubts," he writes in the last year of his long life, "we have decided to presuppose the existence of only two basic instincts: eros and the instinct of destruction . . . The goal of the first is to establish at any time larger unities and preserve them. The goal of the second is, on the contrary, to break connections and destroy things . . .. In biological functions both basic instincts combine mutually or they act the one against the other."[602] Obsessed as he was with sexuality, he frequently dealt with love, hate, jealousy, shame, and so forth. From an erotic perspective he was also interested in anguish, melancholy, depression and sadness, among other feelings. And not abandoning his pansexualism he dedicated to envy a few tangential and valuable pages.

The original Freudian thesis is that envy is the source of the social. He does not believe, as W. Trotter held,[603] that the gregarious instinct is something primary, but something derived; it is born "out of the envy the first born feels at the intrusion of his new brother."[604] According to Freud, this "primitive envy" could have been ended by getting rid of the newly born; but since this is not possible, the child is forced to form community with others, and thus "a collective feeling of community is formed that is later on developed further in school."[605]

Is there a categorical imperative in this ethic derived from an impotence to monopolize paternal love? "The first demand of this reactional formation is to treat everybody equally. . . . Since one is not able to be the preferred one, let no one else be either."[606] Our basic impulse to love those who gave us life produces envy, and this originates egalitarian sociability. This, according to Freud, is the autogenesis of the gregarious instinct in man, and other analogous feelings answer a similar mechanism: "Companionship, the spirit of camaradery, etc., are also derived without any doubt from this primary envy."[607]

Is the uneven distribution of property the cause of envy, and in general, of the bad intentions of some men towards others? Freud's answer is a negative response to Marx: "I am not concerned with the economic criticism of the communist system; it is not possible for me to investigate if the suppression of private property is opportune and convincing; but, on the other hand, I am able to recognize as a vain illusion their psychological hypothesis."[608] And which are the reasons? With the suppression of private property "the differences of power and influence"[609] will not disappear; above all, "they would find a substitution in the privileges derived from sexual relations that would become the source of the most intense envy and the most violent hostility among human beings."[610] Freud's pansexualism led him to a radicalization of envy, but not to error. It is highly probable that there will be envious people as long as a woman prefers one man to others.

Abel represents the country, while Cain stands for the city in certain Biblical exegeses. In the country a certain solitude is possible, while in the city sociability is inevitable. From this point of view, society has an envious origin; but it is also like an affective game of chance. Freud does not believe that this constitutes an anecdotic relation; but rather an intrinsic foundation of the political solidarity of envy, and thus his radicalization of an egalitarian pretense that is essentially envious. According to Freud, society is born of the collaboration between eros and the destructive instinct; this is a synthesis of contraries in unstable equilibrium in which envy plays the main role. This deep and provoking step has had no followers in the wide womb of the psychoanalytical school.

5. Unamuno

Miguel de Unamuno (1864–1936) wrote, at times casually, at times with enormous depth, about everything human, and left in his essay *La Envidia Hispana* (1909) and his novel *Abel Sánchez* (1917) a detailed description of envy and hate.[611] Unamuno calls the passion of envy "a psychic morbosity,"[612] a terrible plague,"[613] "an intimate gangrene,"[614] and "deadly cancer" of the human spirit and very specially of "the Spanish soul."[615] He calls envy "the National Spanish Leprosy,"[616] and "the ferment of Spanish social life."[617] Unamuno believes that Spain is the country where the first commandment reads: "Hate thy neighbor as you hate yourself,"[618] and this trait follows the colonizers across the Atlantic: "This our ancestral wound, twin sister of fighting leisure, our grandparents transmitted to the countries of Hispano America, and there it has flourished, its stench in bloom, even more than amongst us."[619] Unamuno's conclusion is apodictic: "We are, collectively, envious people; we Spaniards on this side of the

Atlantic, and you, our descendents on the other shore."[620] He used to call Madrid "Envypolis."

Unamuno, however, acknowledges that envy is a universal fact: "Whoever believes that all his misfortunes are the result of the envy of others is himself envious. Are we not all envious? . . . This is our original sin."[621] He sides with Aristotle affirming that envy is not felt "of the visitor, but of the people of the same village, group, among themselves; not of the older person, of the one from a different generation, but of the friend, the equal. The greatest envy is among brothers . . . Envy, decidedly, is a form of being related to others."[622] There is also an echo of Nietzsche when he asserts that even when an action is criminal, it "frees us from the bad feeling,"[623] that is, from envy and hate. He agrees with Schopenhauer when he writes: "Envy is very subtle and most inventive in finding sweet words and praises,"[624] and "malicious tricks" in order to "level the praise showered on others."[625] These are observations that come out of the experience of life Unamuno had.

Unamuno is very clear in bringing out the causes of envy: "It is born out of spiritual idleness,"[626] "it is the daughter of mental shallowness and of the lack of great intimate projects,"[627] it is the result of "spiritual greed,"[628] and "it is the companion of dogmatism."[629] Spiritual idleness is not for Unamuno some form of quietism or doing nothing at all, for this idleness is compatible with an intense vital activity and serious studying; "an idle intelligence"[630] is not easy to interpret except that for Unamuno any mind is idle that is not occupied as he prescribes. In any case, Unamuno stands alone in many of his assertions, for there is almost unanimity in affirming that envy is a complex psychic phenomenon, among people who contemplate each other, compare, measure and try to overcome felt inferiorities by manipulating facts and values. Unamuno himself, as so often happens through his works, contradicts himself when he mentions as habitual envious people, clerics, scholars, and certain writers, all very intelligent, to a higher or lower degree, but always "intellectually active."

Unamuno follows in the footsteps of the tradition that links Cain—the original envious—with the origin of the city, and thus he generalizes: "Envy was, is and will be the strongest foundation of civilian fraternity."[631] This intuition, with Freudian echoes, precludes the thesis of Schoeck. Finally, Unamuno establishes a political relation when he affirms that "Envy is the mother of democracy,"[632] for "peace and democracy produce, almost necessarily, envy. All democracies are envious."[633] He suggests the motives for such results: idleness and egalitarianism. These give rise to an inability to adjust to inferiorities and difference: the envious "cannot suffer that others distinguish themselves,"[634] and as a consequence they try to bring them down. The demands for egalitarianism from the many to the few takes place in different areas of human acting. Unamuno points out two: politics engaged in the democratic method, and ideology appealing to values already accepted. He is explicit about this latter case: "The origin of any kind of orthodoxy, in religion as well as in art, is envy.'"[635] Unamuno singles out the social effects of envy when he suggests that egalitarian politics and ideology try to erase any form of distinction.

Unamuno's contribution may be summarized by recalling a topic that is as ancient as the statement of Ibn Hazm: "In Spain the wise man is envied with twice as much animosity as in any other country of the world."[636]

6. Scheler

Max Scheler (1874–1928) represents the revindication of the feeling of envy without falling into an irrational vitalism. He cultivates all philosophical disciplines with a special dedication to emotive and moral life.[637] He deals with envy thematically in his book *On Resentment and the Moral Judgement of Values.*[638] According to Scheler values are apprehended in a direct manner, not through reason, but through pure feeling. In this way affective life, so disdained by the intellectualisms of every period, is raised to the forefront of philosophical interest.

Envy, according to Scheler, "rises from a feeling of impotence towards achieving an end by the mere fact that someone else already possesses it."[639] This is a passion that "has a determined object,"[640] and which "disappears when the good I envy becomes mine,"[641] and which is "more spiritual"[642] than others, like anger. There are degrees in the feeling of envy: "The most impotent envy is at the same time the most fearsome";[643] thus "existential envy, that is the envy inspired by a person not so much by what he has, but by what he is intrinsically."[644]

Scheler places envy among the "emotions and affects that are normal by themselves and belong to the essence of human nature."[645] Does this mean that envy deserves a moral qualification of neutral or positive? Neither; Scheler denies that envy may be counted as one of the "forces that develop civilization," for "envy does not tighten but relaxes the acquisitive will";[646] it is rather a "counterimpulse"[647] that reaches out against positive values. How can we, then explain that envy belongs to nature while it is an impulse with no positive function? The philosopher does not answer this important question.

Envy, according to Scheler, is one of those emotions that when not discharged but systematically repressed, produces a "psychic intoxication"[648] known as resentment, a term coined by Nietzsche and which Scheler reworks completely. There is repression "where there is no place for a moral victory (as in vengeance, for example, or true forgiveness), or when there is no adequate action or expression of emotion in external provocations, for example, insults, waving of fists, etc."[649] This analysis, which resembles the analysis by Freud, presents serious difficulties. A moral victory would be to achieve what one envies; but if this fails, where would catharsis be in envy? Scheler does not solve this problem. Would something like a curse or the evil eye take place? Experience fails to show that such emotional discharges free us from envy. The outcome would then be that if envy is connatural and it remains usually repressed, then resentment in the envious is inevitable. Scheler does not reach this conclusion, but it does flow easily from his premises.

The main thesis of Scheler is that envy affects ethics. Any form of resentment that becomes intoxicated with envy renders the individual incapable of achieving the pursued value. It is then that, according to Scheler, a chain of reasoning takes place through which what is envied is denied any value, then whatever is related to that value is also devalued, and, finally, "a universal denial of all value"[650] is reached. The resentful proceeds to "injure, lower, diminish"[651] that which cannot but make him feel impotent, and this leads him to deny objective values, and to change their hierarchy. This mental manipulation creates false moralities. Scheler believed that some of the wrong ethical teachings of his period, "egalitarianism,"[652] "universal philanthropy,"[653] "the subordination of vital values to utilitarian ones,"[654] and "democracy"[655] were the result of this resentment. This "overturning of all values,"characteristic of modern times, has its origin in the "victory of the less vital, the pariahs of human kind, and resentment is its root."[656]

Though Scheler does not make the claim, it flows from his premises that the emotions derived from resentment, envy, and vengeance are the two most important. Envy is to be condemned not because it is self-punishing and antisocial, but because, according to Scheler, envy subverts the moral order in the individual and in society.

7. Klein

Melanie Klein (1882–1960) is a heterodox Freudian, specializing in child psychoanalysis. Her extensive works are not very systematic and her terminology imprecise, thus to present her thought is tantamount to an interpretation. According to this author, anxiety in children, particularly depression, emerges from a "primary disassociation,"[657] or subconscious contradiction that occurs in the first three or four months of life. In this early disassociation we find envy, an emotional phenomenon, which in this manner gains the clinical character of being radical and causal. She defines envy as "the annoying feeling against another person who has and enjoys something desirable, the envious feeling being that of taking that good or harming that person."[658] It is not, therefore, a passive state of mind, but rather a "destructive dynamism."[659] Thus, the author puts it together with "hate."[660] This concept of envy is closer to passion—in its traditional sense—than to emotion.

The main contribution of Melanie Klein is her formulation of the hypothesis of the origin of envy. According to this author, envy consists in a process that takes place in the subconscious of the new born when her mother's breast is missing, the "first envied object."[661] "This frustration leads to the fancy that milk and love are deliberately denied or postponed for the child's own benefit. Inherent to envy is not only the desire to possess, but also a powerful urge to ruin the pleasure others might have from the desired object."[662] One wishes to enjoy one's food and also destroy it. This paradox supposes a schizoid situation that breeds bad conscience: "One of the deepest sources of guilt is always linked to envy of the feeding breasts and the feeling of having ruined their goodness as a consequence of the attacks of envy."[663] The author suggests that "envy is perceived as the greatest of all sins for it attacks and harms the good object, fountain of life."[664] In sum, envy, as a conflict not yet overcome, and as a guilty feeling, is the cause on which we must work in order to remedy child anxiety.[665]

Which are the defenses against envy? The author suggests that they are "infinite,"[666] like the "idealization . . . and exultation"[667] of what is envied. She also suggests the contrary: "devaluation."[668] We may also "inspire envy in others,"[669] or "avoid the contact of people."[670] But the most efficient therapy is to promote "gratitude, for it contributes to happiness, frees from resentment and envy,"[671] and inspires the opposite impulse, "love."[672]

This theory is a psychoanalytic curiosity of little exegetic value. In the first place, the unconscious processes in children three and four months old cannot be proven and cannot be deduced from subsequent behavior. Secondly, it is not methodologically right to project onto the healthy population certain exceptional situations of child pathology. Thirdly, for those children not raised at their mother's breasts, would one then have to transfer Klein's analysis of the maternal breasts with all her sexual connotations and asides, which has been omitted not to complicate the issue, to the feeding bottle? Fourthly, how can a three or four month old mind conceive of the complex idea that the mother withholds her milk for the benefit of the child? Fifthly, if envy happens because we have a weak ego, and everyone envies, would we have to conclude that psychic normalcy does not exist and that it cannot be defined? And finally, the gratuitous and unbelievable hypothesis of Klein on the origin of envy hardly explains anything about the development and function of the envious feeling.

8. Schoeck

Helmut Schoeck (1923), professor of sociology at Munich, is the author of *Der Neid. Eine Theory der Gesellschaft* (1966). In 1979 he published five more critical essays on socialist egalitarianism[673] where he takes a political position derived from his previous critical stance.

Schoeck provides a panoramic survey of literature and thought, above all of ethnology, to reach the conclusion that envy is a "universal [*allgegenwart*]"[674] fact, and that the claimed social harmony of primitive groups, like the illusory golden age, is a "myth."[675] Envy, he sustains, is connatural to the human species: "The biological data of our existence make it very improbable that anyone could develop without the possibility of envy."[676] But this extensive and plural claim does not make it possible to be very systematic. In order to build the doctrine of this author it is necessary to select sentences spread over all his works and, overcoming certain paradoxes, be able to articulate them in a coherent body.

On the one hand, Schoeck affirms "that the envious man is the negation of the foundations of any society,"[677] and that envy "of others is always, by nature, an unending, negative and unproductive feeling."[678] This is the traditional idea of the antisocial character of envy. But on the other hand Schoeck affirms that "envy cannot be considered only as a negative phenomenon,"[679] for at times "it is an incentive [*Triebfeder*] for positive accomplishments,"[680] since "only envy makes possible any kind of coexistence";[681] "without envy society cannot be organized."[682]

How does the author justify such a novel thesis? He only presents in passing an argument that he does not develop. He presupposes that "any form of association rests on certain automatic social controls,"[683] among which he mentions reporting to the police in a more or less anonymous way, or to the IRS. This "mutual and spontaneous supervision of some citizens over others, this social control, owes its efficacy to the envious impulse [*Neid faktor*]."[684]

The solution, therefore, is not to suppress envy, for it is inevitable, but to "domesticate and channel it."[685] And how is this done? Schoeck only mentions it in passing. We must "control envy as much as possible and divert it towards those values that are decisive for the survival of society"[686] but he does not mention these values. A remedy against envy is to "disarm it with concepts that are either religious or that rationalize inequality."[687] We must, finally, mediate "social inhibitions [*Hemmung*]"[688] of envy, for "it is not possible to imagine any-kind of organized existence if we are unable to suppress to a great extent the envy of everyone towards everyone."[689] To what degree are we going to control, disarm, inhibit, and suppress envy? The author does not describe the larger part of that envious impulse that we are supposed to control, or is he able to limit "the minimum of necessary envy"[690] that may be allowed.

Without determining prerequisites, Schoeck's program suffers from excessive imprecision. His thesis comes down to this: envy cannot be eliminated, it is very negative; but a certain dose is necessary for the operation of the mutual and spontaneous controls that society requires. Except for the universal fact of envy, all the other extremes of this project are too ambiguous and very problematic. We will deal with them in the second part of this book.

Among the positive contributions of Schoeck the most important is, agreeing with Scheler, his analysis of the envious origin of egalitarianism, socialism and democracy. "The utopian desire of an egalitarian society cannot have any other origin than the incapacity of its members to deal with their own envy and with the supposed envy of the less fortunate members of that society."[691] With the exception of Marxism and some socialist groups, no other movement has traveled as far in order to ground the new society upon the virtue of envy."[692] "It would be a miracle if the democratic political process would ever renounce to the use of the envious motivation [*Neid motiv*]."[693] "The cultivation of this feeling [envy] is characteristic of the "agitator" or the "the engineer of envy."[694]

We find that Schoeck provides more interesting insights in his scholia and in his information than in his main thesis.

X. Conclusion

It may be deduced from this essential historical recapitulation that there is general agreement on two points: the envious condition of human nature and the radical evil of the feeling of envy. Some authors point out also the antisocial character of envy. It is, however, surprising that the literature about such a universal and negative tendency is so scarce. There are few writers who have dealt with the problem and, in general, their observations are brief, isolated, or marginal; quite often they only repeat topical ideas. This reticence on the part of the theoreticians shows that there is a resistance in the human species to face openly this generalized tendency to envy. It is like a specific modesty that makes it more difficult to clarify the question and remove the impulse. Human kind has reacted towards envy with more ignorance and concealment than towards sex. Such an ethical problem, which has such extraordinary inroads into individual and collective happiness has habitually been dealt with hypocritically and almost in secret. The main methodological conclusion to be reached at this level of the debate is that up to now there has hardly been any will to debate this issue. It is, perhaps, for this reason that we find ourselves so distant from the ideal that Fray Luis de Leon chased so eagerly: "neither envied nor envious."[695] This is, therefore, a fallow field in need of energetic, intellectual seeding.

B. THE ANALYSIS

I. The Problem

Humans have at their disposal three basic systems to guide them in the world: the instinctive or conditioned, the emotional or sentimental, and the logical or rational. They share the first two with other species and the last is, on this planet, their exclusive property. The origin of emotions, an obviously inferior one, is their first qualifying note. Feelings show, among others, two fundamental deficiencies: they may confuse or even blind the discursive faculties and they supply rudimentary, mixed, hardly communicable, and even false information about reality.

The poet Alexander Pope, giving a metaphorical, popular version of an idea that the Greeks borrowed from the wisdom of the East, wrote that reason is the helm while passions are the winds of the soul. It is evident that many times we reason, led by love or hate, fear or anguish, that is, by our feelings; but this is not enough to deduce that the mind remains static and inactive if it is not moved by feelings. The truth of the matter is that thought is a continuous activity that the impassive spirit does not stop, but rather liberates and purifies. Impassiveness is the ideal climate for the advance of reason.

To choose from among several opinions only based on the likes and dislikes they initially inspire in us, that is, to be guided only by affectation, is usually a mistake. Feelings give us very inadequate information about reality and are useless to predict, with a minimum of approximation. The emotional interpretation of reality is so imprecise and subjective that, in practice, it cancels itself as a cognitive formula.

In their daily lives, both males and females are still predominantly affective; when they occasionally become intellectual, they use myths, ideologies, topics and passwords—the famous prejudices or "idola" of Bacon—with such repetition that their rationality is minimal. Pure reason finds refuge with certain exceptional moments in the activity of a few who become the true active subjects of the rationalizing process that history uncovers. The formal "logical" existence of the larger part of humanity, besides being erratic, reduces itself to the consumption of other peoples' reasonings, and this is already a notable progress in relation to primitive people. Even though both are rationally extremely poor, there is a hopeful distance between the archaic chants of the shaman and the contemporary slogans of the demagogues. If biological and cultural evolution continue, as is very likely, the emotional life will be taken over by the logical life and thus humans will come nearer to the sempiternal ideal of the pure spirit.

Envy is a feeling and therefore it is something that does not belong to the higher level; it is, besides, such a universal fact that it has been proclaimed to constitute an instinctive inclination of the human species. Envy, however, has become one of the most rationalized of the affective phenomena, such that it rather resembles, with more refinement and complexity, a mental phenomenon. But it is not, as a consequence, a feeling that is logically and vitally more valuable than the others. On the contrary, it is one of the most negative feelings, for the one who feels it and for the one who inspires it. This relative rationality and this complete malignancy show that this is a phenomenon that hides jealously and that has been missed by the sciences. For hundreds of thousands of years *homo sapiens*, with a strange mixture of fear and shame, has taken for granted and avoided dealing with envy, unable to make a decision and face it with the *logos*. This is what we are trying to do now.

II. Conceptualization

1. Definition, Origin, Typology

Envy is neither wanted nor known: it is felt. It is neither volition nor knowledge: it is feeling. Feeling is an ambiguous stage of pleasure or displeasure. Envy belongs to a group of feelings that are painful and are intentional, since it is a displeasure provoked by something from the outside. It is not a localized physical pain, nor a psychosomatic emotion or intense commotion; it is a general displeasure, weighty, durable, and its corporal reflection is hardly noticeable or perceptible. What in its cause distinguishes envy from other unpleasant feelings?

From the time of the classics it has been said that envy is pain at the good of others. Aristotle himself mentions those goods [τά ἀγαθά] that, like riches, incite envy. But he is not quite accurate. No one envies an abandoned treasure; one simply desires it. For something to be envied it must have two conditions: it must be valuable and it must belong to someone else. This "belong to someone else" is essential: there is no envy without an ownership. And why is it necessary that the good have an owner? Because what is envied is not the particular good, but the joy that it normally carries with it to its owner. The preoccupation of the envious is the happiness of his neighbor. But not all forms of happiness are envied: it is also necessary that the envious person misses the extra happiness that the other enjoys. Envy requires a relative emptiness of happiness and finally the acknowledgement that it cannot be filled in an acceptable space of time. Envy is the pain one feels in the presence of someone else's happiness, a superior, desired, inaccessible, and unreachable happiness.

This lean phenomenological description of envy reveals that we are not dealing here with a state that, like hunger, is motivated from the inside. It is not an innate instinct or impulse: it is an intentional feeling one reaches after a rather complex mental process made up of judgment of fact and value plus reasoning. Let us reconstruct this logical course, more or less conscious, ordinarily tacit, which usually degenerates into a habit and that may even become an almost reflex reaction.

Our starting point is the evaluation of an exterior fact: a quality, a position, an inheritance. If that value belongs to a person it is taken for granted that it provides that person happiness. The next step is a comparison that leads to the discovery that one is or one has less than that other person. It is not difficult to measure a hierarchical difference or quantifiable resource; but this is not our case, but rather it is the pleasure carried with it. How does one measure the unevenness of happiness? Not objectively, for everyone is happy in his or her own way and there is no doubt that greater power or greater riches do not necessarily carry greater happiness. What usually happens is that the subject takes the place of the other, and reaches the conclusion that in such a hypothetical situation he or she would be happier. There is an artificial mental substitution in order to formulate such value judgment. It is also possible that the subject might feel so unhappy that any supposed happiness of someone else might appear to him superior. In both cases there is an awareness of an inferior happiness and a relative scarcity in relation to other people. This opinion may move the subject to make a greater effort to reach an analogous position: this is emulation. But it is possible that, despite this strong desire, the subject may feel incapable of reaching such a position.

This incapacity may be subjective, if it involves the recognition of a personal ineptitude, or objective, if the good that someone else's happiness produces is not repeatable or transferable, like the color of one's eyes. When such impotent inferiority cannot be assimilated, the result is unhappiness. This painful feeling at a supposed superior happiness of another is envy.

What is the cause of envy? Adler states that it is the will to power. A child is by nature an organic and functional being inferior to the adult. This fact, increased at times by family and academic relations, creates a feeling of inferiority that gives as a result an impulse of contrary sign, the will to power. An adult who has not been able to overcome this infantile inferiority complex will remain diminished in his mental capacities; and if, on the other hand, his desire for domination is not tempered by a feeling of human communion, this adult will turn out proud, greedy, hateful, jealous, and envious. "Where there is thirst for power and superiority, [it is] frequently the case that envy will appear." This description by Adler, though partially insightful, is not accurate to the facts.

The desire to neutralize the uneasiness at one's own inferiority by reaching for the standard of the best is emulation. But envy aims at suppressing the pain caused by our own frustration in bringing down the other person. Emulation moves to lift oneself, envy to break other people. The envious one does not find dominant the desire to be more, but rather to make the other less; there is no will to improve, but rather to level all. The prototype of the *Wille zur Macht* is the Nietzschean superman, the impetuous, spontaneous, defiant, and creative, while the envious is fearful, hypocritical, a flatterer, sterile. The will to power does not cause envy, but when such a feeling searches for freedom it orients feelings towards political values and leads to envy of particular social positions.

Not all envy is grounded in the will to power, nor in an inferiority complex, for the sufferer of an inferiority complex does not feel inferior to someone about something, but to the majority in almost everything; he is not a person, as opposed to the envious one, who finds himself occasionally in a subordinate situation, but rather someone who considers himself in a state and constitution of inferiority. It is not the same to be substantially inferior or to find oneself accidentally in a position of inferiority. Whoever suffers from an inferiority complex lacks self-impulse and tends to be shy and resigned, while the envious person tends towards despair and resentment. Envy does not come to life out of a desire to dominate but rather out of a desire to survive.

Is envy generated by the limitation of material goods? Our planet does not hold one single infinite material good: some are scarce, like gold; others abundant, like air. The criterion therefore cannot be absolute, but relative and in such a case envy would provoke material goods to be less available. But this proportion does not hold; for example, something as rare as jewelry is less envied than something as common as superior authority. It is, however, true that there is no envy if there is no lack of something, and this for the ultimate reason, among others, that everything is limited, or to be more technical, because contingency is almost a transcendental quality, a characteristic of everything mundane with no exception. But, on the other hand, it is not true that where there is scarcity there is envy.

The essential condition for envy to arise is not an objectivity of scarcity, as so many think, but rather a subjective inability to have. There are scarce goods, like gold, and nonetheless they are made available everywhere to everyone. In the majority of cases the problem of the envious person has nothing to do with the fact that some good is more or less limited, but rather that he wants it and it is practically unreachable, not because of scarcity but rather for a lack of the necessary capacity to obtain it. There is, however, a possible archetype in which desire and unreachability are both contingent on scarcity: the essential goods of a primitive society. In the paleolithic family, women, old people, children, and sick people depended for their lives on the game brought to them by the hunter. Within such a circle it is not inconceivable that while some took care of their hunger, others would torture themselves thinking that the happy situation of some was the cause of their own hunger and even their death. Could one trace in these oblique and impotent looks the first case of the envious, evil eye? We cannot exclude the possibility that the original and more frequent feeling of envy may be found in the archaic limitation of one's own primary goods or their consumption by others. This would constitute a primordial envy or uneasiness at survival that was threatened by the enjoyment by others of an indispensable and limited good. But this possible hypothesis, that I consider the most probable, does not allow us to establish a necessary causal link between limitation and envy in those early circumstances and even less so in the present ones. The true link is established through unreachability.

Is it possible to sketch a typology of envy? Yes, in a schematic manner. Attending to its object, envy may be existential, social, or patrimonial, if a person is envied because of his qualities, position, or possessions. Existential envy is grounded on the conviction that the other is happier because he is more intelligent, energetic, capable, elegant, etc. The envy is almost existential, caused by qualities that are not congenital; but they are so intimately embodied within the nature of the envious person that they become a part of his own makeup, like a habit—thus sanctity and some other capacities. Existential envy is rather uncommon for it tends to explain unnatural inferiorities through destiny or chance and this favors a fatalistic attitude and therefore the resigned acceptance of the adverse imbalance. But if existential envy is not directed or deactivated through some form of reasoning it becomes exceedingly rigid and stubborn due to the strength and immobility of its object, and it is very damaging for it affects the very essence of the envious person.

Social envy is grounded in the belief that others are happier because of the position they occupy in the community due to their privileged birth or their promotions. In the first case, it is a kind of envy bordering on existential envy because it is a received envy and partially shares in the characteristics of the former. In the second case, it is an acquired envy because of efficacious acts and for this reason similar to patrimonial envy; it is flexible and less lasting. Social envy may be collected and aimed at a group, generally against a social class or social level. In such a case it may be shared, as we shall soon see, and tacit, or express associations are formed of people who coincide in envying the same superiors as, for example, the bourgeois parties against the aristocratic. All forms of envy are political agglutinates, but social envy is so by nature.

Patrimonial envy is grounded in the belief that the other is happier because he is the owner of a larger amount of goods. Money is here the predominant good for it allows the acquisition of other goods, though not all, for some are *extra commercium.* What cannot be acquired generates a particularly afflictive and chronic feeling. Patrimonial envy is primary, felt daily, and is more common.

Concrete envious feelings are mixed because, in fact, there is a tight connection between what one is, the place one occupies, and what one owns, and also because the envious person establishes mental connections between being, power, and having. However, the emphasis is always on one of the three basic dimensions of an enviable objective.

In its origin envy proceeds from pride, from the will to power, or from greed. Pride underlies personal inferiority and gives rise to existential envy. Egocentricity is less common among the excellent than among the mediocre and may appear as very radical among the lowest levels. This is an endemic form of envy in certain collectivities that, like the Spanish one at certain periods, overvalued dignity and arrogance.

Social envy is born from the desire for power. The desire to climb makes any imbalance painful in the hierarchy of nobility, or in governing, or in authority at all levels. There is pure social envy in some exceptional polititians, but it is joined to the existential envy and even more so to the patrimonial one, in which case we are dealing with a desire for power in order to possess.

Patrimonial envy rises out of greed or appetite for things and is the most vulgar and most encouraged by the modern consumer society. An unbridled publicity unleashes demands that might be possibly satisfied and also those that might not be satisfied, and this generates an impotence that becomes the launching pad of envy. The standardization of products and activities levels all desires and, since vocations and tastes do not disappear, it concentrates the demand on the same goods and this promotes comparisons and makes more obvious the balance of inferiority. For example, if someone has their dominant desire directed to a car and compares their own car to a more modern or luxurious one, they feel a deeper inferiority than the person who compares two objects of dissimilar ends, like his tennis racquet with his neighbor's violin. Egalitarian powers, characteristics of monopolistic capitalisms (and in particular those of Marxism or of the state), tend to unify supply and demand, while not necessarily leveling consumption; on the other hand, egalitarians simplify all models and make the differences more obvious and envious. Qualitative uniformity in the market of communist countries has awakened the most elemental envy, the quantitative patrimonial envy, extending it to the vast field of products for primary needs.

Depending on the number of subjects, we may distinguish between individual or private envy, and shared or public envy. This last requires a certain degree of communication and declared or covert leadership. Public envy cannot be organized nor disseminated without a certain amount of exteriority but since the feeling cannot be acknowledged it needs a covert legitimization that usually appears as an egalitarian ideology, with charity or justice as fronts. While individual envy may be simply secret, collective envy must be hypocritical.

2. Axiophile Envy

It is said that no one envies adversity but goodness: virtue, riches, success. Plutarch expresses this with a seductive metaphor: one envies "the shiny [λαηπρός]." No one doubts such an affirmation and yet it is highly problematic. If envy is a painful feeling, how can it be produced by some good? The good—that is, what one desires due to the pleasure it brings—how can it also be disagreeable? It would be a contradiction that is not resolved by supposing that the envious is a kind of moral invert who feels repulsion for the good and thus he does not envy what produces unhappiness.

The truth is that the formal object of envy is not a good; it is, rather, the unaccepted impotence to be able to achieve the superior happiness of others. What generates the feeling of pain is clearly negative and a lack: an impossibility, an inferiority, a frustration, an absence of hope. One does not envy any good as such but only insofar as it belongs to somebody else. Envy does not spring from the aversion to some good but rather from the contrary, from the apprehension of something valuable—fortune, beauty, power—that is vehemently desired but that one is unable to achieve. The envious person neither ignores nor rejects values; just the contrary: he watches out for them and spies on them, he desires them, and he is so oversensitive to them that he suffers just imagining the pleasure they bring to their present owner, and which he lacks. It is not true that where there is good there is envy, but it is too true that where there is envy there is the apprehension of something valuable. In this sense envy is axiophilia, but resentment is not.

When a feeling grows, because it is self-induced or internally developed, and it is not greed leading to some kind of action or is not overcome through reasoning, resentment follows. We are dealing here with the squaring of hate, vengeance, and, above all, envy. This species of intimate, emotional multiplication is one of the more complex affections of the human psyche and, therefore, it is more common among the intelligent and complex than among the stupid and simple.

The most characteristic features of resentment are its obsessive insistence, its interiority almost exempt of somatic reflexes, the intensity of one's own impotence, and, most especially, the complex method one discovers in order to survive and eliminate it. Let us break down the different moments of this maneuver in the chosen archetype of envy. The phenomenological analysis made it appear that the envious adventure begins with a judgment of value about some good: "The enjoyment of *that*—quality, position, possession—brings happiness to someone else." Now then, the complex mental operations of the resentful one consist in breaking down this initial judgment that started the process by an energetic manipulation of judgments about values. The recipe consists of negating that *that* may be valuable. For example, to feel envy towards someone because he is loved, one need only convince oneself that to be an object of love is not valuable. This attack to the root brings down the whole argumentation of the envious person. But the machinations of the resentful person do not stop here; he needs to explore his success. If to be loved is not valuable or good, is it simply neutral or bad? The autonomous dynamism of such an energetic psychic position and the powerful mental inertia of the effort already carried out to negate some value propel resentment towards a final movement consisting of the affirmation that *that* is a counter-value; that is, that to be the object of love entails, as an example, oppression and selfishness. This would be the final, schematic proposal: "Whoever enjoys what I lack is guilty because his assumed good is an evil." Nietzsche called this desperate, potent, and last measure *Umwertung*, a neologism that literally translates as "transvaloration." In its pure sense it means to run around or "turn inside out" a value, denying it and affirming the contrary; it is an inversion of values.

With this decision of extreme logical violence, resentment achieves two purposes. The first dissolves envy, for how can one be more happy if he possesses a counter-value? He must be a poor soul, worthy of compassion or scorn. The second and more advanced purpose is one of vindication: "those who declare as valuable that which makes me unduly unhappy because I lack it are guilty of proclaiming a counter-value." In this way the envious person transforms the exemplar into a scandal and the envied into an outlaw; thus the old self-punishment is turned into the punishment of another.

This inversion of values is not only efficient in the case of envy, but it is also applicable to all states of inferiority through bad conscience. The guilt feeling at the transgression of the norm becomes a satisfaction at the fulfillment of duty through the theoretical inversion of the precept. And simultaneously, the tacit or expressed judge who appeared so on account of his assumed exemplarity is thus reduced to the condition of a convict. As, for example, the one who, on account of his assumed meekness, makes me feel guilty of a supposed vice of anger and despotism, is condemned by me and my moral inversion of cowardice and weakness. The ideal limit of resentment is to make the other believe that whatever he considered virtuous is really depraved behavior. This is the culmination of the inversion of values; as when in the hypothesis of resentment, the one envying the rich is made to feel guilty for not being poor, and asks everyone's forgiveness for his superiority.

But the result seldom succeeds in its double purpose of liberation from a pain suffered and of revenge for a damage caused. In fact, the one feeling resentment never succeeds in fully convincing himself that what is valuable is a counter-value, and this doubt obstructs the emancipatory operation. Besides, he does not succeed in convincing everyone, including his victims, that those judged exemplary by everyone are really perverse. It is not easy, therefore, to exit from resentment on account of its peculiar dialectic; because of it, one stays resentful forever.

In summary: envy is pain through axiophilia, and resentment is an effort to catharsis through axiophobia. Envy is the counter-affection of an unsure argumentation, and resentment is the refutation of a painful reasoning through the inversion of its premise. The mental exchange of resentment doubles envy with complicity and consumes a very large amount of interior energy.

3. Hidden Envy

One may admit to pride, avarice, lust, anger, gluttony, and laziness and one may even boast of them. There is only one capital sin no one admits to: envy. This is the dark, hidden, eternally masked sin. One tries to hide it from others with multiple disguises; its symbol ought to be a mask. The envious person avoids seeing this emotion as it is and buries it in the subconscious or rationalizes it in order to distort it. People conceal their envy and, furthermore, disown it.

What is the cause of this cover up? To say that it is an atavistic habit would not answer the question but would place it at our origins and there we would have to restate the question and solve it. Since all instincts perform some function, what is the answer then? Even if envy were not a conscious reaction but an acquired habit or a congenital tendency, would the question still persist as to why it is kept in hiding with such general obstinacy? The silence surrounding envy is not an undecipherable enigma, it has a clear though never before formulated etiology. The envious person cloaks this emotion for two main reasons, one technical, the other moral.

The first is a tactical motivation. What is envied is usually inaccessible, something that cannot be duplicated or transferred, like talent or beauty. When we deal with something that is interchangeable, like money, the envious person feels envy because he considers himself impotent to obtain it. For this reason envy does not cease unless the envied person loses his money. Only then does the cause of envy cease. This outcome may be left to chance, but if the envious wants to participate actively in the process, efficacy advises that he lie in ambush. Social usages allow only for the dispossession of those goods that are unjustly held back. Envy, however, is suffering caused by the goods of others because others own them, not because they enjoy them unjustly; for this would not be envy but indignation, something quite different, and an emotion that may be externalized and is considered to be noble. If envy were made public then any action taken to remove its cause would be deemed socially illegitimate. To publicize such an emotion would automatically disqualify the intention of satisfying it and cancel it. In order to work against his victim under the best conditions the envious person must watch his feelings and pretend to have others that are more acceptable and effective. The most frequent strategy is for the envious person to disguise himself as charitable or just. This pretense is a tactical must, for if the secret were made public it would become neutralized in practice.

In all the other vices of the soul publicity does not deprive them of authority and may even be an asset. The proud person sees his distance from others increase when they realize his pride. People stop asking from the avaricious person. The fame of the sensuous person is a complementary lure. People become afraid of the irritable person. The voracious sybarite is a stimulus to his possible hosts. And the lazy person is in demand only when no effort is expected. Publicity is the Achilles' tendon of envy: when it is uncovered it loses its sting.

The other reason explains not only the secret of envy but also its self-deception. An interior judgment condemns the envious person and embarrasses him. But why does not this bad conscience occur with other vices? Because the envious person does not have excuses here. In all the other capital sins there is a positive dimension that also partially serves as an excuse. The proud person has true qualities and self-confidence; the avaricious person has ambition, austerity, and discipline for saving; the sensuous person has tenderness and vitality; the irritable person has strength and courage; the glutton has health and prodigality; the idle is elitist and ingenious. But envy does not have, even tangentially, a single valuable note. Envy is totally mean and negative as much for the active subject as for the passive one; it is pure evil for there is no justification whatsoever in suffering at the happiness of others and enjoying their misfortunes. Envy is a perverse emotion without the least mixture of goodness. The depth of one's undeclinable moral conscience does not permit seeing oneself as objectively bad, except in relation to some past action and then it is accompanied by repentance. Envy, besides, is not an act that ends once it is executed; it is rather a continous action, a continued anemic state that we need to try to distort mentally while we are in it, in order to escape the repulsion people feel at seeing themselves acting perversely *in actu*. The absolute evil of envy is the ethical reason why whoever suffers it must keep it hidden even from himself.

To hide envy is not just a simple psychological datum, it is rather a human decision that results from a complex rational process. From this perspective it is easy to see envy as originating through a reasoning process rather than from an elemental instinct, like sensuality or aggression. One does not envy because the genetic code so dictates. Envy is the most intellectual of our emotions, not only because its hormonal cradle is lacking, but also because, despite its false premises, its origin is in reason. It is born out of a syllogism, and other syllogisms induce us to cover it up, and thus it is found, like reason, intermingled with sophisms.

Such a cerebral passion has been able to survive, almost untouched, all kinds of moral admonitions; but it may tumble down if confronted systematically with conceptual criticism.

4. Confusing Envy

Envy cannot be made public but such airtight silence does not make it an emotion with purely internal results. The envious person is moved to undertake certain maneuvers to reduce or suppress his assumed inferiority in happiness. But since this operation must resist detection, the passion must be covered up with techniques that lead to confusion.

The most passive and cautious technique is silence: the envious pretends to ignore the goods, the position, or the qualities of the envied person. If confronted with them he pretends ignorance, surprise, or lack of interest. It is not true that he may erase the envied person from his mind by an energetic act of the will, rather, while having him present, he pretends not to know of his existence. In the womb of minorities the shared envy is usually translated into conspiracies of silence: *nec nominetur in vobis*. There are a large number of thinkers and artists to whom their contemporaries have denied not only their recognition but even their disagreements. It is an attempt at elimination by spiritual ostracism, a persecution by omission, the most hypocritical of all; it is envy disguised as contempt. Envious silence is the art of destroying the self.

If due to objective or subjective reasons silence is not possible, the envious then becomes hypocritical by underlying and multiplying the negative and making marginal or simply omitting the positive. Nothing human is perfect and therefore one suffers from insufficiencies. With an extraordinary discriminatory subtlety the envious overlooks what is done well and rummages for what is lacking: he finds intellectual mediocrity in athletes, physical weakness in geniuses, aesthetic insensibility in scientists, lack of knowledge in artists, extravagance in innovators, vulgarity in traditionalists, and so on. A pejorative intention covers all his judgments: if thought is deep it is obscure, if true it is dull, if brilliant it is an exaggeration, if devastating it is sophistic, if convincing it is dialectical, if exact it is incomplete, if beautiful it is not rigorous, and so on. And when there is no alternative but to admit to some merit then there is still comparison with the ideal, to which it should or could have arrived. This is called maximalism, an antihistorical attitude which is always unreasonable and unjust. The envious hypercriticism is the art of reducing in size what is great.

The next step is the attitude *ad hominem:* the work might be more or less good but the author leaves much to be desired or is simply to be despised. But what if the envied person is not vulnerable, might he not have a defective ancestor, a brother who is a rascal, an unfaithful wife, or a son who is a scoundrel? By discrediting the author or his intimate surroundings the critic pretends to socialize his work and, above all, undermine his well-being so that the felt inferiority in happiness becomes even more so in misfortune. Once the envious has achieved the misfortunes of El Cid, or Cervantes, or Quevedo, the conquest of Valencia, or *Don Quijote* or *El Buscón* are of less consequence, for they are no longer goods for the happiness of others but potentially his own. The envious defamation is the art of debasing excellence.

Beyond this there is still slander, a fraudulent invention of perverse behavior. This is the most risky of the confusing techniques, but the envious prefers to be called slanderous rather than envious. If he is not able to postpone, lower, or accuse he will substitute the actual good with an imaginary evil. Silence denies the existence of the envied, hypercriticism denies value, defamation underlines the defective, but slander is the invention of servility. These are the four cardinal roads that, under the pretext of rigor, transform the other's superiority into insignificance, imperfection, deficiency, or perversity.

These tactics point out the refined astuteness of the envious. We are able to see from this perspective that this is a trained feeling and a catharsis of extraordinary complexity and subtlety. Neither its input nor output are spontaneous or elemental as all instinctive emotions are, but rather they are complex and elaborate as all superior functions of humans are. The maturation of such an emotion and the course of its unfolding reactions point to a high degree of rationalization.

The practice of confusing methods creates mental habits that turn against the envious. What starts as an intention to deform results in a deformed mind. There are envious people who can only see what is broken, corrupt, false, and reach a point from which they are unable to return not because of malice but because of invincible inertia. They are simply spellbound. Finally, the envious loses all sense of reality; he can enjoy almost nothing for he stumbles over what is valuable while he is consumed by curiosity for what is negative. Envy ends up imposing an acute intellectual myopia and a selective inverted ethic, the root of a growing frustration, disenchantment, and misfortune. Not everyone who is bitter is envious; but omnivorous envy leads to bitterness and isolation. Lastly, the self-confusing action of envy is an intellectual self-punishment that brings with it an affective displeasure.

In summary, the envious is a mediator who tries to set up covering screens and deforming mirrors between the envied and others, and in the end, between himself and his surroundings, losing thus all objectivity and distancing himself from the world. Envy, insofar as it is confusing, tends to misinform, draw caricatures, isolate; is biased and antisocial; it is an emotion with very little intellectual effectiveness; instead of bringing light and interpretation, it darkens, falsifies, and distances reality.

5. Universal Envy

Following the rebellion of the angels and original sin which, in a certain way, was envy of God, Genesis narrates the first crime committed by Cain who envied his brother Abel. This old narrative is evidence, in symbolic terms, that envy starts with the origin of the human species. Moralists in all periods of time have testified to the universality of envy, and the same has been done, since the last century, by sociologists. Envy is omnipresent and ubiquitous.

What is the reason for such universality? It has been said it was due to a *motus*, an impulse or instinct, that now is called behavior control. If envy were an instinct, it would be simple, congenital, spontaneous, stereotyped, determined, functional, permanent, necessary, intentional, and able to perform within a vacuum in order to liberate its immanent tension. But we have already seen that envy implies a complex logical process and hence a high degree of rationalization. Besides, it is acquired, reasoned out, appears in several forms, unleashes under diverse stimuli, is negative, temporal, may be avoided, and requires an object. It is a behavior that cannot be reduced to instinct and therefore the explanation must be different.

The cases for the universality of envy are not biological, but intellectual and we need not look for them in our vital operations, but in our mental ones. Within the logical process previous to feeling there is a decisive point of inflection: the comparison of the envious with the envied. This interpersonal contrast is exclusive to humans. Each one of us needs to have an idea of ourselves and, when we live in society, this idea is built through comparison, principally with our neighbors. This contrast allows us to know if we are tall or short, strong or weak, ugly or handsome, intelligent or stupid, etc. And while we take measure, since there are not two people who are equal, we also measure in relation to inferiority or superiority. We all place ourselves and identify ourselves in relation to others. This confronting procedure is, at the same time, unavoidable, for it is founded in the structure of human knowledge.

An infinite and perfect being would know everything directly and at once: an absolute, exhaustive, simultaneous, and infallible intuition. But human knowledge is always relative, fragmented, progressive, and subject to error. Within the context of this investigation an important note to stress is epistemological relativism. As Kant pointed out, human knowledge is written down in space and time. Now, every point in space is determined in relation to others: any typc of localization is relative to some other points of reference arbitrarily chosen, everything stands at a certain distance from something known. We do not even know if the universe has a center and boundaries. The same may be said about time, which is defined by a before and an after and which we take to be eternal: every moment is discerned as posterior to another, and without which it could not be dated. We know neither an hour nor a place that is absolute, and we determine them by their relationship to one another. If all human knowledge is spacio-temporal and if place and time are fixed by us through comparisons, it is obvious that human knowledge is intrinsically relative, though truth need not be.

The relativity of knowing appears in all areas and specifications and from all perspectives. It is not necessary to exhaust them; it is enough to produce some examples. The logical category of relations is the fundamental one; as Hartmann pointed out it is a supercategory and, as Amor Ruibal demonstrated, it is almost a transcendental category. Judgments of existence are affirmation-negation, and the inclusion of meaning entails exclusions: what is this is not that. Every precision is a separation of something from something else and it is possible to define only by fencing this from that. Science is the integration of distinctions. Numbers have value due to the place they occupy in relation to other numbers. Any computation of quantity entails a measure of more or less weight, more or less extension, more or less temperature, etc.; computation of quality entails more or less utility, more or less goodness, more or less beauty, etc; all such measures are relative to models or scales of valuation. Every value judgment is equivalent to a comparison between two extremes more or less courageous, more or less elegant, etc. To measure intelligence one needs to compare it to the overgifted or the undergifted. All dimensions are polar and there is no judgment without coordinates and degrees. And, finally, a thesis and an equation are only true within a system, that is, placed coherently in relation to the others. Wisdom is reflexive and all knowledge is a crossroad of relativities that refer to an absolute that in itself is unknowable.

The comparison humans make of themselves with others therefore answers this need for polarities in a logical imperative—for it is in this manner that we are able to figure out who we are and what we are worth. It also answers an existential imperative since every normal human lives from his own self-consciousness; self-ignorance, like amnesia, is a pathological situation. Thus, the interpersonal comparison from which envy is born is not a hobby or a weakness certain people have; it is a demand of the relative character of human knowledge and, therefore, an inexorable fact. And given the fact that people are not duplicates, it turns out that some are inferior to others, at least in certain aspects. Since no human is superior to all in everything, the awareness of a partial inferiority is a situation no human can avoid.

If envy were simply an awareness of concrete inferiorities, the feeling would be universal and even necessary. But this is not the case, for potential envy becomes affective only when the subject is unable to overcome his inferiority or to assimilate it. No one is capable of overcoming all of his inferiorities and no one is capable of assimilating all of them at once. Hence the universality and contingency of the fact of envy. It is this *quantum* of impotent and unassimilable inferiority that in some persons amounts to a minimum, and is marginal and temporary, while in others it is immense, central, lasting, and is the reason that envy is universal.

6. Prefabricated Envy

Following Aristotle we repeat that one envies "those nearer [ἐγγύς] and similar [ὅμοιος]," concretely, brothers, relatives, neighbors, those of the same profession and class. Freud suggested that the first envy rises between brothers at a tender age. This characterization of envy as an emotion relative to those around us is inexact. There is, no doubt, envy among those of the same blood, colleagues, partners, and neighbors; but it is not a relation grounded in genetic or professional relations, in games or at home, nor even in simply living together. All those forms may exist and yet not give rise to the feeling of envy.

The necessary condition for envy is not one of physical, but mental contiguity; it is not coexistence, but knowledge. Given the saying *Nihil volitum quin praecognitum* [nothing wanted unless previously known], one must affirm that only that which is previously known is envied. The emotion of envy is born out of a judgment, more or less true, about the happiness of the other. Normally the other is a neighbor, for proximity is a direct incitement to knowledge; but it is also possible to know indirectly of what is distant, even if it is not seen or touched. This path was widened with civilization. There were periods when the only sources of information were nature and the spoken word. Then one could affirm without fear of inexactitude that envy was concentrated on the neighbors. But in the measure that the amount of knowledge received through the testimony of others has today increased, in the same manner, the capacity to envy the unlike and the remote has also increased.

Contemporary people are subject to a massive supply of information through the mass media; consequently, people can have opinions about the happiness of those they have never met or groups of people to which they do not belong; and, as a result of these feelings, they may envy. This possibility becomes a probability if, as is habitual in the mass media, information is distributed already "focused" by a partial selection, an intentional editing, mystifying, or simply a bias that, in our case, is directed to bring out the differences among individuals or estates. It is therefore obvious that in opposition to what has happened under other circumstances, the larger number of envious feelings are now directed, not against those nearer and alike, but against the distant and different.

One of the main characteristics of this mediated envy is that it does not only ground itself in the existence of others never seen, and only described by some intermediaries, but also in a value judgment provided by outsiders. The same mediating agents are those that assure us that the other is happier and that this fact implies a diminution of our own possibilities for happiness. This is how ideologues and the preachers of egalitarianism promote an emotion of envy that, since the end of the eighteenth century, has not stopped gaining in scope and intensity.

In our time, the larger portion of the current envy is not based on proximity, for people live rather isolated and mutually unknown in the womb of immense multitudes. Rather it is based on the tenacious preaching, laboriously and systematically carried out by a minority, that with such a ploy pretends to rise to power or, simply satisfies its own resentment against the winners. People who have hardly anything in common with the man on the street arouse envy against unreal people who do not even resemble the descriptions given. This is a ready-made, serial envy whose object is so distant that it becomes depersonalized to the point of losing its individuality. One does not envy this or that person, but an abstraction, like "the rich" or "the elitists." Envy is promoted against those collective names, not because of what they are, but because of the adjectives imparted on them by the resentment of ideologues: enterprising people are called "exploiters"; the best are called "privileged"; the bosses are called "authoritarian"; the happy ones "selfish"; and so on.

To envy what is different, remote, and impersonal (as it has previously been incriminated and marked by the inquisitors of difference and the apologists of equality) is a species of envy that comes to us prefabricated, a very popular type of envy in our time and one that hardly resembles the one Aristotle observed.

7. Self-punishing Envy

Envy, like all other painful feelings, does not produce a localized physical pain but rather a diffuse discomfort. Contrary to other feelings, like depression, envy does not have an unconscious and autonomous origin but a conscious one; it does not spring from a mysterious interior, but from a known external stimulus or from the mental actualization of such a stimulus. One must think of the envied to feel envy, just as one must think of the hated to feel hatred. What truly distinguishes envy from other painful feelings is its necessary link to discomfort; it does not afflict us intermittently or occasionally but is absolutely inseparable from displeasure; it is reflectively painful by nature. The fact that it carries within its own womb its own punishment, explains why it is compared, though improperly, to oxide, waste, or gangrene.

In terms of equity we must admit that if envy is malignant it also carries with itself a punishment, that is to say, it is self-punishing. And the greater the envy the greater the punishment. This proportionality, and not just the self-punishment that envy carries, makes us conclude, if we pay strict attention to the envied, that envy is the only "just" vice. But we must consider that the envied may be also adversely affected. And since self-punishment does not cancel out the envious feeling, nor, eventually, the subsequent hostile actions, it could be considered as an immanent justice *ad intra*; but not externally and socially for the envied is never protected, nor insured, nor compensated by anyone.

Envy may also disturb those who witness it without participating in it, a category that certainly includes its victims. There is always an uneasiness in the envied. Why? More than out of sympathy or compassion for the other's displeasure it is out of fear at the reactions of the envious which, when exteriorized, always become aggressive: expropriation of the good, marginality, hypercriticism, defamation, slander. . . . Even when envy does not translate into action it is always a threat. The envied is aware that there is a permanent, potential aggressor even when he ignores the place, the hour, and the way of the possible aggression. This absence of precision about danger becomes particularly unnerving; this is the anguish of the envied under a hidden danger that is also prolonged and uncertain. The evil eye and the curse, evils attributed to the envious, have as a side effect the anguish of their indeterminateness. To know or have the presentiment of being envied brings out a wide range of uncomfortable situations, from a simple discomfort and uneasiness to paralysis.

Does a feeling that afflicts and causes affliction have any pleasurable connotation? More than pleasure, it is a feeling of liberation that overcomes the envious when envy is satisfied; but as long as envy lasts there is only pain. The same does not happen with enjoying someone else's harm, which at times is paired with envy. There are two reasons for this association. The first is that both feelings are simultaneously contrary and complementary. The second, more solid reason, is that both proceed from a comparison between one's level of happiness and someone else's and both exclude sympathy. Joy at the harm of others springs from superiority, while envy springs from inferiority. They are two very different feelings with different types of malignancies. Envy operates on the pretext of a supposed lost good; while enjoyment at other people's sufferings lacks any real or imaginary justification.

III. Evaluation

1. Disfunctional Envy

Do feelings perform useful tasks within our vital economy? They do so in at least three main ways: they produce happiness, help us to gain orientation, and help us react to our environment.

There are feelings that carry pleasure within and, therefore, are forms of well-being. Happiness and unhappiness are the two main species of the affective state. Is there a possible form of happiness that is not affective or sentimental? Theologians attribute to angels an intellectual and volitive enjoyment gained through knowledge and love; it is the happiness of the blessed. It might not be wise to exclude as a possibility the fact that evolution, up to now, has been a progressive substitution of *pathos* for logic, and that humans could become pure *logos* without any mixture of emotivity. But in the present state it is obvious that feelings perform a main function in relation to happiness; they constitute the main translation of human happiness.

All feelings carry with them pleasure or displeasure; there are no neutral emotions. For this reason, feelings guide human behavior since they induce us to avoid the unpleasant and search for the pleasant. Often enough, what is agreeable coincides with what is adequate and beneficial, and what is disagreeable with what is inadequate and damaging, as, for example, a putrid smell. Cognition and affectivity are two very different environments, but contrary to what is usually held to be the case, they are not opposed to each other in absolute terms, and they, in part, blot each other out. Feelings also perform an elementary and diffuse task as carriers of information. There is in animals intense and decisive activity that is sentimental and that acts as an embryonic form of cognition. This function still lingers in *homo sapiens,* though it is slowly receding and is at times so off the mark that it has lost all orienting character.

There are feelings that unfold somatic reactions and psychic attitudes that lead to predictable behaviors. Darwin pointed out that these interdependencies are, in many cases, functional: thus anger, for it incites to aggression, and fear, for it moves to flight. The biological determination of feelings in intersexual relations is even more overwhelming, especially in procreation. In certain cases, emotions appear as mechanisms inherent in the system of life itself and they are justified and explained for their contribution to the conservation of the species.

Envy does not perform any of these functions. It is, in the first place, a painful feeling. Where there is envy there is never pleasure; there is always displeasure. The joy at the suffering of others is not the climax of envy, but rather its extinction because of the disappearance of motive, and it is a very different kind of feeling whose only homology may be found in the contrary. The self-punishing character of envy keeps it from carrying any happiness. If a feeling is justified on account of the happiness it carries with it, envy would then be the most aberrant of all affective vicissitudes.

Secondly, envy does not provide any valid information about the surrounding environment. On the contrary, it presents the superior person as an enemy and a scandal, and not as a friend and a model; it narrows and darkens the vital horizon, instead of opening it up and shedding light on it; it identifies the envious's path of happiness with other people's, and this produces self-ignorance and depersonalization; it does not bring nearer, but rather distances and obstructs the knowledge of others; and finally, it is obsessive and self-absorbing, depriving, thus, the envious from all sense of reality and decreasing discursive reason. Ariston rightly wrote of Keous that envy was a "blindness of the soul" (Frag. 13.4. Ed. Wehrili, p. 34), dazzling or ophthalmic. If the justification of a feeling were merely that it supply us with accurate information about the surrounding environment, envy would be considered one of the most counterproductive, for it is specifically a misinformation.

Thirdly, does envy predispose us with adequate reactions? Envy tends to diminish the happiness of the envied, but does not thus increase the well-being of the envious; quite the contrary. Still, one could ask if in the long run, envy, to the degree that it deprives the other, does not enrich the envious. The depriving capacity of envy, however, is very limited. Besides, the good lost by the envied seldom, if ever, falls to the envious. But even in this exceptional supposition, does it compensate for the suffering during the prolonged wait? And in the improbable eventuality that it did compensate, would it not have been of greater gain to put to use the emulation that is cancelled by envy? In the pure selfishness of the tension between the "I" and the "you" the utility of envy is contemptible. In all other areas the feeling of envy is of the highest impertinence and inadequacy: it does not incite to create, but to cancel out; not to establish hierarchies but uniformities; envy does not move toward anything positive.

The envious person neither gains happiness, nor is oriented nor predisposed to positive action; he suffers, becomes misinformed, and is prone to negative behavior. From an individual point of view the feeling is not only superfluous, it is counterproductive. Does envy develop into a function that is socially advantageous for the community, even if it is painful to each of its members? According to Freud sociability comes out of envy: envy is the radical impulse, while sociability is the result. This process takes place in the favorite scenario of the Viennese psychiatrist—during infancy. Here is the hypothetical reconstruction: the child receives with envy his new brother, and since he cannot get rid of him, he becomes his associate in order to share equally the parental love and goods. But the facts do not confirm such an affirmation. Before the younger brother is born, the first born was already within the familial society and was holding tight to it. Even if he never stopped being an only child he would have continued being sociable because his gregarious impulse was fostered prior to the appearance of any new member of the group. And there is still more: why is fratricide such an aberrant form of behavior if the first impulse is to get rid of one's brother? Why is Cain's figure exceptional and not archetypal? The feeling of envy requires the existence of at least two people, plus some form of relation between them, namely, a community. People may live together without envy; but there is no envy without community, therefore envy cannot be the origin of community.

It is, on the other hand, an illusion to suppose that the first feeling of a child towards his brother is envy—one of the most complex and intellectualized of feelings. What does the first born know about the happiness of the newlyborn? And who has been able to prove that he suffers on account of that happiness? Experimental psychology has been able to prove that one of the first feelings of the infant is jealousy towards any candidate who shares the attention of his mother, namely, the pain at losing a monopoly on happiness; but this is not envy. Let us suppose that this is a question of terms and that Freud thought jealousy to be the root of the social. But this is also a false thesis for jealousy presupposes community and a jealous Robinson Crusoe is inconceivable. Furthermore, the envious band together against those they envy; but outside the tragicomedies, where do victims and those that cause jealousy form associations? Jealousy is a feeling that is more alienating and antisocial than envy.

And, finally, love and parental goods are not a quantifiable fortune that children may distribute among themselves. Love is a flow that the lover freely bestows and that no one from the outside can force or distribute. Something similar could be said about parental goods; they are also sporadic, extremely free, and fluid. In order to stand by the rules of the egalitarian distribution, will the first born not accept a gift from his parents until his younger brother receives a gift equal to his and vice versa? This is an unbelievable presupposition that is denied by experience.

None of the points of the Freudian argument hold so it is understandable that the thesis has not had a positive echo. It is just a speculation without a real foundation, and it is only the author's prestige that justifies a critical revision.

Society is the primary fact, for every human is born of parents and survives for years due to them and the gregarious instinct of staying with them. And this is a viable community without the least vestige of envy. In the same way that love and pleasure are solitary feelings, envy and jealousy require a society as a *conditio sine qua non*; they do not create it, they need it.

Though envy is not the origin of sociability, could it not serve as the glue that holds it together? Could it be an involuntary and sacrificial way of serving others? According to Schoeck no society can be formed without envy for envy is the motor of the mutual and spontaneous supervision that some citizens exercise over others, that is, social control. The thesis implies a series of hypotheses that I find to be ungrounded.

Is the discipline of a group maintained by the mutual control of some members over the others? No. The empire, not the spontaneous associations, has formed and sustained the great political unities. There is not a single exception to this rule, from Sumer to the Soviet Union. And something similar happens with smaller unities. If we remove the officers from an army, the troops will disband and plunder. The death of the father means the separation of the brothers, unless one takes his place. Social cohesion is not born out of the interaction of the citizens, but out of authority. There is no society without law, and this is a coercive norm established by the highest authority with the help of judges and a police force. The universal, juridical self-tutelage is a utopia in part anarchist and in part democratic. Mutual control may be more or less intense, but it is not the cause of social order. Is it, at least, its essential condition? It is neither; for within any form of government, the despotic or the simply authoritiarian, discipline has been maintained without mutual controls and at times, with the tacit or expressed resistance of the citizens.

It is not usually the case that those who are governed try to control one another, but that they try to control the government, though generally without much success. Besides it is silence that is spontaneous in human groups, not the denunciation of one another; and rather than accusation, complicity is the norm. This attitude is already prevalent in the family and early schooling. To be denounced by someone not involved in a dispute is exceptional, but when it happens, is it due to envy? Here we have another unfounded hypothesis.

If anyone informs the authorities of some action against the law, he usually does it seeking self-protection, reparation, or restitution. The motive is usually self-interest insofar as it is protected by legal order. There is also, though infrequently, testimony by witnesses on illegal acts; the motive here is not envy but civil solidarity, the will to collaborate in the exercise of the law, or simply the reward. Hence the fact that prosecution witnesses of a crime need to be subpoenaed and even coerced. What feelings of envy does anyone give vent to when reporting a murderer, rapist, thief, or pyromaniac? Against which supposed superior happiness or inachievable happiness is he rebelling? Is he rebelling against the happiness of the parricide, sadist, or pyromaniac? There is no room, within such contexts, for envy. The whistle-blowers are moved by money, by the promise of immunity for their own crimes, or by the competition. In the underground, tensions are usually resolved by an internal settling of accounts. No one denies that envy may lead to certain denunciations, such as cheating on taxes or stealing, but do these sporadic accusations sustain the governing power and the property of the state? If paying taxes were a matter of denunciations from neighbors, very few would pay them.

Social controls, besides, cannot be anonymous as a system. On the contrary, with the exception of the executioner who is a mere instrument, all petitions from authorities are nominal and public, as are the declarations from witnesses in front of a tribunal. Envy, on the other hand, hides and its tactic is silence. Only occasionally does one dare to throw a stone and hide the hand that threw it, but in general the opposite is the case. Because of its own inconfessability, envy does not allow the establishment of an efficient social control; when in exceptional cases it operates in this manner, it can only be considered as a hint of a hypothesis at work, for the presumption of truth in the envious is minimal.

It is true that there is not envy where there is no community, but false that communities are formed thanks to envy. The feeling of envy does not join but separates, it is not social but antisocial. There are communities based on love, interest, or necessity; envy is only the ground that joins the occasional and negative solidarity of the envious against the envied, and these associations seldom last on their own; they require a demagogue.

Envy is not the support of communal life but does it contribute to a more just life? This egalitarian thesis is the outcome of the following syllogism: justice means equality, envy promotes equality, therefore envy is just. The major premise is false, for justice does not consist in giving the same to everyone, but to each according to his merits. The second premise is also false. The envious is not at all bothered by general inequality, nor by the inferiority of others; what tortures the envious is his own inferiority and his desire to transform it into superiority over the envied at any price. The feelings of the envious are at the margins of equity, and in practice his behavior is objectively unjust for he is not in the least concerned about depriving the other of what he justly owns, and he never stops to consider the possibility that he has no right to what he desires. When the envious joins those who promise him equality, he does not do it out of generous philanthropy, but out of mean selfishness and with the hope that a set of favorable circumstances will rescue him from his particular impotence and his bad conscience. The genuine, just protest is not the one proclaimed by the envious, but rather by the indignant person whose motive is not his personal inferiority and his own anger but an abstract ethical criterion proportional between the merit and the reward. Envy is a feeling proper of greedy people, indignation of the altruist. Egalitarian ideologues, alchemists whose philosophical stone is envy, mount their speeches on uncertain postulates, paralogisms, and *petitio principii.*

But even though envy is alien to the virtue of justice, and even if egalitarianism is unjust, does it, in fact, contribute to the egalitarianism of the community? Isolated envy is not operative in the social context, but when collective and organized, like the French or the Soviet Revolution, it has produced notable changes in the social stratification. But these changes, rather than promoting egalitarianism, have in fact produced an inversion of the differences; they have persecuted, dispossessed, and humbled the envied groups and have replaced them by the guide system of the envious. And besides, the immediate egalitarian effect of these transfers on the masses has been more rhetorical than substantial, as proven by the Napoleonic new aristocracy and the so-called *nomenklatur.* Contemporary experience demonstrates that the large egalitarian mutations, always consisting of the rise of the proletariat to the middle class, have not been the fruit of the overthrow of certain aristocracies nor of the distribution of their patrimony, but rather of economic development. A simple comparison between

East and West establish that the powerful motive for this development is a hierarchical emulation and not an egalitarian envy.

In 1932 Eugenio Raiga wrote a book whose main thesis was as follows: "The feared and fearful strategies of envy react against the arrogance and contempt of the privileged, they moderate their pride and lead them to a modesty that, in spite of its lack of sincerity, is welcomed and allows the rest of the people to feel that they are not thrown into the pit. Vulgar envy, with its marks and horrors, performs thus a social function for in this manner it answers the demands of the common life." Could this be the justification for this growing feeling? No. Modesty is a virtue that consists of not overvaluing oneself or exaggerating our own value, namely, in the control of the most ingenuous of human proclivities. But envy has the opposite effect: the envious multiplies his own inferiority; it is only through envy that he reaches the belief that he is part of the privileged. The true fact is that to feel oneself the object of envy is an invitation to immodesty. Besides, modesty is a virtue that admits no duplicity as it is a true conviction, while the usual defenses against envy are only disguises, simulations, or impostures, and even the most satanic pride may hide behind these. The tricks used to hide that which the envied invents are unthinkable in the isolationism of a Robinson Crusoe. A solitary person may be modest, but envy is not possible without the company of others. Modesty may be reached through self-examination and self-discipline, while a life of duplicity is reached out of fear of others and astuteness. These are two different worlds. In summation, envy does not produce modesty, but deception, and it is not possible to defend that deception as a social good that justifies its instigator.

In synthesis, envy is a disfunctional emotion, as much from the viewpoint of the individual as from the group.

2. Mistaken Envy

The Stoic philosophers held that passions are irrational [ἄιογος] and Hume held the contrary belief that passions are not unreasonable. The truth of the matter is that, in order for envy to appear, the data of the senses must undergo a complex mental operation. Envy is a feeling that arises out of judgments and reasonings and requires the use of a deductive intelligence; it is exclusive of rational beings, and *homo sapiens* does not share it with other beings. An unthought envy is impossible. In a strict sense, it cannot be held that envy is irrational; it is the most rationalized of affective states after resentment.

How can it be explained that reason, so rigorous and utilitarian, is able to produce a feeling that is painful and, simultaneously, counterproductive and negative? There is nothing in humans that is infallible, and envy is handled by an intellect that makes mistakes. There are factual as well as dialectical errors. The whole process starts with the proposition: "This person is happier than I am," which embraces two separate mental moments, the appreciation of another's happiness, and the comparison with one's own: "This man is happy" and "His happiness is greater than mine."

Happiness is a pleasurable feeling caused by the balance between what one desires and what one possesses. It does not entirely depend on objective goods, but more so on the desires of the subject. The subjective factor is essential here. For this reason one of the Epicurean philosophers could write that the greatest of riches is to not desire; this is the reason why there are goods that make some people happy, but not others. There are certain probable generalizations in this matter, but we lack absolute norms to foresee individual well-being. We can only guess at other people's happiness from their pronouncements on the subject: their gestures and words. Happiness is an event that has only one essential witness, and an interested witness at that—a legal situation not conducive to proving much. When someone declares he is happy we may believe him or not, and we shall never be able to prove or disprove it, or even less so, to measure the intensity of that feeling. From our own experience we know that out of modesty or civility we usually hide our pain and pretend to be happier than we really are, and that in order to protect ourselves from the envious we at times diffuse our happiness. These habits make any discourse on happiness even more problematic. Two beings who share a whole life together may be sure that they love but not so sure that they are loved; and they cannot even suppose that they make their lover happy. It is doubtful that we may know things in themselves, but it is certain that our knowledge about other people's feelings is inaccurate, indirect, alloyed, and often enough, mistaken. Happiness is pure subjectivity that can be communicated only in rudimentary fashion, almost ineffable, and almost always concealed. Other people's happiness is, therefore, one of the most unknown realities of our world.

How can anyone come up with the accurate judgment, "This person is happy," when seemingly happy people such as the very rich or extremely beautiful commit suicide, and when very desperate poor people hang on fiercely to life? It is even more difficult to affirm that the other is "more" happy than ourselves, for every quantitative comparison requires a certain precision of measure. How can anyone measure something that is practically unknown in those around us? The envious must renounce all epistemological rigor and substitute his impossible objective certainty for the risky subjective exercise of placing himself mentally in the place of the envied. In the course of this dialectical jump the envious comes up with the following judgment: "If I were him and were in his social or patrimonial position, I would be happier than I am now." The first condition, in its literal sense, is a metaphysical impossibility, for no one can simultaneously be himself and another; if the interpreted meaning is that one's personality will disappear and will be transformed into that of the other, how can one foresee what one is going to feel as the other? This might be known after, but certainly not before, the substantial metamorphosis. The second condition, to hold the same social position and own the same patrimonial goods, possibly could happen in reality; but we could never know which would be our behavior until such an event takes place. Our own experience testifies to the irrationality of hypothetical promises: the saying "If this happened to me, I would do . . ." never happens in real life; the customary behavior is to do something different.

The reasoning developed by the envious process does not stand against even the most elementary criticism. "The other is happier than I am because if I were in his place I would be happier than in my present situation" is a hypothetical, conditional, contingent, and unverifiable judgment with so many chances for error that it would be rash to ground any form of behavior on it.

But the following argument is not any weaker. Once the envious has admitted his assumed inferior way of happiness, he tells himself, "I would like to, but I can't." Firstly, to wish for the supposed happiness of another may be a grave error if that happiness is not as we imagine it to be. Secondly, even if the envied is truly happy, would the envious be as happy in his same circumstances? Thirdly, is that declaration of impotence an impossible task or is it just a lack of will? In this last case, the saying "I wish, but I can't" is self-deception, since the true statement would rather read: "I wish, but I do not want." This simple feeling of becoming aware of doubt or laziness is not sufficient reason for it to become transformed into the torture of envy. If envy sprouts, it is because we commit the additional error of raising our listless ideality to the despair of impotence.

Let us suppose, finally, that the envious is truly impotent in attaining the true superior happiness of the other. In such a case, envy will only appear when a further error is committed—to think that such superior happiness of the other diminishes or cancels ours. However, none of these two effects is true. If an increase of the happiness of some over the arithmetic mean of the population would imply a diminution of the quota of happiness of other members of the same population—it would force us to admit that happiness is something objective and homogeneous, and this presupposition is off the mark: happiness is subjective, heterogeneous, unlimited, and variable. In order to establish that the ownership of goods above the egalitarian average implies a proportional reduction of the possibilities of happiness in others, we would have to accept that a particular kind of good produces identical happiness in each and every one of us, and this is false. The idea that the increase in happiness in some implies a decrease in others is a rudimentary extrapolation of a situation that used to occur in primitive economic structures regarding primary and limited material goods—the superconsumption of some being the underconsumption of others. But those kinds of goods are no longer the main object of happiness, and they will become less so with the cultural and economic development of humanity.

In order for the happiness of others to completely cancel out our own, it would be generated necessarily by the enjoyment of one objectively single good that would simultaneously be a single, irreplaceable and subjective good. This is the romantic situation of a man whose existence is bent towards the enjoyment of one good that is exclusive and irreplaceable and that belongs to another. Only then would there be incompatibility between the two forms of happiness, but are there such creatures that long only for one good and could not care less for the rest of the universe? Even if this were the case, such a pathological obsession would lead to pain on account of the desired but inaccessible good, for it is already allotted to somebody else, but not pain at the expense of others. In order to arrive at such a feeling, one needs to commit the definitive error of believing that the cause of his own deficit in happiness is the desire the other has. But, returning to our romantic example, why should the other be guilty because he is the preferred one?

The counterproductive and superfluous character of envy suggests that it is an absurd emotion. The same conclusion is reached by uncovering the series of errors of fact, judgment and deduction, and the series of uncertain hypotheses that follow one another in the envious process.

IV. Envy as a Political Factor

1. Origin of the Division

The political class, due to the unity of sovereign power and the relative scarcity of its delegations and participations, always subdivides into the two sectors of those who strive to continue holding the reins of power and enjoying the perquisites and those who aspire to replace them. To achieve their respective ends, both sides make use of the following three resources: power, technical capability, and popular support. Power is illegitimate pressure on people and ranges from threats to revolution, including at times the abuse of power. Technical capability is the guarantee of administrative efficacy, particularly in the economic and juridical areas. Popular support is tacit when there is a consensus and there is no resistance, and it is expressed in the streets or elections. The greater the popular support, the more deeply governments intervene in the lives of the people—which is what has been happening in the West since the end of the eighteenth century. This outcome was not directed by the masses, but rather by the bourgeoisie, a political class that replaced the hereditary monarchy and the blood aristocracy.

It is an intrinsic need that the governing minority be divided. But why should the governed be divided? This is a radical question not often formulated—as if it concerned an obvious fact, which it does not. The normal procedure is for the population to form a common front with active or passive resistance against tyranny, and constantly but moderately to demand greater order, justice, or more development when an administration is reasonably receptive. Solidarity is a spontaneous and logical outcome in every specific group, as may be seen from sociobiological studies of animals.

The governed are not political enemies by nature of the political fact; rather they are so because the political class tries with great effort to divide them. The motive is clear: if the governing minority is fragmented, and if the various factions aim for popular support, they will forcibly round up the masses into opposing camps. It is not the case that a few bees want to leave the beehive, but rather that every queen requires her own swarm. If those who govern did not systematically use popular support, there would be little support for demagogues—no parties of the masses. The elite—the more so the less powerful they are—divide societies in order to govern. Let us reconstruct this process.

The limiting hypothesis is that of separatism. A region separates from the main land to satisfy the ambition for power of some prince or of some minority that created the national or independent consciousness in the first place. But here we are dealing with divisions within the state itself. Within any political system, those who govern remain more easily in power if the governed are divided among themselves. Within a democratic system, those who aspire to power need a faction that is the most powerful and largest to back them up. The political parties of the masses are not formed from below but shaped from above; it is the political class that baptizes, programs, structures, finances, and uses them. With the exception of testimonial parties, the criterion for dividing the governed is to draw an imaginary line that puts on one side those usually called "privileged" and that others consider "the best"; opposite them, on the other side, are those often called "the people," who are considered less capable. The goal of parties is to convince the largest number that they are of "the people"; the goal of other parties is to persuade them that their interests are represented by "the best." Though it may sound cynical, the truth of the matter is that the number of "the people" present to vote is more the outcome of propaganda than of the social reality. These distinctions, like those homologous to them of the Right and the Left, though they have a foundation in reality, are relative and inaccurate.

The class struggle, as the fight between the "bourgeoisie" and "the proletariat" is known today, is basically another invention of the political class. This class is the one that moment by moment defines the shifting limits of those supposed classes, indoctrinates them about their supposed interests, measures the intensity and place of their confrontations, and in the end also encourages the shift from one political party to another. The common means employed for promoting the union of the larger numbers ("the people," "the mob," depending on the observer) and their confrontation with the smaller numbers ("the privileged" or "the best," depending on the perspective) is collective envy.

Why appeal to deleterious envy rather than to creative emulation? For the reason that emulation does not accentuate the division, and division is what interests the polarized political class. Emulation distributes energy along the whole group and does not promote the formation of incompatible factions. How does one divide into two or more groups that mutually exclude each other those who have participated in a marathon or a javelin competition? This is an impossible task, for emulation joins without discrimination, without exceptions. An ordered competition that determines a gradation within a hierarchy that runs from the winner to the last competitor homogenizes all the participants and flows into a continuous list with no breaks. And the same happens when, instead of individuals, we deal with sports teams, since all the players are interchangeable.

Envy, however, confronts the loser with the winner; it distances and divides. But if this is so, how can it be used as a social union? Envy as a bilateral relation is in truth a means of separation, for it opens an abyss between the "I" and the "you," the abyss of the unassimilated, inferior in happiness. Contrary to what happens in emulation, the envious person does not feel any solidarity with the envied about anything. Emulation needs the other, while envy separates the envied from the others, and the envious person progressively isolates himself from his own world. Envy does not inspire rivalry and exemplarity, but incompatibility and loneliness. How can a feeling that constitutes such an antisocial attitude be used as a political adhesive? It does so by establishing an alliance among those who share common envies to carry out negative actions against the envied, as their passion dictates. Indirect and divisive actions with indirect efforts are devaluation, discredit, and calumny of the envied; and among the open strategies with direct efforts are aggression and expropriation.

2. Social Justice

Demagogues appeal to envy because its universality makes potential victims of all the people and because the invincible inequality of our own personal capabilities and of the irremediable limitation of many social goods makes it inevitable that the majority will feel inferior to certain minorities. The promotion of this envious feeling of inferiority is the dominant political tactic, at least in the present age. The demagogic promotion of envy, as with everything else that refers to this unpublishable feeling, is not carried out in public but under cover. A contemporary disguise of collective envy is what is called "social justice." How does this ideological and derivative argumentation run? A fundamental postulate is established that the more just a society is, the more equal its members are in opportunities, position, and wealth; and immediately it is established that the party will fight without rest to achieve such "justice." The appeal of this axiom and of such a program is evidently unbeatable for the envious, since it promises to abolish the unassimilated inferiority that causes them so much pain. Equality is a paradisiacal promise for the envious, the definitive incentive.

A first consequence of this ad hoc concept of justice is that those in positions of superiority are evil exploiters and those who feel their position is inferior are innocently exploited. This corollary sounds like heavenly music to the envious person who sees his own pain as required for the happiness of others and his resentment therefore as fully justified. Those who *appear* to be the best are really the worst. The second corollary is that the goods of the superior need to be expropriated and distributed among the inferior. The forced dispossession of the superior and able and the subsequent enrichment of the failures and impotents would fulfill the supreme ambition of the envious. And even though in practice one's own promotion is not achieved, it is possible to attempt and at times it may be possible to achieve what is truly essential to envy—the humbling of the envied.

The call to crusades against the superiority of others, as, for example, by

Marxists, has a large following not because the envious and the resentful are a majority but because potentially they may become so, and thus egalitarian ideologies continue to promote such emotions. If, in addition, inequality is emphasized, if it is called arbitrary and even unlawful, if a gratuitous redistribution is promised, if the guilty conscience of the envious is dissolved into collective irresponsibility—the party or the class—and if it is made to appear that all this rests on a moral foundation, it is obvious that the number of the envious will not only multiply but that their envy will intensify. Egalitarianism is the opiate of the envious, and demagogues are the self-interested distributors of its massive consumption.

This is how envy has become the decisive factor in contemporary political confrontations, with rare exceptions, as for example in the United States of America, where emulation has surpassed envy. If this factor were removed, history since the Revolution of 1789 would become unintelligible, and even more so since the Communist Manifesto of 1848.

According to Hayek, "Social justice rests on the hate towards those that enjoy a comfortable position, namely, upon envy." This stark thesis needs to be understood within the context of his most daring book, *The Mirage of Social Justice* (1976). The expression "social justice" starts, according to this great liberal thinker, by being a redundancy since justice is found only for and in society. Besides, it is a notion that lacks a rigorous meaning, since no one has been able to determine, except in the marketplace, what would be the absolutely just distribution of the patrimony and income in a mass society. Only personal behavior may be judged ethically, according to Hayek. The net result of competing economic forces will always be more satisfactory to some than to others; but this is neither just nor unjust. To try to measure the morality of the market is like measuring the morality of chance or of a stone. Finally, the realization of what is called "social justice" requires economic planning and delegation to the public powers of the authority to assign work, rewards, and salaries to every citizen. Within a totalitarian system, this monopoly is equivalent to the tyranny of only one party; and within a democracy, it implies the tyranny of the majority, for in order to please its electoral clientele, it must expropriate the minorities. This is how theoretical social justice may turn out as effective inequity.

This analysis by Hayek is largely accurate. It is obvious that the theory of social justice has not gone beyond declaring some ambiguities such as "the elimination of excessive inequities," "the suppression of privileges," "redistribution," "let those who have more pay," and so on. But with the exception of the utopian egalitarians who claimed an impossible equal quota for each citizen, no one has been able to bring forward satisfactory formulations. What, after all, is the universally just salary? What is the just personal capital? What is the just participation of the private sector? What is the just amount of taxation? These are some of the basic questions never answered. It is evident that any planned and coercive distribution of social goods entails the suppression or adulteration of the marketplace, which will force the market to strain and function incoherently and in spurts. It is also true that interventionism leads to increasing controls and therefore to the progressive elimination of private initiative, and actual liberties end up being destroyed by totalitarian models. Furthermore, so-called social justice promotes inequities and is despotic in socialist governments, while it is biased in favor of the party and expropriates in social democratic governments. It is, therefore, a poorly structured justice, one that is ineffective, antiliberal, and dubitably just. It is remarkable that in our time people take as unshakable such an extraordinarily problematic idea.

It is not possible to hold, in the realm of essences, that social justice is simply a manifestation of envy. Whoever acts justly must give to each his own. In this sense, the distributive dimension of justice has a rational and not a sentimental foundation. But what such political parties as the Marxists usually call "social justice" is the policy of inspiring the less productive to demand that the state carry out transfers of goods by expropriating those who produce more, humbling the superior to satisfy the inferior. This maneuver is no doubt a political use of envy. The generalization of such a practice very often makes it possible for the topic of social justice to become the pharisaic institutionalization of collective envy or a tacit concession to placate it.

Justice is the adjudication of social goods in proportion to the returns of each member of the community. Egalitarian distribution without regard for individual merits and demerits is inequality rather than justice.

3. Ideological Correlation

The more developed a society is, the less ideological its politics are, for in such a society collective problems are objectively stated and they are solved not with emotional and simplistic recipes (ideologies) but with rational and technical procedures. In those states, however, where an appeal goes periodically to voters to pronounce themselves through votes in favor of one of the two or more competing party oligarchies, the voters need to be mobilized. But the masses are not moved with detailed and rigorous programs, since their rational capacity for discernment is very limited; they are mobilized with simple mental images that function as substitutes for classical ideologies. These elemental motivations, closer to publicity slogans than to exact definitions, are mostly made up of the image of a leader, recipes of general economic interest, and some primitive emotion. Among the latter, envy is, after nationalism, the most important.

It may be said that in general the members of a political class are as envious as the society to which they belong. Spanish people are more envious than Germans, and Germans more so than Americans, for example. But the question here is whether there is any correlation between ideologies and the use of envy for politics. Classical liberalism and socialism, the two fundamental ideologies in the transition between the nineteenth and twentieth centuries, have continued to develop and become more diffused, though they have managed to keep their names so that people may refer to them. Their twilight ambiguity has reached the point where they no longer serve as the coordinates of supranational reference. The political pundits have fallen back on an older and broader dichotomy, the "Right" and the "Left." These terms, despite their relative imprecision, correspond to the two large alternatives of our time: a society with a private economy or a society with a public economy.

Do the Right and the Left behave differently regarding envy? The leaders of the political Right show less solidarity and are less unified than those of the Left. In the books of memoirs by politicians on the Right, those who receive the heaviest censure are not their adversaries but fellow rightists. A member of the Right who converts into a traveling companion of the Left is encountered more frequently than is the opposite. This type of behavior is in part a consequence of a larger measure of individualism and pride; but in the main the leaders of the Right are more envied than those of the Left and envy flourishes more within rightist groups—which is the supreme weakness of the Right.

On the other hand, when leaders of the Right try to stimulate collective emotions, they do not appeal to the envious for a practical reason: the majority of voters of the Right regard themselves as belonging to the camp of the envied. There is also a theoretical reason: the Right always regards collective envy as negative. On the other hand, envy is the main effective ingredient of all motivations the leaders of the Left distribute to their infrastructures. "Make the *privileged* pay" is the main slogan; the egalitarian topic is reduced to just that. This strategy has the advantage, among others, that it is not as difficult as creating wealth or jobs, but it translates rather into the simplicity of raising the taxes of the most capable and of those who work with the greatest productivity. To punish the best is always more feasible than to produce the best. The easiest electoral promise to fulfill is to satisfy the envious by punishing the envied.

It is paradoxical that the political sector that suffers less internal envy than others appeals systematically to envy as a political motivation, while the party oligarchy that prescribes social envy is the one that suffers more internally on account of envy.

Conservatism and revolutionism are two styles or dispositions that in certain historical moments may become doctrine; but they are basically two methods for solving political problems. The conservative method consists in perfecting the human circumstance without destroying what is valuable; this is a realistic prudential progression. The revolutionary method consists in eliminating what exists and replacing it with something new—supposedly the best; this is an idealistic, bold, and substitutional operation. Is there any relation between envy and these two opposing ways of tackling the *res publica?*

Envy produces dissatisfaction both in the one who suffers it and in the one who inspires it; it is therefore twice negative from the point of view of knowledge. It also insulates, in that it separates the envious from the envied and even stimulates the latter to physical seclusion; it is, then, also from the social point of view, twice negative. It even induces the envied to inactivity, and causes the envious to degrade and at times annihilate the envied. From one side it inhibits and from the other it isolates; from the point of view of action, it is doubly negative.

This plural negativism of envy makes it a useful instrument for those who plan demolishing acts, and this is even more the case with the revolutionaries' act, for this is their only definite act; the second act, the constructive act, they seldom accomplish. Our logical and historical analysis makes it evident that envy is the typical resort of revolutionaries, while it is almost inconceivable that conservatism, whose method rejects pure and simple destruction, would resort to it. The conservative style is totally opposed to envy; conservatism counts on emulation, competition with others, and ultimately on creativity.

4. Egalitarianism and Orthodoxy

Organized envy usually crystallizes into egalitarian norms whose origin is found not in custom but in government. This is a kind of uniformity from above: egalitarianism through coercion, either ideological, economic, or social. These three facets are complementary and Marxist-Leninist doctrine proclaims a utopia based on this triple equalization: that all think alike, that all belong to this one class only, and that all share a similar patrimony. Ideological egalitarianism requires a supreme definitory urging, an education, the means of communication to the masses that are centralized and directed, and an implacable censure for whatever is not the official ideology. This in short is cultural dictatorship, the ultimate weapon of egalitarianism. The envious find within this system a firm protection against originality, against free intellectual exchange, and against noetic superiority. Power alone is allowed to think; the rest can only be simple reformulators or applicators shaped by the same mold. To distinguish oneself is to fall into heterodoxy. For this reason, any thinker worthy of the name has been labeled within Marxism "deviationist." Even within democracies, there are certain dogmas that allow the labeling of those who disagree as "maladjusted." The envy of the intellectually mediocre establishes a canon so that it may denounce and condemn the independent thinker. The unity of the envious imposes an "orthodoxy" that not only frees them from the effort to create and makes it easy to overlook the absence of creativity, but forces those who were formerly privileged and envied to an agreement, so that they may come to some pronouncement like the following: "Do not envy me; I am not different. I am equal to you, I believe your catechism is true, and I condemn to moral exile all those that are not members of this club." In this manner, "the privileged" have apologized for being outstanding and have promised to change their ways. This ruse neutralizes the envy of the establishment and allows free access to the communication media and to the budgets. "Either the syndicate of orthodoxy or the ghetto" constitutes the dilemma that summarizes the tactic of the most refined manifestation of collective envy.

But this is not the solution. Within the same league of the envious, and apart from their coming together to debase the envied, there are other unsurpassable inferiorities and other deep envies that resemble the *odium* that people say exists in a convent. Envy is incurable.

5. Social Development

Nietzsche wrote that a country is the roundabout way [*Unschweife*] Nature takes to arrive at a few great men. I think it is true that the highest function of the group is to give birth to excellent individuals. For this reason, the quality of a society depends on its capacity to produce eminent personalities. A genius gives pride to family, school, and nation; mass-man does not. Contrary to what might be deduced from democratic propositions, the value of a nation in history, from classical Greece to the state of Israel, does not come from its numbers but from its quality. The greatness of a person depends on his genetic structure (health, intellectual capacity, perseverance, etc.), his development (learning habits, and so forth) and his public recognition (social promotion and public service). The origin of these three factors is social. The more eugenic a group is, the greater the biological possibilities of selection; and the better education is, the greater the development of the innate aptitudes. It may be said therefore that society is a womb in the biological sense insofar as it gives birth, in the pedagogic sense insofar as it educates, and in the political sense insofar as it exalts. Envy intervenes with increasing negativity in each of these three stages. Envy shunts aside the intelligent, the strong, and the virtuous and does not encourage their reproduction; the isolation of the superior man is anti-eugenic. Scholarly envy towards the best and most studious promotes laziness and loss of interest in studies; egalitarian education delays the best. Social envy, finally, creates impediments to the public recognition of the best, to the promotion and use of their work. The efficacy of envy is greater in society than in school, and greater in school than in a couple; the larger the extension, the greater the negativity. For this reason, social envy has the greatest destructive capability.

In summary, the more envy there is, the less the collective capacity to generate great men and the less the sociobiological quality of the group. The self-punishing character of this passion is evident even on a communitarian scale: the more envious a nation is, the smaller the number of eminent individuals, and therefore the less apt to create, to advance, and lead in history. The crisis of the governing minorities in Europe in the second half of this century and its consequent decadence are the result of the progression of social envy due to the work of egalitarian ideologies.

We must bear in mind another correlation: the importance of those three factors becomes more relevant with the degree of cultural evolution. Pushing the best aside is very difficult in small groups, and natural selection has many opportunities. On the other hand, the larger and more complex the group, the greater the lack of communication resulting from envy and the greater the number of possibilities for exiling and ostracizing. In primitive societies, the amount of cultural patrimony transmitted was very limited, and with the exception of magical esotericism, there was small difference in knowledge. As the fields of knowledge increased, education became imperative in the process of hierarchical creation or egalitarian envy. And, finally, genius is spontaneously acknowledged in primitive groups and is used immediately; on the other hand, the promotion of mediocrities and the humiliation of the eminent is made possible in more evolved societies by an envious technology geared to publicity, not the public. This makes it possible to conclude that, as a nation becomes modern and civilized, the negativity of envy becomes stronger and its sociobiological danger is intensified. Envy canceled fewer great men in Europe in the sixteenth century than in the twentieth, and one of the reasons America has become so powerful is that it has been able to instill a morality of emulation that neutralizes the growing possibilities of envy.

V. Envy, Hierarchy and the State

1. The Role of the Minorities

The direction and rhythm of human progress do not depend on the masses, even when they add up to hundreds of millions; they depend on superior minorities. The great historical jumps, like those of classical Greece, Christianity, the Renaissance, the French Revolution, or the Industrial Revolution were due to a few and not to the masses. The same happens with great national progress, including such contemporary instances as the Meiji revolution (Japan) and Sun Yat-Sen's in China.

We have archetypal examples in Spain. The Caliphate of Córdoba reached its zenith with Almanzor—Ibn Abi Amir—and a few years after the death of this leader the empire became fragmented into a large number of decadent kingdoms. The people were the same; only the leaders were different. Toward the end of the reign of Enrique IV, Spain found itself at the lowest point of its history: anarchy, poverty, corruption, discredit of kingship. Only two years after his death, Isabel and Fernando (Isabella and Ferdinand) brought peace to Castile. By 1497, they had already achieved national unity, and in 1480 the Parliament of Toledo institutionalized the first modern state. Within those fifteen years, the citizens remained the same: only the leaders changed. Instead of corrupt cliques, there was a selection of the capable. A kingdom that had come tumbling down in 1474 was by 1480 a great monarchy that brought an end to the reconquest of Spain and discovered America.

Why? For the simple reason that, since the appearance on this earth of *homo sapiens*, the supreme stimulus to progress has been the ability to use reason, and those who embody it more perfectly are the creative minorities. All men are rational; but only a few use reason with a high degree of innovative efficacy. If progress depends on the best use of superior intelligence, it is obvious that one of the main goals of any form of social organization is the promotion of the highly gifted, placing them at leadership levels within the selection and hierarchical distribution of the members of the community. One of the primary objectives of the state is to organize the work of citizens so that each one's capacities may be put to the best use. How can such an important goal be accomplished?

2. Hierarchical Ordering by the State

The social development of the group demands a simultaneous division and specialization of labor. Little by little, warriors, farmers, craftsmen, and merchants stand out. Each task allows for more and more specialized subdivisions. But within each task, masters and disciples soon appear; and among those, the excellent, the mediocre, and the deficient.

The modern state has not been a simple spectator in this process of specialization and hierarchical ordering but has assumed the role of referee. Education is the first field of hierarchical ordering. The state grants scholarly and academic degrees and in this manner orders the graduates hierarchically according to their degrees: Doctor, Master, Bachelor, high school diploma, and so forth. In fact, the difficulty of the tests required establishes a hierarchy of degrees. The teaching institutions establish another hierarchy; degrees from one university are considered higher than the same degree from another. At times, it is the state that opens centers for the formation of elites, like the famous Ecole Normal at Paris, which in fact creates a higher caste of Frenchmen, the "*normaliens.*" National education is not only a pedagogical institution; it is also an institution that establishes hierarchies.

Public administration is another form of hierarchical ordering. The state classifies its civil servants into superior, intermediary, and subordinate. Within each body, categories are created, and within each category seniority and merit are acknowledged. Promotions and *curricula vitae* are signs of a hierarchical order within the structure of the state. Even the protocol for admission obeys hierarchical laws. Higher degrees and greater knowledge are needed for higher positions, and there are lists compiled as a result of tests with a number one at the top followed by all the others. The mechanism for promotions is also hierarchical. The scales go from corporal to captain to general, and so on. Political appointments also have a hierarchical scale: minister, secretary of state, undersecretary, director general, and so on. Salaries are fixed according to the position held.

The state has promoted hierarchies in the private sector through the granting of nobility titles, decorations, and other types of distinctive honors. The state grants rewards and administers punishment: Medals are a merit, penal records are a demerit. The state, through positive norms, bestows authority in the workplace and establishes incentives, exemptions, and a large number of other means to promote individual effort and the subsequent social hierarchical ordering.

This hierarchical function of the state is primordial and most essential. Why? For two reasons: one is factual and immanent, and this is physical necessity; the other is ethical and transcendental, and this is justice.

The first reason is obvious. The fact of division of labor and unequal capacities implies certain hierarchies that the state may rationalize, radicalize, reduce, or invert, but never cancel. Human society—as well as animal society—is constitutively hierarchical, and the state must start from this radical fact.

The second justification is transcendental. Living together requires norms and the state is the instrument capable of dictating and imposing them. This is the primary reason for the existence of political power. But norms cannot be created by the sheer arbitrariness of the legislator; they must be just. There is no state without law, and law is a reference to justice, the ought of action. The ultimate foundation of justice is not a question for clarification at this point. In any event, one of the essential dimensions of any conception of justice—to give everyone what is his according to his merits—is the distributive justice of goods and positions. It is an essential imperative of government to distribute citizens hierarchically with justice.

This hierarchical function of the state is not, therefore, the outcome of chance. It is not even the happy invention of government or of legislation; it is an imperative derived from the nature of society and the idea of justice itself. It is conceivable that a state might hierarchically order its citizens with inequity; but it is inconceivable that a state would renounce this hierarchical function of ordering. One of the essential notes of the states is this hierarchical ordering of its citizens.

Within Hegelian thought, it would be the monopoly of the state to establish such hierarchies; from the viewpoint of a rational realism, the conclusion would be otherwise. The state may establish hierarchies through an arbitrary decision, independently of the objective qualifications of candidates. Such an action may have a transitory efficacy but be deficient, for the reason that it grants a power—*potestas*—that lacks the corresponding authority—*auctoritas*; it is pure coercion. This phenomenon is not exclusive of certain constitutional models. Nepotism is found in absolutist systems. Within democratic systems, the most frequent outcome is inequity in the distribution of and access to hierarchies and public funds by the members of the party.

Within the ethics of natural law, the legislator does not introduce law out of nothing; his function is limited to adapting the pre-existing natural law to every positive norm. For this reason, certain dispositions are unjust. In such a context, the different codes are temporal actualizations of permanent potentialities. Something analogous happens with the hierarchical function of the state, except that in this case the whole process takes place on an existential plane. What is already an anterior reality—the special capabilities of some citizens—should be juridically acknowledged and protected.

Human hierarchies stem from innate aptitudes, depending on the phenotypical scheme of the individual; thus society makes it possible with its educative means for the individual to develop those aptitudes by his own effort. Heredity, the environment, and the will are the causes for the unequal capacities among people. The hierarchical function of the state is prior and conditioning insofar as it stimulates the dynamism of social differences; but it is posterior and subordinate insofar as it acknowledges these aptitudes, makes available the means to practice them, grants the deserved power, and increases, maintains, or reduces it as the objective capacity increases, maintains itself, or diminishes.

The state defines justice but does not create it; nor is the state the only cause for social stratification. The hierarchical function of the state is not so much to create as to promote, acknowledge, and guarantee justice.

3. The Function and Division of Powers

The true inventor of the doctrinal scheme founding the "demoliberal" state was John Locke, and he is also the author of the division of power. His theory, as completed and developed later, became crystallized as the famous trichotomy: the legislative, the executive, and the judicial powers. An objection of principle has been raised against it: sovereignty and political power in its pure form are one and indivisible. And other factual objections have also been raised. There are also other powers, like the moderating power of a king or a president, the constitutive power of a constitutional tribunal or assembly, or the administrative power of the bureaucracy. A final pragmatic objection has also been raised: The theory is impossible to bring about since at times the legislative branch executes (when it gives its vote of confidence to the cabinet) and the executive branch legislates (when it dictates decrees of general application).

The trinitarian doctrine of the division of powers is untenable both at the conceptual level and at the level of facts, as happens with the majority of the postulates that serve as foundation for the social model of Locke and his epigone Rousseau. For this reason, the trinity of powers had to be substituted for the doctrine of the division of "functions" of the state and the distribution of those powers to certain branches. This distribution, coming in the shape of innumerable constitutional forms, tends to control despotism and guard some of the liberties of the people. It is not an exact theory, but a fluid legal resource that may be adaptable to presidentialism though not to parliamentarism, and that works respectably well at times though at others it does not. The ideologues of inorganic democracy point out the intrinsic virtues of the triple division of powers, not realizing that their model tends to serve rules of the party, a party-rule, and that the oligarchy of the majority party controls the chief of state, the parliament, and the government, and, depending on the organic structure of the magistracy, may also influence the constitutional tribunal and even the normal dispensation of justice. "Party rule," which *de iure* goes back to the classic theory of the division of powers as an untouchable dogma, *de facto* contradicts that theory's claims—at times as much as an absolute monarchy. The leader of the majority party performs the moderating function of controlling the legislative, the executive, and part of the judicial branches even though this is done through distinct agents.

The division of the functions of the state and their distribution into several branches brings in the obvious technical advantage of a division of labor and of specialization; it allows also for the independence of the judges who may take recourse against the administration, check the interference of sectarian politics against the citizens, and come closer to the sovereignty of the law or of the law of the state. This is an ethical advantage. This was an ideal not envisioned by Locke and has not only not been fully realized but is constantly threatened by despotism of the majority parties. This is the archetypal case of the so-called popular democracies.

The hierarchical function of the state is not still another function to be added to the constitutive, moderating, political, administrative, legislative, and judicial; it is rather a common quality of the activity that is the state. When a constitution is written down, a hierarchy of organs and norms is established. When the different activities of the several institutions are moderated, then questions of competence are not considered, as when political decisions are made to give promotions to some over others and goods are transferred to them; when administrative dossiers are resolved and some are more favored than others; when there is legislation and some receive rewards and punishments greater than others; and when sentence is passed on a case and some are granted a subjective right that others are denied. The hierarchical function is not one of more power; it is a transcendental property of every act of the state. It is an inherent aspect of the exercise of power.

4. Just Hierarchical Distribution

The hierarchical distribution is in part the work of the society and in part the work of the state. Hierarchical distribution by society, like the fame of a doctor, happens slowly, spontaneously, and at times hazardously. But the hierarchical distribution of the state, like the appointment of an ambassador, may be immediate, voluntary, and purposeful; thus it may be more susceptible to rationalization and ethical evaluation. It is discussed below.

A hierarchy is just if it corresponds to merit. The ideal position of each citizen from the standpoint of the state would be that which renders maximum social benefit. The optimal use of human resources should end up as a meritocracy. Such an ideal hierarchical distribution by the state requires certain objective criteria for measuring individual capacities, a functional determination of work in the several branches, and a corresponding reflection of these in the different echelons.

The distribution of human resources that the public administration needs is not usually done with economic criteria that lead to bureaucratic parasitism, low productivity, and unjust taxation. We are not dealing here with the formal acceptance of a timetable but of real necessities. Public administration, in general, tends towards parasitism and gigantism. In order to determine the number of employees, the state must come up, as private enterprise does, with strict functional criteria, rather than with criteria that are inflational or charitable. The exceptional public offers of work during periods of unemployment are no more than a cover-up of the problem, with the added serious dangers of mortgaging the future of the budget and closing the door to future generations.

Given certain needs, we must proceed to the selection of adequate personnel. The more just procedure is public competition with equal opportunity for all and with objective and invariable criteria of evaluation applied by tribunals that are capable and independent. Given the limited number of employees and the different echelons, the adjudication of positions must follow objective criteria of merit only.

Deviations from this hierarchical function of the state result in partial evaluations, imbalance between capacities and jobs, and arbitrariness in promotions and compensations. The main motivation for this deviation is not corruption or even nepotism; it is political favoritism. Public offices are no longer for sale, but very often they are adjudicated to the "nearest one." There exists, no doubt, family or affective proximity; but the greatest danger to a just hierarchization is the political proximity of the fellow believer.

5. Party Rule and Selectivity

A state made out of parties and party rule is the form that, after two hundred years of degenerative evolution, representative inorganic democracy takes. The actual power within such a model does not belong to the leader, the chambers, the intermediary bodies, or the people, but to the oligarchies of the parties. As I have pointed out on another occasion (*La Partitocracia*, ed. Instituto de Estudios Políticos, Madrid, 1977, pp. 154 *passim*), the main characteristics of party rule are: (1) the disappearance of independent deputies, for the parties control the making and electing of the candidates; (2) the impoverishment of the political class, for it must be docile to the leader of the party; (3) a partial robbery within the electorate, for its operative possibilities are reduced to the limits offered by the parties—at times only two; (4) the conversion of the deputy into an instrumental number, since he has to pronounce himself according to the discipline of the group; (5) the devaluation of the legislative chamber as it is controlled by the government of the majority party and reduced to the margins by the extraparliamentary majority that makes it possible to control it or change it; (6) the concentration of the power of the state in the leader of the majority party; (7) in sum, party rule or "partocracy" vacillates between the dictatorship of the oligarchy of one party and an anarchy where there is no majority or coalition among the minorities.

This system works out quite satisfactorily in the United States with the corrective of the presidential veto, in Great Britain with the aristocratic corrective of the House of Lords, in Switzerland with the corrective of the local and regional depoliticization, and so on. But it does not work at all in many other contemporary states. Like any constitutional model, it is neither good nor bad in itself; its efficacy depends on how it is applied to the circumstances of a concrete society at a determined period.

The supreme imperative of all economic activity is the optimization of resources in order to obtain the greatest yield from the available social capital. This ideal is fulfilled mostly by the extremely complex mechanism of the market. But as Hayek has shown, it is not fulfilled by the intervention of the state and even less so by parliament, for it tends to increase the participation of the public sector in the economy. This leads to certain misappropriations and decreases in social revenues and, because political parties tend to use public funds not for investments that accrue greater economic revenue but that accrue maximum political revenue, it translates into transfers of money to the electoral clientele. Political parties do not establish economic priorities or determine the assignment of resources according to criteria for the national common good, but for the party good—and therefore unjustly. The partocratic selection of the beneficiaries of the budgets of the state is very deficient. And what about the human selection of distribution of echelons within the state's hierarchy?

Political parties perform two types of selections: political class and public administration, namely—oligarchies of the party and civil servants. The party selects the leading minorities by means of the candidates for election. The system of parliamentary groups of a party demands that its members vote mostly on partly lines; the deputies of one group must pronounce themselves according to the norms of the leader. In parliament, the deputies of one party, with the exception of some from the center, are not thinking heads, but rather numbers to form a minority or a majority. It follows that ideological docility is one of the most important qualities to be found in anyone aspiring to a political career, for this is the guarantee that his declarations and vote will follow the party lines of the leader. This submission is almost assured in those without personal opinions, and they make the best candidates, with the most probable discretion and fidelity. But people of this type, who hold the functions of their intellect in suspension and whose main preoccupation is to survive, are usually not the most gifted. This is the main reason the political class selected by the party oligarchy is, with rare exceptions, a class of mediocrities. A quick survey of contemporary parliaments shows the great extent to which this sociological law is true.

How do parties select civil servants? The natural inclination of political parties is to saturate with fellow believers the ranks of public administration. To this end, when they are in power, they try by legal means to broaden the legal possibilities of the free assignment of state and local employees—not so much those on temporary work, but those on permanent contract. When this is not possible, those in power make use of procedures that achieve the same ends, like the merger of independent bodies, early retirement, the enlargement of the different ranks and posts, the consolidation of those under temporary contract, selective examinations, and, as a last resort, the manipulation of the courts. In this way, even when elections and political power are lost, bureaucracy still remains on the side of the past administration. Meanwhile, members of the party are rewarded with public funds, devotion to the party has grown deeper, and even those who are merely doubting or are opportunists receive stimulus to join. This is a clear case of enlarging one's own political clientele by means of favoritism. This is obviously not a criterion that agrees with the common good or with justice, for it promotes party followers even when they are not capable, with the consequence that the best are pushed aside.

The teaching profession constitutes a special case. The parties inspired by Marxism have adopted the tactic of coming to power not through the massive support of the proletariat, but through the cooperation of so-called intellectuals. It makes little difference that such a tactic contradicts the postulates of historical materialism. Its practical application runs through the controls shaping public opinion, educational institutions, and the means of mass communication. The university is the main center of this activity since it is the "alma mater" of the whole educative process, and the parties try to make it a branch of the state and fill its positions not on the basis of scholarship and knowledge but party affiliation. When these parties feel insecure with respect to their hold on power, they oversaturate the positions with appointments that make departments top-heavy and deny promotions to future generations. In this way, the disciplines become politicized and lose intellectual dignity. Those who rebel against ideological subservience, ordinarily the best, are ostracized or eliminated, and the transmission of culture is left in the hands of the commentators on the party catechism. Objective science thus becomes egalitarian. This is one of the most serious outcomes of the hierarchical function of the state: injustice to the teachers, the students, and the truth. This is the road to the diabolical utopia Orwell described.

Besides the distribution of civil servants, party favoritism works directly and systematically in the selectivity of those higher ranks where decisions are made and thus in the hierarchy of the state. This favoritism is possible even within those bodies that are more strictly controlled by rules, like the military or the legislative branch, and the efforts of this policy are the promotion of the less capable and the demoralization of the best. In this manner, certain bodies that were the pride of the state have become broken down. In any case, the result is distributive injustice, a waste of human resources, and the unfulfillment of the hierarchical ordering of the state.

6. Envy and Inverse Selectivity

The envious person does not acknowledge that anyone is more worthy than he is. He is therefore radically antihierarchical, and, as Madam de Staël wrote, prefers the equality of hell to the gradation of heaven. Those parties that recruit voters from among the envious promise egalitarian societies in which the state will not only renounce its function of organizing its citizens according to a hierarchy of merits but will destroy all types of hierarchy. When the oligarchies of those parties gain power, they feel the need to accomplish part of the totality of such a program. The procedures are usually the same.

Equality is easier to achieve by devaluing all the officers rather than by promoting all the soldiers. And what happens with the military is equally applicable to any type of hierarchy. Besides, the suppression of minorities is, because of their smaller numbers, less difficult than the education of the masses. Furthermore, these negative actions have the advantage that they may be realized without producing anything and without exercising any creative effort. For this reason, they are within the reach of the least capable. These technical possibilities are enhanced by the politics of pleasing the massive clientele of the envious. This explains the fact that all egalitarian activities are in the hands of the inferior and are carried out from below by decapitating those on high.

The political parties that choose to break down the state rather than order its hierarchies usually start by dismantling the elitist groups of public administration. Some are suppressed, others are merged with auxiliary branches, or the standards of administration may be lowered or infiltrated by political appointees as leaders or by adding massive promotions of mediocrities. Those who, because of their services, are at the top of the echelons are retired prematurely, purged, or sent into hibernation. Salaries become uniform to make sure that the best do not have economic superiority over the inferior or the experts over the nonexperts. In this way, the state's bureaucracy loses its definite shape and becomes a shapeless and homogeneous pool where everyone is reduced to an interchangeable number. This is the paradise of the envious civil servant.

The next step is to break down the whole society. The radical attack is focused on education; the centers that educate elites must be suppressed and the gifted must be forced to keep a low profile and keep step with the deficient. Then the structures of authority must be made to disappear. The head of the family is accused of paternalism, the president of the company is accused of exploitative ambition, the hardworking or more qualified is accused of being a loner or trying to please management. Everywhere, everyone is encouraged to use uncivil and plebeian manners, including fashion and language. Moral and aesthetic values are denied with the ensuing permissiveness and confusion. And when social rejection occurs, then cynicism takes over: "It was a mistake" or "It will not happen again." But it happens again. The state's means of communication and the official rewards offered are the main instruments of this ethical subversion.

But this is not the end. The triumphant envious person is not satisfied with lowering the best; he must humiliate them by placing them under the supervision of the inferior. The order of the hierarchies is inverted, and so are merit and qualifications. The failed and resentful employee is promoted. Incompatibilities are multiplied so that he who can do the most remains inactive for the longest time, and the outstanding person returns to the crowd. The most impudent actor is rewarded and so is the most informalist painter, the grossest language user, the most dissolute preacher. The most secret and private becomes the most respectable, and the monstrous becomes normal. What was once considered good is now considered evil, and vice versa. This upheaval of values is the goal of resentment and, rather than being the culmination, is the supreme transfiguration of envy. This program is presented, with a sublime hypocrisy, as a "change" or moral renewal.

The supreme social crime is that it is the state that performs this inverse selection, for it is contrary to its proper essence. For this reason, such operations are always transitory. The egalitarian rulers, after they have destroyed the values of a nation, end up sacralizing an ideology and rebuilding a hierarchy—the *Nomenklatur*—that is qualitatively inferior to its predecessors, more closed and rigid, and inclined to terror in order not to become the victim of its own egalitarian tactics. The guilty societies feel condemned by nature to pay, for generations, a heavy duty on account of the unconditional surrender to envy and resentment that they exploited to gain power.

7. Favoritism and Meritocracy

The history of public administration is the history of a fight between the tendency of those in power to appoint the civil servant for personal and arbitrary reasons and the rational imperative that selection be made institutionally and on the basis of merit and qualifications. The first method is that of free designation, and it corresponds to a patrimonial conception of the state. The politician feels that the country is his to use, and he exploits it in favor of his relatives, friends, and fellow members of the party, expecting full submission from them as compensation. This is a personal relation between "I appoint you so that you serve me" and "I serve you because you appointed me." This is an arbitrary political contract.

The second procedure is meritocracy or employment regulated by aptitude and according to objective criteria with equal opportunity for others: Impartial referees evaluate the candidates, and promotions and appointments are decided as a function of seniority and rank. This is an institutional relationship: "The law appoints you so that you may serve the community" and "I serve my people because this is my moral and legal duty."

To the degree that public administration becomes more rational, arbitrariness in appointments diminishes and meritocracy increases as do the regulations for promotions. This has been the historical line followed by the states, with some episodic setbacks, regardless of their constitutional model. Rome is an example. A gradation of honors that enforces a hierarchy is established with the appearance of norms, like the laws of Villius (180 B.C.) and Cornelius (80 B.C.). The order of progression is as follows: quaestor, aedile, censor, praetor, and consul. In order to become a quaestor, it was necessary to have been in ten military campaigns and be thirty years old. To become an aedile, one had to be thirty-seven years old, forty to be a praetor, and forty-three to be a consul. The legate or commander of a legion had to have been a senator. To become a proconsul, one had to have been a consul. This *cursus honorum,* with variations according to certain periods, was for the Republic as much as for the Empire the spine of Roman administration. In this way, the acquired rights were protected, services rendered were rewarded, nepotism and corruption were controlled, training and experience were used, and the dignity of the institutions was preserved.

The Spanish kings, through a series of controls, progressively limited their discretionary powers. This process of rationalization accelerated when Bravo Murillo, a moderate among moderates, brought out the decree of 18 June 1852. This is how he formulated his motives to Isabel II: "Neither your Majesty nor your Ministers take the power to appoint employees as a right established for your own benefit, but, on the contrary, as a duty difficult to execute that forces you to look for the appropriate persons that are most able to carry out the public charge." This decree established entrance examinations for all employees, with the exception of those who, like judges, the military, diplomats, and professors, already had their own regulations. It also ruled the ranks for promotions. This norm was only partially applied until the cabinet born of the "progressivist" revolution of 1868 overturned the decree and established total arbitrariness: "The Ministers . . . appoint and promote freely the employees of their respective dependencies." The rationalization of the public function continues to be the actual model in use—with exceptions during the Restoration I and the Republic II and by means of the Maura law of 22 June 1918—and finds its culmination with the López-Ródo law. The contemporary history of Spain proves that administration is more effective when it is less arbitrary with its appointments.

The state based on law substitutes general, permanent norms for politically autonomous will, thereby reducing arbitrariness in the access to public appointments. Since all democratic states claim to prefer the state based on law, it might seem that there is a necessary correlation between democracy and meritocracy; but this is not the case. Sila's dictatorship was based much more on merit than Republican Rome was; and in Spain the same is true with the Catholic kings and with respect to the Republic. We cannot ignore the fact that the dependence of democratic governments on the people forces them to mount their electoral machinery, appointing friendly employees at the national, regional, and local levels. Hence the fact that multiple-party democracies are no less inclined to arbitrary methods in hiring practice than absolute monarchies. The process of regulation of the public sector is separable from the constitutional model, and its efficacy is the result of the degree of rationalization of the state.

The rationalization of the state has supposedly reduced bureaucratic party rule to a minimum—the so-called political and temporary posts. Both processes, however, are so common and elastic that they have kept retarding the acclaimed meritocratic process. The number of political appointments increases or decreases differently in different countries. For example, the governors or prefects are professional civil servants in France, while they are not in Spain. Governments that nationalize different economic sectors include, within the roster of political appointments, the leaders of management of public companies; and federal states multiply political appointments in proportion to the autonomous centers they politically hold. Where interventionism increases, the rationalizing tendency to enlarge meritocracy and reduce party rule decreases.

We need to add to all these factors a campaign against the official tests for appointments or promotions. In the case of university chairs or professorships, the system of tests or "oppositions" for selection has certain extreme features that have been caricatured; but is there a just system that is objective and equal for all candidates before a tribunal of peers capable of establishing a hierarchy of aptitudes? If we suppress open and objective tests for access to a public post, regardless of the effort involved in written or oral tests, we fall back into nepotism and cronyism, or even worse, into the politicization of the state's bureaucracy, from judges to admirals and diplomats.

Arbitrariness in appointments hides arbitrariness in promotions, transfers, freezes, and destitutions. One of the most written-about persons of the last century was the "dismissed employee." In nineteenth century Athens, the employees dismissed as the result of a government crisis used to gather at "Lamentation Square," a place of sorrow that keeps its name to this day. In Madrid in 1840 a book appeared with the title *The Cry of the Dismissed*, and in the first Restoration even newspapers were published to defend the dismissed employee from the arbitrariness of the politicians—for example, *El Empleo* (Jobs) and *Los destinos civiles* (Civil appointments). The state's bureaucracy was at the mercy of the whims of those in power.

The consequences of such an institutional inversion are grave. One is the generalization of the spoils system or the distribution of the budget as if it were the spoils of war for the governing team. Another consequence is the diminution of effectiveness of the administration. Yet another is the difficulty of rotation among the political parties, for, given the immobility of the civil servant, how it is possible to govern with a sectarian and adverse bureaucracy?

There is a great deal of talk about neutralizing the armed forces but hardly any at all about cleaning up the public function. The rationality of the state requires: (a) selection through objective, competitive, and open evaluation of the candidates; (b) continuity in civil service and also respect for the rights achieved; (c) professionalization; (d) reduction of the number of posts that ministers or their cabinets may arbitrarily use for political reasons and the demand that other high-level political appointments be made from people belonging to competent bodies of proven ability; and (e) for the rest of appointments, decisions based on regulations rather than the whim of politicians.

The professionalization and rationalization of public administration is a rational imperative of the hierarchical function of the state.

8. Conclusion

The abominable spectacle seen in the last century of continuous traffic of civil servants after an election—the friends of the victors were given the jobs, the losers were dismissed—made it imperative to establish certain objective criteria for greater rationalization of admission to those jobs and promotions in public administration. This procedure set off a process of regulations that, with ups and downs, has reached a high point in certain countries. In this matter, the Spanish political change has meant an important step backward, and in some sectors this step backward has moved all the way to the reign of Isabel II, famous for the politicalization of administration and a general decadence.

Singula quaeque locum teneant, Horace proclaimed. The right man in the right place is the political kernel of Anglo-Saxon democracy. Each one in his place, according to merit, is a fundamental imperative for any form of government, and it is up to the judicial branch to establish impediments to unjust favoritism or the envious ordering in the distribution of power and responsibility. And this ordering must be a rigorous one, particularly in those governments that naturally tend to a partial selectivity and, on occasions, to an inverse one. For example, party rule requires certain norms for admission and promotion to civil appointments that need to be extremely rigorous so that objective criteria prevail in order to reduce arbitrariness to a marginal anecdote and raise individual merit in the respect of the public. This is not just a demand of social justice and reason; the hierarchical function of the state is the key to the progress of the human species upon this earth and in history.

VI. The Defenses

1. The Flight from Envy

The envious never speak of envy, and those that are envied hardly ever mention it—philosophers have hardly touched it. While not a taboo, envy is certainly indiscreet, inconvenient, and almost forbidden. This is paradoxical for it is a universal phenomenon and, nevertheless, silenced, a great problem and yet avoided. Envy weighs heavily over the social life of people, and we all covertly take positions regarding envy: some promote it, others fight it, the majority avoid it. Why do humans take precautions against envy? Perhaps the reason is, as for the people from primitive and classical societies, the fear of the fascination of evil. Even among those people more empirically inclined, the buried remains of such a belief still endure. The cardinal motive, however, is less commercial at the present level of rationality in contemporary societies. Envy promotes harmful and hostile behavior, and this is what needs to be neutralized.

The primary defense is to hide one's own happiness. In principle, it might appear that it would be enough to say nothing about it, since happiness is pure, internal subjectivity. Nonetheless, people do not feel safe with such a line of action so near to them, and they raise around themselves a wall—not a physical wall but a moral one which varies in perimeter and height according to each person; this is what we call "intimacy." What is included within this enclosure? Generally, it is not our work, for according to the Biblical curse, it is more afflictive than pleasurable; rather, our leisure is the source of happiness. And so with love, the center of all earthly adventures and shaper of the nuclear space of intimacy. The next barrier is that of the family and of friendship, since our possible leisure and intensity of its use depend to a large measure on our economic resources; our personal finances become another separation we build to distance us from the others. Love, friends, and money are reserved matters because they raise envy, but they are fully shared among lovers for envy of one another is inconceivable. Intimacy is the space of happiness which we close to the curiosity of others, not so much out of modesty but out of a need to reduce the occasions of the envy of others. This is the universal and basic self-defense we use against envy, and if this feeling did not exist, would it not be senseless to have this wide and opaque space of our intimacy?

In the common man, this region of restricted access is relatively small and permanent, while in the cultivated man it is wide and varied because part of his work coincides with his leisure, and this deals with peculiar and uncommon activities. We may say that, all in all, to improve oneself is to open new horizons of happiness and, therefore, the possibility of happy occasions is greater in the wise than in the ignorant, in the disciplined than in the unruly, in the superior than in the mediocre; at the same time the sensibility towards pain is also increased. This distinction, because of its newness and visibility, awakens greater curiosity. It is for this reason that the best are called upon to increase their public service and, simultaneously, to hide larger and larger portions of their lives to protect themselves against the envious, thus forcing this permanent contradiction. This strange situation creates two extreme types of reactions: the logical one of isolation, and the pathetic one of contempt and challenge.

The Stoic advice to the situation is loneliness in friendship, and this corresponds to the Apollonian self-sufficient and reasoning man. The extreme position would be to become a complete hermit, the absolute flight. On the other hand is the greedy Dionysian hedonist, whose passionate position counsels the dominion over others and over action; exhibitionism is the total presence here. The former fears envy, the latter awakens it and challenges it. Between both ends we find a large mass of people who are experts at consuming dosages of isolation with portions of belittling of others and of ostentation. This is a case of a calculated risk of the advantages and disadvantages in order to maximize success by dodging envy. This kind of person will not act publicly unless he first measures the potential for envy. Intellectual society would be unexplainable if the dense narrative of defensive and challenging reactions against envy were left out.

2. The Simulation

Next to the strategy of hiding happiness—a passive attitude—there is the strategy of using disguises, that is, showing pain where there is joy. The rich person emphasizes his worries, the powerful his responsibilities, the intelligent his doubts, the lover his jealousies, the winner his disappointments, the admired the treasons against him, and so on. The directors of spiritual life have suggested a solution in covering up—to pretend that there is family misadventure, an illness, a frustration, or the inability to disarm the envious. I heard an actor say that the critics praised him more after the news spread that he was sick. Gracián used to advise eminent Spaniards to widely advertise a small indiscretion so that the envious would feed upon it and leave the rest alone. With such simple strategies people try to force others to pay no attention or, on occasion, to inspire in them joy at the misery of others or commiseration—anything is better than allowing envy to appear.

When the happy circumstance is impossible to hide or to divert, the envied must use extreme resources. One is to humble himself and ask the pardon of the envious; another is to convince them that he is only an instrument of their well-being. Both tactics are habitual among politicians and famous people. The democratic leader uses both recipes simultaneously: he begs for the vote of the envious and at the same time convinces them that he is simply their representative. The final goal is the persuasion of the envious that the superior is not his rival but rather a happy servant, a truthful occurrence in many cases, but this is another question.

Environmental hostility and the limitless human ambition are the reasons why there is so little happiness, but envy is the reason why happiness is less apparent. Envy is the threat that at times inhibits, and that always encourages hiding of human happiness. Humans, when surrounded by envy, tend to show a mediocre happiness, crossed with dissatisfactions; and this would be the impression that a naive observer would have of humanity; but, would it not be true to affirm that there are many evanescent happinesses and also a prolonged depth of bearable pain?

The obscuring, as much as the diverting of happiness may have collective protagonists. In general, groups superior in quality, position, or wealth, the roots of presumed superior happiness hide from the inferior groups and constitute closed circles of collective intimate areas. They have at their disposal their own places of reunion, and these are not easily accessible to others. Their customs and habits are peculiar to them and they practice endogamy. They create a unique world of symbolic forms, including linguistics. The greater the difference between one group and the rest, the greater is the confinement. Like the forbidden city in imperial Peking and the Kremlin in Soviet Russia, carried to the limit, the elites would commit esoteric suicide. Contrary to what demogogues preach, the fact of the isolationism of these groups does not come out of pride, nor their guilty complex, nor a supposed and undefined "classicism"; it is rather a defense against envy. This is the reason it is found at all levels, including the inferior ones, and this is the reason it is a universal phenomenon and compatible with publicity within its own orbit. The ivory towers of the envied increase their social isolation and the real inferiority of the envious. This is a complementary form of inexorable self-punishment.

This cloistering is different from what Nietzsche called the "pathos of distance," that is, a no-man's land that every hierarchical position tries to place between itself and the inferior one to make the assault more difficult and idealize the qualities of the group. The greater the power, the larger the distance from it. This distance is particularly habitual and operative at the peak of the scale, and values are expected to become incarnate with more purity and fullness. Thus, distance, rather than protecting from envy, serves as an exemplar to an authority.

When envy is particularly intense, groups also take recourse in disguises. The high Arabic bourgeois spread their riches towards the interior of their houses, while the external walls showed poverty. The Andalusian patio is a remnant of this habit. The austerity of the monastic walls contrasts with the sumptuousness of the cloisters. From the Church and the state down to the small corporation, these collective groups tend to make a show only of institutional luxury, for to the degree that it appears without a head or its title is anonymous, to the same degree it is more difficult to envy. On the other hand, they jealously cover up the wealth of their members and only publicize a facet of their work. The archetypal example is that of the elites created by party rule, where images of individual austerity are publicized and public display of luxury is reserved for the functions of the state. Such displays of double personality are disguises, since in any kind of human existence there is a natural state of simplicity, and not even the more divinized monarchs could live permanently in *statu maiestatis*.

It has been repeated since Machiavelli that politics is rhetoric and often enough a swindle. Is it, perhaps, on account of a constitutive falsehood in politicians? Of course not. The governed are deceived for many practical reasons; but one of the most important is to neutralize envy against the leading minority. The principles of legitimacy—divine right or consent, the techniques of representation—organic or inorganic, the freedom of information—private or the state's, etc., are legal fictions with more or less foundation, thought out or divulged in order to carry out the important goal of containing the envy of the people, which, if it overflowed, would lead to an ungovernable anarchy.

3. Courtesy

Is courtesy a plot to appease the envious? Courtesy is a form of behavior that, while not compulsory, is external and performed to please people. To use discretion is essential here, for, otherwise, it would not be courtesy but simply the fulfillment of a duty. As an external behavior, it is sufficient that it be materially executed, for, in contrast to love and charity, it is not required that the act coincide with the feeling. These stereotyped courtesies are optative rites in certain places, and there are also courtesies that are simply personal.

It was Flechier who first affirmed that certain practices of courtesy are formulated to appease the envy of others and disarm it. Tips, reciprocal invitations to celebrations or collective invitations to celebrate a happy occasion, the sharing of home and food with the guests, and, in general, compliments ("please," "bon appetit," etc.) and sympathy are examples of these rituals. Such a heterogeneous list of presumed nonfascinating spells requires a casuistic analysis.

If we examine, for example, the most universal "tipping situations," it is difficult to imagine that the person guiding a patron to a theater seat might envy him, for he has many occasions to see the show; waiters do not easily envy the diner, for they have access to the same food; taxi drivers cannot envy [the fact that passengers travel in the streets by car]. Which are, therefore, the envious elements that we try to neutralize with a tip? Are wedding or anniversary invitations to neighbors or acquaintances issued to placate a supposed envy or with the desire to increase happiness through an increase in numbers and joy? Is the offer of a cigarette or a drink to a casual acquaintance an answer to the fear of being envied or to the desire to avoid loneliness, or is it to cement a friendship? And what about those stereotyped compliments? How can they virtually stop envy if the person presumed envious knows that those formalisms have lost their true meaning? When the host says, "This is your house," who could believe that such a statement is a real gift of the house he enters? And, finally, since the majority of the rules of courtesy are used with people whom the assumed envied person is not going to see again or who are easily identifiable, how can such doubtful envy cause anxiety?

Courtesy, in general, is not a means to destroy envy: it is rather the lubricant to smooth social relations, the symbol of respect towards others, a declaration of solidarity and sympathy and, therefore, very distant from selfish and dividing envy.

Does the envied protect himself by doing favors to the envious? This is an old question already negatively answered by Plutarch. Our experience of charity and generosity has already confirmed the classical opinion. Neither Christianity or philanthropy have extinguished envy; socialism under the pretext of a just distribution, has obviously done nothing more than increase it. The power to benefit others is a fountain of happiness and a clear demonstration of superiority over the beneficiary. When the envious receives favors from the envied he feels that his inferiority in happiness increases and thus intensifies the feeling of envy. Besides, the normal imperative to be grateful contributes to a deterioration of the state of the soul. Envy annuls gratitude, for it is incompatible with it. For this reason, the ungrateful, envious person finds himself burdened with an additional guilt that he tries to remove with the usual inversion of values. This discharge of the conscience of the envious requires self-convictions like these: "He gives out of what he owns with injustice, what he does not need and less than I deserve." Such ethical manipulations, so characteristic of resentment, add anxiety to the envious. To reward those capable of gratitude, or to reward anonymously, may increase solidarity and the total of happiness; to give to the envious is to multiply his antisocial desires and his misery. In order to cure envy, the envied does not need to be generous—he must be miserable. This is the only thing we cannot ask from humans who are intrinsically and essentially made for happiness.

If, in this context, altruism is useless, envy promotes selfishness; if simulation works, then it promotes deceit.

Envy is the main reason that social life is a lie and that people live in ivory towers.

VII. Overcoming and Suppressing Envy

1. The Possible Options

Is there anyone who is superior to everyone in everything, particularly, in happiness? It is possible. But the rest, at a determined moment, are equal to virtually all humans, and are inferior to many in countless aspects, and probably in happiness. It is, therefore, obvious, that if inferiority in happiness produces envy such a feeling would constitute a necessary evil for the immense majority of humans. Experience proves, however, that not all inferiorities in happiness give rise to envy. There are, for example, innumerable parents who do not envy their children, but sacrifice themselves even more so that the children exceed them in happiness. The conclusion is evident: the consciousness of inferiority in happiness does not necessarily entail a feeling of envy. If there are acceptable inferiorities, the problem may be reduced to discovering the ways for such acceptability. Whoever is able to assimilate his inferiorities will be immunized against envy. How can this be achieved? Before we go deep into this we must examine a previous question: why does inferiority in happiness cause us misery?

Happiness is a state of being created by the satisfaction of desires, and every human act is moved by a sovereign impulse to reach the highest possible degree of well-being. We only wish for the good we know and, for this reason, we tend to desire what we do not possess and we presume it brings happiness to others. The superior happiness of others, insofar as it is known to us, is the main source of desire, and any pending desire is the source of misery. The contemplation of a real or presumed greater happiness—the measure that it manifests our own dissatisfaction with others—entails pleasure. This feeling is an essential trick of nature for it stimulates humans and leads them to advance. The cultural evolution for our species would have been very slow had it not been for the weight of our personal, relative inferiority. The working mechanism of such inner sorrow is evident. *Homo sapiens* would still be waiting for a genetic mutation to be able to leave the paleolithic if humans were totally insensitive to the superiority of the imagined or real happiness of others. Desire is the basic energy of human evolution. From this point of view, the ethics of asceticism, though capable of more happiness than the Faustian, are radically involutive as in the Oriental and Stoic versions. Whoever does not desire cuts himself from the creative dynamism of nature. Does he escape a trap or does he cheat? This large moral question demands another volume.

The pain at the possibility of being less may give rise to three main attitudes: a positive one, which includes the effort to achieve what one desires; a neutral one, which is the acceptance of our inferiority in happiness; and a negative one, which is the desire that the other lose the good we desire. The first is emulation, the last one is envy. The first one requires effort, the last one does not, except when misery prolongs itself and is doubled: pain at our own dissatisfaction and pain at the happiness of another. We fall into envy for a lack of effort, out of laziness, for a self-obsession that leads to a feeling of impotence. Vital entropy diminishes in the envied and increases in the envious. Envy, insofar as it is a self-abandonment and surrender, is initially easier, though later on one must pay a high price for such weakness. The crossroad is at this point: to fight to become more, to simulate inferiority, or to abandon oneself to envy. Let us start at the first option.

2. Emulation

Emulation is not a heroic attitude but an ordinary one, for it proceeds from a radical instinct of the species, the desire to be more. Humans find themselves with a personal genetic code within a concrete world. These are the two given factors of existence, the rest we make ourselves. We do not play out our history according to an already prefabricated role given to us by others. The largest portion of our biography is not an inheritance, but a creation. In this sense, the self is created and we are all *self-made men*.

The leading desire of children is to become "grownups," and adolescents are asked continuously, "What do you want to be when you grow up?" In this apparently trivial question throbs the transcendental and universal conviction that humans work out their own project of existence. This is the reason why such a question has become a ritual one. Humans "are" not fixed, which is a remarkable difference from the rest of nature; they "want to be" this or that. Some decide it with rigor and viability, but not a single young person conceives of his future as a pure work of chance. One is born under concrete circumstances and with a concrete constitution, but what one eventually becomes, though conditioned by one's own abilities and capacities, depends entirely on one's actions.

Is it possible to find out what people want to become? It looks like an impossible task, for every person is a nonduplicable individual with attitudes, tastes, and particular aspirations. Priest, soldier, poet, scientist, business man? The list is endless. But this infinity of vocations does not mean the question cannot be answered. In spite of the plurality of concrete enterprises all humans coincide in a radical and specific vocation that no one has emphasized with its due importance; we all want "to be more." Let us try to clarify and unfold such a thick and tight expression.

All humans aspire to become more in their areas of action. They also aspire to become better known in their profession and to have a larger portion of people recognize their growing merit. Every profession is conceived as a succession of promotions. People as disparate as the artist and the chairman of the board agree on this. All wish to become and "be worth more," to rise in the hierarchy of efficacy and consideration.

But they also desire to possess things. The saying "you are worth as much as you own" mirrors the indubitable fact that, contrary to other members of the planet, humans are technical subjects; that is, they use instruments that run from the jawbone to the computer, and therefore, personal superiority depends in part on the team and the instruments one uses. Hence, one of the ways to be more is to have more. This is not a superiority that is personal as much as patrimonial, and in no way ignoble, since instruments are a product of the intellect. Humans, to the degree that they are within the social economy, strive to "have more" in order to "have more power."

It is true there are people, like the philosopher or the mystic, who are dedicated to what the Greeks called the life of theory. And it is possible to find among them those so distant from earthly ambitions, who do not search for material goods and even renounce the inclination to let their compatriots classify them according to any type of hierarchy. Are these exceptions that negate the general law? No, for neither detachment nor modesty imply a renunciation of the specific human vocation to become more. The follower of mystical practices looks for deeper knowledge, and the most spiritual of the mystics desires to come closer to God without delays on the way. These are their peculiar and most ambitious ways of becoming more.

The basic desire of humans is not the simple increase of the external patrimony in order to increase their power. There is a successive deepening of desire. To begin with, the conservation instinct impels us to last; this is the primitive way of being more—lasting a longer time. Later we try to increase the number of our useful goods; and still later we seek knowledge and virtue. These are growing levels of intimacy and substantiality; knowledge and decency are habits that become embodied in the subject and, in this way, his perfected nature. The desire to be more does not stop at the level of the accidental, but extends into the substantial. Man has become more and more *sapiens;* he strives to become superman in the world and reach the heavens as blessed spirit, that is, to become an angel. This is the genuine "to be more," for it is ontological.

What distances us most from the inferior animals is our determined will to be more. Those gains at the disposal of humanity are the fruit of a very strong impulse, in the best members of the human race, to be more. This is a very fruitful thrust, and it gave us fire, cities, science, and laws. All that is great in history comes out of this impulse to improve one's self and others; and that is, therefore, radically unegalitarian, though it is enriching to others in the long run. Self-perfection and self-emulation are the two sides of the expression "to be more." A vital creative thrust weakens envy. "Be more" is the categorical imperative of evolution, and *per accidens,* also the absolute antidote of envy. But it is not possible, always, to be more than others due to the circumstantial and constitutive limitations we have. We need to accept and assimilate, therefore, numberless inferiorities. But how? In the first place, by overcoming them with other superiorities; in the second, feeling happiness at what is valuable even if it belongs to others; in the third, with a feeling of solidarity with the whole species; and finally with sympathy.

3. The Work Well Done

There is not a single normal human who lacks abilities, predispositions, and opportunities to perform some type of activity to an eminent degree, namely, better than the majority of those around him. This is a superiority derived from a specialized vocation and from a will to improvement and excellence. This generalization is based on the moral of "the work well done," embodied during centuries by the artisans' guilds. This precept was tacitly repealed by the French Revolution, which liberalized and broke down the hierarchy within the crafts until they ended up in anarchy and, later on, by the Industrial Revolution, which mechanized production and made out of workers objects without personality. The responsibility for the work well done moves, in an anonymous and mass production, from the working masses to the planning elite. Were the multitudes who abdicated their creative capacity to the routine of a factory aware that by renouncing a personal work of quality they were also abolishing one of the best ways to neutralize envy? Two egalitarianisms, the legal and the mechanic, narrowed for the masses the path of "work well done" throwing them down into the pits of universal inferiority, and therefore, to the redoubled temptation of envy. We cannot wait for a total mechanization of the work place in order to humanize work; we must return the lost individuality to the working effort, if not in its qualitative aspect at least in its quantitative one. We need to multiply those systems of production that allow workers to be recognized by name, and salaries and promotions should be again determined by merit. Promotion due to seniority only, egalitarian remunerations and the lineal raise in salaries are the case for the dissolution of the morality of the work well done, and consequently, for the inflation of envy. This is a vicious cycle: envy demands equality, and equality promotes envy. "Do what you do, and let it be better than anyone else's" is the liberating slogan from the inferiority of envy. The creative and happy attitude is to substitute universal uniformity with a generalized distinctiveness.

4. What is Valuable in the Genitive

The envious person suffers from color blindness in his appraisals: he is capable of acknowledging value in so far as it is his or can be made his, and tends to deny it if it belongs to others or is unreachable. A good vaccine against envy is to acknowledge everything that is valuable, independent of its possessor. The application of this maxim stumbles against one cognitive obstacle. There are certain qualities, like humility, that Christians consider valuable, but non-Christians do not. There are forms, like abstract paintings and dodecaphonic music that some appreciate and others do not. And there are behaviors and facts that, depending on the observer, deserve apologies or praise. The evaluation of logical, ethical, esthetic, religious, or merely useful values is not fully objective and it undergoes changes in time, space, the tribe, or the individual. But this does not mean that the ethical color blindness of the envious is incurable. It is not necessary to eliminate subjective discrepancies in the appraisal of the valuable; it is sufficient to remove the tendency to become obsessed with those values that belong to another. A redeeming mental surgery needs to be performed on the genitive particle "of." Is it not absurd to feel envious pain at the qualities of a human while he is alive to celebrate them after he is dead? This behavior, typical of envious countries toward their best citizens, sheds light on the problem: the envious becomes blind to value only when it belongs to another. Why does the reader or listener rejoice with the happiness of literary characters? Because he knows they are fictitious and this allows him to objectively admire their qualities without assimilating feelings of inferiority. The happiness that appears in literature is a happiness that does not belong to any particular "you"; art places it in the nominative, and reason may achieve the same. We need to cultivate the appreciation of the good qualities of others. From childhood we need to stress this interest, this respect, and this joy for the merit of others. Whoever enjoys other people's qualities will never feel envy.

5. Solidarity of the Species

The biological evolution of *homo sapiens* is practically imperceptible for hundreds of thousands of years. Instead, cultural evolution has been intense and in some areas, such as science and technology, it has been extraordinary in the last hundred years. What is characteristic about cultural evolution is that the genetic code does not change; only the environment changes. The enriching of the environment perfects human life. The amount of knowledge multiplies, as does art, institutions, and the means of production, so each coming generation finds a more ready and refined team of co-workers. The protagonists of this process of inventiveness and accumulation are not the consumers, but the scientists, the artists, the statisticians, and managers in collaboration with those who have learned to save. The active subject of human progress is a superior minority. Without Socrates, or Aristotle, how many centuries would cultural evolution have had to walk backwards? Though this may be true, envy condemned Socrates to death and Aristotle had to emigrate to save, if not his courage, at least his philosophy. Envy, insofar as it aims to bring down the heads of the eminent, has delayed more cultural evolution than the glacier periods.

History will progress at a prodigiously fast pace, as if it had just escaped from a gravitational field, when these destructive feelings will be eradicated from the human soul. Consumers, who form the greatest majority of humanity, will be persuaded that they owe their lives to the drug dealers and their financial supporters who have packed drugs for the masses, and that whatever makes easier their daily fight against nature is thanks to the control exercised against those who know more, organized more, and saved more to contribute the necessary means of production. We should feel joyous admiration, instead of painful envy, toward those who, because they reach high peaks of superiority, enrich their country and are able, therefore, to enrich mankind. The material patrimony and the cultural heritage, though administered by a few, may enrich the whole human race. The envious's vision is myopic in the extreme for it reduces the field of observation to a bilateral and unfavorable relation and is incapable of contemplating the whole fertile field. The more envious societies are, the less fertile and unified they become, and as a consequence they become poorer. Here we find, again, a vicious circle: poverty leads to envy and envy leads to misery. We need to strengthen a consciousness of true solidarity between the superior and the inferior. We must congratulate ourselves that in our midst we come upon gifted people and winners, for their works will benefit everyone. The joy at what is valuable is another antidote against envy. The dark feeling of envy disappears when the myopic and narrow personal perspective is abandoned and we raise our gaze towards the collective horizon for only then do we realize that even the most egocentric of truly gifted persons, however unwillingly, performs a function that benefits the rest. We need to cultivate those conditions that will make possible the birth of the superior among us and we need to stimulate his creative capacity, elevating him with admiration and not burying him through envy.

6. Sympathy

Envy is a "feeling against" and its antidote is an intense emotional attitude, a sympathy of "feeling with." To sympathize must not be understood in its literal sense of hating with the one who hates or feeling anguish with whomever feels anguish, but rather in the sense of participation, though less vividly, in the joys and miseries of other people. It is, therefore, to feel compassion with the one who suffers and joy with the one who rejoices. Compassion entails an initial contagion of pain that easily changes into a satisfaction of love, consolation, and desire to help the other person. Commiserating sympathy is not, therefore, a permanent state of pain. And, obviously, congratulatory sympathy means rejoicing at the happiness of others, a pleasurable feeling that we add to our own happiness. These two basic forms of sympathy are more spontaneous, simple, and natural than some forms of "antipathy," like envy that stands out because of its intellectualism, artifice, and complexity. The feelings of others are logically unknowable; but their signs—likes and dislikes—are transferable through gesture and language. Other peoples' feelings are "com-passible" [felt together] even when they are unintelligible. Therefore, whoever rejoices when others rejoice will never envy. And what about love?

Absolute lovers share everything and form a coherent, affective system. If there are no dualities there are no comparisons, not even agreements, and there is no room for envy. But this loving plenitude is an ideal limit towards which real lovers strive. Mallarmé, who believed that such final unity could never be achieved in this world, said that "love is the misfortune of being two." Love is a journey towards a dreamt unity and it does not weaken envy completely, as some Neoplatonists have proclaimed. The possessive lover may envy those spaces of happiness that belong only to the beloved; indeed, a lover may envy with more fury than anybody else. In such a context, we also find connotations of a neighboring feeling: jealousy. Envy is pain at someone else's happiness; jealousy is the pain we feel when we fear that someone else may interfere with the monopoly we have over the person who makes us happy. The envious wishes to deprive the other of something, while the jealous person feels dispossessed of someone he feels belongs to him. Envy between lovers is mixed with jealousy for it starts from the conviction that all the happiness of the other is not shared and that there is something that belongs to us, that someone owes us.

Besides those subjective changes that are to be found in emotional stages, we also find the elimination of objects. Envy is extinguished when the envied stops being present in the consciousness of the envious, either because he is dead, or forgotten, or has been substituted by another. The last case is not common, since it is possible to envy simultaneously an infinity of people, and it is not true that a larger envy removes a lesser one. The total extinction of envy takes place only when the envious comes to the conclusion that the envied is no longer happier than he is. When a comparison of mutual happinesses reveals that we are superior in happiness to the other, then envy loses its rational support and disappears. No one envies the unhappy or the less happy. Dante condemned the envious to hell; but he presumed that there they would not continue envying each other.

In conclusion: the misery of envious inferiority may be overcome through emulation, perfective specialization, enjoyment of values regardless of who owns them, consciousness of solidarity with every creative effort, and sympathy. But this program of healthy expansion requires that the demagogic prophets of resentment be replaced by generous and clear spirits.

VIII. Conclusions

Envy is the pain we feel at the happiness of others, a happiness that is seen as superior to ours, that we desire, that is inaccessible and cannot be assimilated. The cause of envy is neither the desire for power nor the limitation of wealth; it is, rather, our lack of satisfaction based on a complex reasoning. The historical origin of envy might be found in the preservation instinct of the nonhunters in the primitive societies. Today's envy is existential, social, and patrimonial, and each is based, respectively, on pride, the desire to emulate, and greed. There are also individual and shared envies.

The envious appreciates values, but it pains him that others possess them and are made happier by them. The resentful person, on the other hand, denies values and even sees them as countervalues.

Envy is the only capital vice that no one confesses so that they may operate more effectively against the envied and also in order to deceive themselves, since humans have a spontaneous consciousness that envy is an evil feeling.

The envious covers his affliction with an infinity of disguising tactics. The main recipes to lower the envied person are excessive criticism, defamation, and calumny; silence is the way to eliminate the envied socially. This negative habit ends up causing mental daltonism and myopia in the envious.

Envy is a feeling felt at all times in all places. This universality cannot be explained through an innate instinct, but rather because humans learn through comparisons, and, therefore, humans come to an idea of themselves through comparisons with others, and thus they feel inferior to many, in many respects.

One only envies what was previously known, which usually is what is near, but not necessarily. We may also envy the happiness of someone distant through a fictive or real description. The promoters of enviable images and the instigators of the feelings of envy deliver to their clientele a prefabricated envy; this is the way of the demagogic mass media.

Envy is not a feeling brought about through direct sensations, but through a reasoning that leads to envy; for this reason it is a feeling that is intrinsically self-punishing. The envious punishes himself, necessarily or willingly. There is no pleasure in envy.

Envy does not perform one single useful function in our vital economy. It does not bring pleasure, but misery; it does not provide exact information about the environment, but inexact; and it does not move towards rewarding actions, but to negating behaviors. Envy is not the motor of society; it separates and isolates. It is hardly useful for the mutual control of the members of a community. It is not an impulse leading to justice because its egalitarianism is neither altruistic nor fair, but selfish and vindictive.

The complex mental process inherent in envy consists in a series of hypothetical, unbelievable, or false judgments and in incorrect deductive reasoning. The envious feeling is linked to a series of errors of fact, of evaluation, and of reasoning. A rigorous analysis of the mental makeup of envy diffuses it radically.

Though envy is antisocial it may be manipulated to bring together the envious against the envied. Such alliances do not happen spontaneously but are promoted by demagogues who underline the inferiorities of some with respect to others, call them inequities, and further promise egalitarian utopias. An *ad hoc* interpretation of distributive justice serves as pseudo-legitimation to such social upheavals. When the leaders of the envious come to power they use politics of expropriation through nationalizations, for though progressive and discriminatory taxation they impose official ideologies in order to gain an equality of thought. Egalitarian programs are incompatible with freedom and they require increasing economic interventions, hypertrophy of bureaucracy and, as a last recourse, totalitarian methods. In the end, egalitarian utopia does not come about and a new class appears that, with political and economic power in its hands, reaches a greater superiority than any other within a liberal context; and finally, envy reappears in the ruling class and at all social levels.

The majority of people avoid being envied for they fear the hostility of the envious. Some take recourse in flight, namely, in isolation, and thus they widen and wall up the area of their "imtimacy." Others pretend they are not happy or only a very little, and some even humble themselves and ask forgiveness of the envious. When envy is avoided in groups, these do not run away but protect themselves within the cloisters of clubs reserved for members only, and, on occasion, they also take recourse in pretending. Courtesy is not intelligible only as a tactic to disarm the envious, though insofar as it lubricates social contact it may also discourage certain envious reactions. The envious does not become less so on account of the favors the envied pours on him.

Any type of inferiority in happiness gives rise to envy, and this shows that the feeling may be overcome. One way is emulation, which consists not in feeling pain at the happiness of others, but in trying to achieve it. Another is to achieve some kind of vocational specialization and thus compensate for certain inferiorities with the superiority of our chosen and mastered activity according to the ideal of the work well done.

Values do not stop being valuable because they belong to another; they are always valuable. When our judgment assents to this truth, it makes possible the indirect fruition of what belongs to others and envy loses its ethical ground.

Superior humans are normally the most creative, and every human creation is a common good, for it enriches the patrimony of humanity. To the degree that envy stops the best, it also impoverishes all of us. A reasonable "selfishness" forces us to value the most gifted. To convince oneself of sharing in true solidarity with the whole human species is an insurance against envy.

In summary, envy is a general, deep, sterile pain; but it is one of the few that is absolutely removable. It is suffered on account of mental myopia, and an intelligent education may cure it.

C. CREATIVE INEQUALITY

In the two most grandiose, secular temples of the West, the Doric monument dedicated to Lincoln and the Ionic monument dedicated to Jefferson, we find chiseled in marble a sacramental formula that seems taken from Genesis: "All men are created equal." The same words begin the United States' Declaration of Independence, written in 1776. From here, these words were taken to be part of the *Magna Carta* of contemporary society, the Declaration of the Rights of Man in 1793: "*Tous les hommes sont égaux par la nature.*" From that time on, different constitutions and political preachers have continued to spread this dogma. Well, this dogma is neither true nor illuminating. The truth is that all men are born unequal and that society tries to make them equal by means of laws and customs. Inequality is the inseparable companion of freedom and of nature, and there is no equality without arbitrariness and coercion.

I. Introduction

Equality among people is an old illusion that, on a par with that other illusion of happiness, appears everywhere, but with stronger deliberation in our Western culture. Its three decisive movements are Christianity, demo-liberalism, and socialism. These, in turn, translate into egalitarianism in religion, in politics, and in economics.

The old world is a world of territorial gods; each tribe has its gods, who are at times the exultation of historical heroes or national sublimations. This religious regionalism is not limited to the frontiers of a village: there are local, familial, and tribal divinities, and there are multiple local reminders of the major divinities. The first thing to become collectivized was theology, maybe due to the fact that the earthly patrimony was so poor that the only possible treasure to be contemplated was to be found in heaven. The opportunity for worldly and other protections was at the hands of each one's god, and depended on the outcome of their Olympic rivalries, though everyone wished for their god to be the most powerful and benevolent. Some people considered themselves chosen by the divinity and instead of sharing this privilege with others, they used it as their flag for external wars.

It was in Israel—the collective subject of an old theological tradition—that Paul of Tarsus proclaimed the theory of an egalitarian religion: only one God for everyone and of everyone. The chosen people were now guilty, and the previously rejected Gentiles were now the chosen ones. With a revealing reiteration Paul calls himself an "apostle of the Gentiles" and "the minister of Christ before the Gentiles." In one of his most personal letters he writes to Timothy: "I tell the truth and do not lie that I am ordained a preacher and an apostle, a teacher of the Gentiles in faith and verity." Faithful to this evangelic message and even more so to the command to teach the Jews and the other "nations," Paul writes at the beginning of his letter to the Romans, "I am debtor both to the Greeks, and to the Barbarians," that is, I take care of both cultural areas of the early Gentiles. Paul preaches his new revolutionary gospel against the messianic nationalism and the theocratic exclusivisms then in vogue: "Is God only the God of the Jews? Is He not also the God of the Gentiles? Yes, he is also the God of the Gentiles, for there is only one God." (Rom. 3:29). This egalitarianism was a rational one, for if God is Love He cannot be conceived as a friend to some people and the enemy of the rest; this was a beautiful call for it made brethren of humans in cult, customs, and hope; and it was possible because its comparative stand was not a worldly perspective but a divine law with celestial opportunities. This religious egalitarianism extended first to the Empire and then beyond.

The medieval and modern worlds are the familiar monopolies of political power. Royal dynasties were in control of power and this power was transmitted through blood: no one with a different blood line could legitimately aspire to the crown. The nobility was another cloistered group that shared the remaining powers with the Church. The bourgeoisie had access to certain plots of power that they tried to make permanent in their successors.

There was even an inherited tradition of artisan crafts and an implementation guaranteed through guilds. Not everyone could become a king, a count, a merchant, or even a blacksmith. One was born to an inequality in labor that could only arduously be overcome. Opportunities were better for some than others. From the womb, people were condemned to unequal positions of social standing and power. Locke and Rousseau faced this situation and formulated a political egalitarianism. According to the British statesman men are "equal by nature" and remain such until they decide to join one or another political community. All decisions must be made by a majority, for then the larger numbers equal the "greater force" of the social body. In sum, each citizen has a vote equal in power to that of the others, so the many overpower the few. Rousseau, who plagiarizes Locke shamelessly, makes a distinction getween natural and physical inequality, and also between moral and political inequality. He accepts natural inequality but discards the physical, for it consists in the "many privileges that some enjoy with damage to others, like being more rich, more rewarded, more powerful." In another place he points out with greater accuracy the four dimensions of social inequality: "Riches, nobility, power and personal merit." Is there an essential relation between natural and political inequality? This question attacks the heart of the problem but Rousseau rejects this possibility, considering it a hypothesis worthy of slaves listening to the conversations of their masters. This, of course, is a demagogic evasion without argumentative power. If people were as equal to one another as animals are within a species, why have humans reached their present situation? "Political inequality, which is almost nonexistent in the state of nature, becomes stronger and increases through the development of the spirit of humans and of their faculties, and finally it establishes and becomes legitimate through the establishment of property and law." In sum, there is "the equality nature has placed in men, and the inequality they have established." How can we recover, insofar as it is possible, the lost egalitarian paradise? We can do so by establishing that no man has natural authority over another and by grounding any kind of authority in the social contract undertaken by those in political power, for this belongs equally to every citizen. Except for the social contract that must be ratified unanimously, all other decisions must be undertaken by majority vote. Political egalitarianism proclaims the homogeneous and permanent distribution of power among all the members of a community. We come into this world as political equals, and this equality cannot be renounced. Modern democracies are built on this concept, very different from the over-manipulated antecedent in Athens, where a small minority of citizens exercised the sovereignty of power over an immense majority of slaves and foreigners. The political egalitarianism fo the Enlightenment was rational insofar as it denied the gratuitous genealogical expropriation of political power; but as to the rest it swung between fiction and utopia.

The French Revolution established political, but not economic, equality. The first article of the Declaration of Rights of 1789 reads: "Men are born and remain free and equal in rights." Babeuf rejected in 1791 what he called an equality "in name, of legislative or grammatical scholasticism." And Marechal, in his *Manifest of the Equal* (1796) accused the revolutionaries with a similar logic: "Equality has turned out to be nothing more than a beautiful and sterile legal fiction." What these men were asking for was the "equality of fact" or "equality of goods" that consists in the equal distribution among all people of everything, including knowledge. They even affirmed that "whoever has more than belongs to him in his equal share of social goods incurs in robbery." The end result was the utopia of communism: neither rich nor poor, neither powerful nor humble, neither governing nor governed. The technical recipe was the collectivization of property, the suppression of inheritance, and the leveling of salaries. Babeuf, considered a traitor to the Directory, ascended in 1797 the same guillotine as Louis XVI: the revolution was devouring itself.

Industrial capitalism gave birth to an increasing minority owning the means of production and to a majority of wage earners that continued to grow in greater progression. This fact, joined to the increase in the technological possibilities of increased consumption, multiplied the economic differences among the citizens and made those differences more visible. By the second half of the nineteenth century these levels tended to rise due to the increase in the concentration of capital and the proletarianization of the wage earners, and to be preserved through inheritance. Marx raised to the level of sociological law what already was an episode of the capitalist process, and tried to give a scientific texture to the utopian communism of his predecessors. To avoid being associated with Babeuf and his followers, Marx rejected demagogic egalitarianism; but, deep down, he was even more radical. Marxist egalitarianism is not only political and economic ("to each one according to his needs") it is anthropological. The subject of the communist society is not the individual, but generic man. This is the famous text: "When the real, individual man will retake possession of the abstract citizen, when in his empirical life, in his individual work, and in his individual relations he becomes transformed into generic being; when man recognizes his own strength as the strength of society. . . . only then will he attain human emancipation." This is, therefore, almost a metaphysical egalitarianism, where man becomes a species, a universal concept, and acquires that property which belongs to the beings of reason, absolute equality. This thesis carries with it another subordinate egalitarianism: labor. This is a theory of work that claims to be a "means, homogeneous and abstract." For Marx the worth of merchandise depends on the amount of necessary work required to produce it; not any one particular form of work, but only the abstract, standard work of a worker as a mean: "with a degree of ability and intensity within determined social conditions." Work, as it becomes something statistical and anonymous, may be perfectly divided into equal parts. This is the suppression of all laboral differences. "The total laboral strength of a society, observable in the total value of all the merchandises, though embracing innumerable individual unities of work, amounts to as much as an undifferentiated mass of human work; each of these individual units is equal to the rest." This type of "abstract" work corresponds to the "generic" man. In this manner, workers as much as their efforts are interchangeable and equal among themselves. In its final phase, communist society would provide total equality to all subjects—generic man—and the total equality of the patrimony: everything according to the quota or collective (capital, power, work, and income). Marxist egalitarianism, despite its protestations of materialism and empiricism, is the most speculative and metaphysical of all: generic man and abstract work are two over-refined abstractions of reason.

Western civilization moves, therefore, at the command of an egalitarian will that is first religious, then political, and finally economic, that is, more and more bound to earth, though in the Marxist system it is founded on transcendental schemes. Ultimately, these three operations aim towards an egalitarian happiness: equal well-being for all. The most radical desire of man is to be happy, and the aim is that each one of us should be as happy as the next. In its ultimate state egalitarianism would mean the end of all privileges and the suppression of all differences, including the subjective ones. If Rousseau believes that all men are born equal, Marx demands they they live their lives equally at all times, in order to achieve equal happiness. Despite appearances, this latter wish is not rational, for happiness is not an objective but a subjective state, only partially conditioned by the surrounding circumstances.

What we are trying here is not a rigorous examination of the viability of these efforts; this will be done in other chapters. But rather we wish to underline the persistence and volume of the egalitarian pretension in the last two thousand years in the West, and above all since the Enlightenment. The last two hundred years in Western culture are unintelligible if we do not examine this utopian egalitarianism. This is a grave and powerfully alive question, for equality is the power base of the most extensive social movements of our time: democracy and socialism. The key to the contemporary age is egalitarianism.

Paul, as much as Rousseau or Marx and their followers, did not envision the problem of equality as a factual one, but rather as a norm to be followed and achieved. They take as avoidable the actual inequality and affirm equality as desirable. The climate so created gives rise to a bad conscience in the detractors of these claims even when they are only speaking to acknowledge the problem. Egalitarianism is presented as a moral imperative that requires not proof, but fulfillment, like an "ought" that is evident in every conscience. For this reason its defenders are more apostolic than analytical, and their doctrinal elaborations more closely resemble ideological postulates than scientific proofs. The schemes provided are not as much a study on equality as a recipe for equality; give every man one vote and let the simple majority rule, Rousseau prescribed; let us collectivize capital and give each worker equal salary, proposed Babeuf. These are not two diagnostics, they are two therapies. Modern egalitarianism is the affirmation of an ideal and the recommendation of a treatment; this is not a scientific approximation to truth.

In the following pages we will invert the method: does equality exist? Which kind of equalities are possible, and which would be the consequences? Such an analysis cannot be based on feelings, but on reason; not on desires, but on facts; its foundation, therefore, will not be ethics, but physics. The most distant, so far, from egalitarian reflection has been natural science. It is true that at the time of Rousseau empirical knowledge about man was so small that even biological evolution was unknown; Marx was not present at the birth of etiology, genetics, biochemistry, or microphysics. The last years have seen spectacular progress achieved through these sciences and it is necessary to restate egalitarianism from a natural scientific perspective and with an interdisciplinary method. Most of the literature on egalitarianism has the air of political conventions, but what this question requires is the cleanliness of the laboratory.

II. The Inequalities

1. Metaphysical Inequality

There are several ways to understand inequality; one of them, and the most radical, is to understand inequality as a synonym for identity. Identity, however, does not have an univocal meaning. There is an identity that is *absolute*, and this is the relation that every being has to itself: the star Aldebaran is identical to itself at any given moment. This kind of identity is established by reason, it is an intellectual operation that could be labelled a noetic repetition or a tautology. There is, besides, a *relative* identity and this is the kind of identity that holds between two beings when one can fully substitute for the other in any context. Is there a species of objects that are totally interchangeable or identical? The answer varies depending on two kinds of possible objects: real objects, that have an external physical existence, and objects of reason, that only exist in the mind. Rome is a real, concrete being, while "city" is an abstract being of reason. We have all seen particular urban concentrations, but no one has seen "the city." The problematic starting point of philosophy is that we live among real beings of reason. Our surrounding environment is filled with things, and we exert our power over them through concepts. Both kinds of objects, the real and the mental, behave in different ways in the face of the egalitarian challenge. Let us focus on the first ones.

The basic characteristic of any *real entity* is its individuality. This notion may be viewed from an ontic perspective, and thus we refer to its nature, or from a logical perspective, and thus we inquire into the way of its definition. In the first case the individual appears as a set of properties that do not appear in any other object; thus, it has something unique. In the second instance, the individual appears as an entity whose predicate fits it exclusively and cannot be attributed to any other object. It is, then, something referred to with a proper name, or pointed out by means of a demonstrative adjective. "That" man is an individual because he is ontically irrepeatable and because, logically, he is the only person of whom it can be said that he is Socrates, the son of Sophroniscus and Phintareta.

Another characteristic of individuality is that it is not communicable; it cannot be accounted for by means of general concepts. Individuality is singular, though it is not simple but complex. Any real object, even one as minute as a grain of sand or pollen, has a numberless amount of notes. Some of them, like the peculiar or nontransferable ones, have no adequate general concepts to express them. Individuality may be described only partially and approximately. It is like trying to form a circle with straight lines, regardless of how many and how tiny they are drawn. The scholastics used to say that the individual is ineffable; but this is not correct for we may refer to it or call it by a proper name; what cannot be done is to transfer to another individual its nature. This lack of communicability is logical in the sense that individuality cannot be defined so that others know it perfectly through concepts. It is also physical in the sense that it cannot be transferred whole to another object, that is, it cannot be copied exactly.

The second class of objects are the *objects of reason*. These do not have nor can they have real existence; they are mere logical artifacts, mental instruments that humans use to simplify, classify, relate, and transform the world. Innumerable points of different dimensions, color, place, and matter exist in reality; but the Euclidian concept of "point" exists only in the mind; this is what we call a "universal" concept, or a determination that may be attributed to several different entities. This kind of concept is not the name or representation of a particular object, but rather the outline of a structure that repeats itself in individuals with sufficient approximation to become operative, and that is called true insofar as it is useful. The deficiency of all universals is that they are incapable of exhaustively capturing reality, since they miss what is most proper to it, the individuality of things. The greatness of universals is that they allow for the building of science. All scientific knowledge is a system of universal concepts, and without them not a single law could have been formulated. For this reason, science is only science of what is general, in the past, the present, or the future. There can be no science of the individual. The fundamental characteristic of those entities of reason, as we call universal concepts, is their repeatability to infinity, their communicability to others by means of written or verbal signs, and their perennial nature, since they may be forever transmitted from one generation to the next.

If whatever is real is individual, it follows that no two real entities are identical: each physical object is irrepeatable and incommunicable. Even though we predicate identity of certain things—like two copies of the same photographic negative—it is still the case that no two physical objects are completely interchangeable. And this is also the case when we consider objects aesthetically, that is, when we bracket their temporality. Besides, whatever is real is given within time, and thus it has an origin, an evolution, and an end. Every real entity is not only different from other real entities, even from those that most resemble it, but it is also subject to its own change and thus it becomes different from what it was; to the degree that it lasts, it does not even continue being identical to itself. A plurality of changes is the main characteristic of the real, and within this environment identity is not possible.

On the other hand, we find certain identities of reason, identical among themselves, like Euclidian points and lines, because of the way they have been constructed or defined. This mutual identity holds only as long as those entities remain as pure mental artifacts; for as soon as those lines or points are drawn on paper or on the blackboard they gain extension, become individual and different from any other point or line. By this fact, they also surrender the theoretical characteristics given them by the Euclidian postulates. The relative identity of objects only happens in the mind and when we affirm the identity of two different realities we are improperly suggesting a deep similarity; but in no way an identity in the strict sense. We are only indulging in an abusive use of the terms. In sum, it is a philosophical axiom that no two real things are equal in the sense of being identical.

It is the notion of equality, however, that is the basis of scientific knowledge. A definition, a judgment, a function, a law, an equation are equal on account of the fact that the verbal equivalent of the sign "=" is the verb "to be." As in the following equalities: man is a rational animal, the angles of a triangle equal two right angles, the speed of light is equal to 299.792 klm. per second, the square of the hypotenuse is equal to the sum of the square of its legs. The reason why these equalities are genuine, relative identities is because their terms are not real objects but entities of reason, so represented for the sake of calculations. Such generalizations, simplifications, or idealizations of the real are useful because at the macrocosmic level the differences that exist between real objects and their symbols are not worth paying attention to.

The equalities that emerge in scientific knowledge are, in the majority of cases, not even relatively equal among the entities of reason; they are simple *equivalents*. Pythagoras' theorem does not mean that the sum of the squares of the legs is identical to the square built with the hypotenuse; what it really means is that the value of the respective surfaces is numerically the same. We are not dealing, therefore, with an equality, but with a quantitative equivalent: the value of the area is similar. These equivalents may refer not only to extension but also to other values, like mass, temperature, weight, velocity, etc.; they may be applied, also, through extrapolation, to beauty, talent, or virtue insofar as they are quantifiable. Thus, we are able to fix the individual's or the group's intellectual quotient. We never deal with the real entities when dealing with equivalents, but with certain dimensions of the same—weight, color, height, etc.—and these dimensions are mental schemata. The equality "Peter weighs as much as John" does not make Peter and John equal, not even in their respective, concrete masses; it simply states that their distributive gravitational pull is balanced with an equal amount of ballast (dead weight). The equalities established by our daily speech, as much as the language of high mathematics, affirm much less than they seem to do: they do not affirm the identity of things, but rather similar or equivalent values that are arbitrarily defined.

The cosmos is changeable because it is dynamic, and it is varied because its real and actual parts are not identical among themselves. The universe is always different from itself; and at a given moment, its elements are different from each other. This will continue being the case until we achieve a maximum and irreversible entropy, a situation that no one has been able to show is necessary. The mind crystallizes and simplifies that fluid multiplicity to make it manageable. First, it reduces an indeterminate plurality of objects to only one universal concept by singling out their common and essential notes and overlooking their individual and accidental characteristics. In this manner one symbol represents a thousand things, fixes them, and makes them easy to manipulate. This is the most prodigious mechanism for simplification known. Secondly, it classifies and orders those concepts by establishing relations, and thus formulating laws, predicting behaviors, and selecting means to attain certain ends. It is an equation like that of generalized relativity about the universe. It is a marvel of mental economy that lifts man to the category of microcosm. Reality is a diversifying current of water and the mind is the channelling dam. There is no more egalitarianism in the universe than the logical one imposed by the mind, and the ethical one dictated by the will. From a philosophical standpoint, equality is a mental fiction grounded on certain structural and functional similarities. Whatever is real is unequal in the sense that no two things are identical, for they change; and in some way, some are superior or inferior to others.

2. Physical Inequality

From the origins of our civilization, science has tried to study the structure of matter by reducing it to something primary and simple like Leucippus's atom or Aristotle's prime matter. Significant advances are only recent, however. They start with the models of the atom proposed by Rutherford and Bohr and these models have only become more complex in the last half century. The planetary microsystem formed by a proton nucleus around which electrons describe their orbits has become richer with more than a hundred other particles that have been classified, from some as heavy as barium, to the intermediary or mesons, and to the light ones or leptones. One of the last particles discovered is called the ipsylon (1977), a remarkably heavy particle with a mass ten times larger than the proton.

Are these subatomic particles truly elementary, that is, the last and indivisible? It is doubtful that this be the case, for among other properties these particles may transform one into the other. The most recent hypothesis is that these particles are made up of other more elementary particles called quarks, of which about six different types have already been classified, and it has been suggested that others still exist, although contemporary technology makes it impossible to isolate them, and they might also be fictitious. Will the list continue? Could quarks be the result of other more primary particles? We are unable to come up with a definitive answer as to the ultimate constitution of matter, despite the colossal strides of atomic physics and mathematical technologies.

Our problem, however, is this: could there be two subatomic particles that are absolutely identical? The difficulty does not consist in isolating one particle and comparing it to another of its own type, but rather in the ability to verify that it continues being itself; and this difficulty is immense, for the majority of subatomic particles are unstable, and there are some, like the pion zero, whose life is measured in trillionths of a second (10^{-16}). Let us take, as a case study, the proton, a particle of indefinite duration and which disintegrates with difficulty. Are there two identical protons? In order to answer this question we would have to analyze and describe perfectly two concrete protons and compare them. Well, the first act is impossible due to the principle of indeterminacy formulated by Heisenberg. According to this principle, it is impossible to determine simultaneously the position and velocity of a subatomic particle. The more we measure for results in one magnitude, the larger the error becomes in the other. The same incompatability holds between the internal atomic definition of time and energy. There will always be errors in the study of these particles, whose product will be equivalent to no less than 2^{π} multiplied by Plank's constant. This error, though small, is very important in the minute world of microphysics. Such an error is not the outcome of the imperfection of the instruments used; it is rather an insuperable, theoretical obstacle, regardless of how well tuned the instruments are. With these clarifications in mind, how can we compare and establish the eventual identity of two uncertain entities, namely, partially unknowable? This is an impossible task. It is not possible to affirm the identity of two elementary particles as a consequence of the indeterminacy principle.

There is still one more impediment. Quantitative mechanics has discarded the intuitive idea that an elemental particle is a very tiny body. Such a hypothesis, which has been very productive in the past, has now been contradicted by experiments in wider areas and at deeper levels. The truth is that there are no such infinitesimal points. There is an ambiguity that makes it impossible to determine where the corpuscle ends and the wave begins. This double measurement of waves and corpuscles allows for the explanation of a multitude of subatomic phenomena: but it carries with it a grave epistomological shortcoming: the equations achieved do not lead to certain predictions, but rather to frequencies, or in other words, the regularities we are able to formulate within the atom are not deterministic, but only statistical. How then can we affirm the identity of two particles whose respective definitions are subject to the errors of an insurmountable uncertainty, and to the chance of a calculation that is merely probabilistic? It is a doubly impossible task.

It is not the case that this is impossible to achieve today, but rather that contemporary physics affirms the present and future impossibility of being able to prove the absolute identity of two subatomic particles. Could we, then, prove the contrary, namely the unequal and irrepeatable character of each and every one of those particles? We cannot do it apodictically, but we can do it to a certain degree.

The general theory of relativity evens, within the atom, matter and energy. It is not enough to abandon the mechanistic hypothesis that elementary particles are bodies; we must also abandon the idea that they are substances; we must conceive them more like events. All this is the result of Einstein's coordinates of space-time. Rather than things, we find, within the atom, events. This desubstantiation and therefore the historization of infra-atomic reality makes us establish a relation between this reality and a general experience; and this is the irrepeatability of each event, that is, the individuality of all that is historical. This individuality exists because in general there are no two events that are equal, and neither is it logical that they might be found within the atom; and because the subatomic structure is not only very fluid, but it is also in succession, and therefore nothing in it is identical. This fact agrees with the merely probabilistic character of the microphysical predictions.

There is still more. Elementary particles are reduced to energy. The energy of a system is valued by its quantity, that is constant, and by its entropy, that is variable. The notion of entropy is difficult to explain in nonmathematical terms. Let us imagine a chamber totally isolated from the exterior, within which we have introduced a hot heater. After a while, the walls of the chamber, the air, and the heater will have the same temperature. The quantity of energy and matter is now the same as in the beginning of the experiment: there are the same amounts of molecules, atoms, and particles. But that energy has degraded and is inactive because heat has spread uniformly and thus entropy has increased. Entropy measures the order and disorder within a system. It would be necessary to bring energy from the exterior so that macroactivity would reactivate itself within the chamber, as by cooling the air or warming the heater. All the thermodynamic real processes, as the one being described, are irreversible, because energy, even when quantitatively the same, deteriorates. Electric power, water, calories, pressures, tend to level out, or what is the same thing, they tend to increase their homogeneity, namely, entropy. We must, then, bear in mind about energy its constant quantity and its entropy, which increases in proportion to the diminution of the hierarchical disposition of the forces present. All systems tend towards equilibrium, to the increase in entropy, and consequently, to the extinction of change. The outcome of all this is that within an active system the energy level of each molecule, and by analogy, of each one of its constitutive parts, is different. There are no two particles of an active system that have the same entropy, that is, the same place in the cosmic history of irreversible processes; and this should be sufficient to distinguish them, even though equal in everything else. The identity of energy level or thermodynamic egalitarianism is possible. This, however, would be tantamount to the death of the system, a situation very distant from the universe and from our planet. Complete, thermodynamic equality in physics is the end of change, total uniformity, cosmic death.

In sum, the physical world is unequal insofar as it is hierarchical as regards energy. There are no two physical realities that are absolutely identical.

3. Zoological Inequality

Curiosity is the incentive of intellectual progress. Humans, those particles of the cosmos, feel incomplete: they need physical energy and intellectual knowledge.

Human questions are answered with a variety of epistemological shades: science, ideology, and myth. Our scientific knowledge is very recent and limited, and this explains the fact that the present repertoire of humans is either questions or ideologies and myths. Scientific information proceeds from a rigorous analysis of facts. Ideological information proceeds from the voluntaristic and affective manipulation of hypothesis, news, and desires. Mythic information is a mixture of ideology and imagination. The scientific study of humans must be factual, not poetic. The theme of equality cannot be solved, as up to now, with the simple formulation of desires: it must be empirically developed. Humans must, therefore, be placed within the context of nature, and particularly at those levels that are nearer to them. *Homo sapiens* is the most evolved species, the highest and most complex sprout of the zoological tree, while also belonging to it.

Until a few years ago, zoology was an inventory, dissection and classification of different species. Now it is fundamentally a study of the behavior of animals. This new approach, though recent, has already had some remarkable results. One of the most important discoveries has been the demonstration that humans are not only similar to the higher vertebrates in their anatomy and physiology, but that there are notable similarities also in their social behavior. This characteristic of our species has been affirmed since Aristotle stated at the beginning of his *Politics* that man is a "social animal." The colonies of insects or polyps have had a mechanistic appearance that cannot be compared to the State, and the changing reproductive animal nucleus cannot be compared to the permanent family. Today, the study of primates and other vertebrates has shown sociological facts of extreme importance.

1. It is false to believe that sociability is an exclusively human characteristic. Virtually all the superior vertebrates form intraspecific societies.

2. The members of these societies are able to identify one another, and have xenophobic reactions against the members of other groups, even when they belong to the same species. It is not, then, a simple physical grouping; it is a society whose members recognize one another and communicate amongst themselves.

3. There are certain individuals within these communities, called alphas, especially gifted for leadership and who transmit to their descendants their superior quality through their genes. The alpha is not necessarily the most intelligent, the strongest or the most reproductive, though these might be helpful factors. The single most important characteristic is that the alpha has the capacity to bring himself to the attention of all the others, lead them, and protect them.

4. There is a hierarchical stratification from the alpha to the omega individuals, and to these we must add the differences that are the outcome of sex or age.

5. There are also, in these societies, certain usages learned from the elders and the best and that are not, therefore, genetically transmitted.

6. There is, consequently, a specialization of functions: some individuals are sentinels, others are retired, others are leaders.

Contemporary studies of animals show that inequality in the animal kingdom is not only typological, but it is also sociological. There are no two identical animals, nor are there two animals of the same rank within one community and one territory. Biochemical inequality and the hierarchy that exists in the superior vertebrates is not a degeneration or corruption; it is a fact that keeps a certain parallelism with the evolutionary process, in the double sense that the more evolved a species becomes, the more complex is the social organization, and that this social organization is most important for the survival and improvement of the species. The more or less infantile literature that used to humanize animals has its origins in this social behavior of animals that predates the social behavior of humans. We need to start with these facts in order to establish, not the desirability, but the naturality of our social usages and the possibility of their reform.

III. Human Inequality

1. Generalities

All humans are born out of two generating cells: the female ovum and the male spermatozoan. Each one contains in its nucleus twenty-four minute filaments, called chromosomes—that is, half of the chromosomes that all the other human cells have. Which half? We have no knowledge of the causes that make some chromosomes enter the generating cells while others do not; thus, as in many other cases of inscrutable complexity, this fact is attributed to chance. In this manner the nucleus of the first cell of the new being is made: forty-eight chromosomes, half from the female ovum, the other half from the male sperm. Each progenitor, therefore, passes on half of his genetic code. A faithful copy of those forty-eight chromosomes inhabits the nucleus of each cell, with the exception of the genetic ones, which will only receive half that amount in order to repeat, in due time, the genetic process.

Genes are found in the chromosomes, and their numbers are unknown. Their numbers are not counted in thousands, although some say their numbers are in the tens of thousands. The genes are the defining corpuscles of the future structure of the new individual. Some genes determine certain characteristics, like the color of the eyes, and others some other characteristics. The majority of the genes act in association, and this adds difficulty to the clarification of the genetic mesh. Many genes are asleep; that is, they reside in the cellular nucleus and may be transmitted to descendants, but they do not affect the external definition of the individual. Thus, one may be the carrier of a gene for black skin color, and appear, on the outside, totally white. Why do some genes stay in the shadows, while others become operative? This we also ignore, although we know that certain genes are dominant and others recessive. The fact is that within the chromosomic inheritance received from one's parents there is already a very detailed program of what the future of the individual is going to be.

In order to be able to compute the possibility that one human may turn out equal to another, we need to bear in mind two combinatory moments: the paternal or maternal genetic cell that only carries half of the chromosomes; and the chromosomes of the cells of the new human that are only a fraction of the new genes coming from either of the two progenitors and that will influence the real appearance of the new individual. To this we must add the eventual mutations or errors in the configuration of the chromosomes. Under such circumstances, if the number of genes that come together were just thirty-two, the possible different individuals to be formed would amount to more than two million; and since humans have thousands of genes, the number of different children a couple may give birth to is almost infinite. And this is so by only paying attention to the chromosomes, and not having in mind other differences generated by the protoplasms of the genetic cells, or the environmental factors of the dynamic maternal womb, or the mutable external circumstances where the maturation of individuals takes place. All this confirms that it is impossible for two humans to be physically identical, not even in the case of monozygotic twins born of the fecundation of one single ovum by the same spern. Each human is an irrepeatable play of a biological card game, a conception that is absolutely original.

This individuality of every human being may also be shown histologically. Within the sixth chromosome of the male there is a small region that defines the compatibility of the different textures, and orders the rejection of alien organisms as soon as they are inserted through contagion or injection. Upon each human cell there are six distinguishing and identifying marks, three come from the mother and three from the father: these two cells acknowledge each other, and in turn, unmask the exotic ones in order to proceed to their destruction. The lymphocytes are the main agents in the fight against any invasion. One of the great medical difficulties is to compensate for this egocentric reaction in order to make possible surgical transplants. So far we have been able to identify about fifty different marks, which would allow for a million different combinations. An individual will be better or worse prepared to repel any form of infection depending on the model of cellular identification he has. This also explains the uneven resistance to sickness by different individuals. This phenomenon is the product of antibodies or immunoglobulins that are numerous. Within one single species, twenty-five different varieties of antibodies have been catalogued relating to different people. Something analogous occurs with the enzymes as their molecular structure and dynamism changes from one human to the next.

There is, then, a signal in each cell which marks its belonging to one individual. Besides, each cell is different from other analogous cells. The experiment of R. Sperry shows, through the inversion of the eye of a toad, that each neuron, after meticulous exploration, reestablishes its connection with the retinal cell; which proves that they have their identity and function and that these are nontransferable. In sum, there are no two cells that are identical, and people are different from the biochemical point of view.

What value do human differences have? Could they be as insignificant as fingerprints? No, human multiplicity is very far from being insignificant in practice. Humans are different not only in style, but also in aesthetical sensibilities; and there are those differences that affect human physical and mental functions. It is trivial to be blond or dark haired, it is not very substantial to be handsome or ugly: but it is less trivial to be weak or strong, and especially to be stupid or a genius; for experience shows that our degree of intelligence basically determines the success of our life. There are, therefore, differences that are dramatically decisive. Are these differences hereditary or environmental? The resolution of this question is of an enormous social consequence.

2. Genetic Inequality

Thousands of years before Gregor Mendel (1822-1884) established his laws of inheritance, people already knew that many characteristics, like racial, physical, and even moral similarities are inherited. In the nineteenth century certain medical experiments on heredity were systematized. In the thirties, in our own century, the volumes edited by A. Gütt, *Handbuch der Erbkranheiten (A Treatise on Hereditary Diseases)* (Leipzig, 1937) were published.

The color of the skin, height, semblance, and blood groups are inherited. Physical malformations, like polidactilia and brachidactilia are inherited. Functional deficiencies, like daltonism, diabetes, hemophilia, hypertension, and homosexuality are also inherited. Illnesses, like microftalmia, deafness, core, and epilepsy are also inherited, as are the handicaps of alcoholism and syphilis. We also inherit the predisposition to certain infections like tuberculosis, enterocolitis, and chest colds; and deficiences in immunology that allow for arthritis, leprosy, certain allergies, and psoriasis. We also inherit certain genetic errors that, because they mistake the cellular self-identification of the organism, attack their own tissues, as in the case of plaquesclerosis, certain anemias, and so forth. Each day new hereditary roots are discovered with many other side-effects. It is already a serious matter to be born weak or strong, healthy or sickly, for this conditions our physical capacity and the duration of our lives. The biological lottery is the inexorable cause of certain tragic inequalities among humans. But if this discrimination were left to the area of sicknesses, its social impact would be episodic and minor. The serious question arises when we detect signs that the psychic makeup of individuals is predominantly defined via the genetic code, and that, therefore, the differences in superior human functions come already genetically given and are, for the most part, unchangeable.

Longevity and vitality have, then, a genealogical component that has not yet been properly calculated, but that is very important. The human psyche is being studied, especially by psychology and psychiatry, providing illuminating results. There are studies on the heredity of mental illness which date from the beginning of this century; Dubitscer gathered in 1937 materials on mental weaknesses, Luxenburger studied schizophrenia and cyclothymia, Conrad provided data on epilepsy, and Stumpfl on hysteria. The percentage of psychiatric patients with family history of mental illness rises, in some cases, to 79%. These investigations have been carried out in the last fifty years despite certain ideological prejudices from anti-racists and Marxists. The studies carried out by Kallmann on identical twins give some very high figures in this regard: 100% of homosexuals, 96% in the case of cyclothymia, 86% in the case of schizophrenia, and 68.5% of schizophrenic twins are children from couples with the same illness. The hereditary character of mental anomalies appears, therefore, to have an hereditary basis that experiments bear out in the sense that human psychic personality comes, to a large degree, conditioned at birth.

Psychopathological studies have also been complemented by psychological studies in regard to the intelligence quotient. These tests do not allow for a complete measure of the whole human spiritual capacity, but they provide data on some of the intellectual capacities that are most operative. The parallelism shown between the estimated intellectual quotient and the posterior biographical success of those studied confirm the realism and utility of the method.

The distribution of the intelligence quotient within a Western population is far from seeming egalitarian, although it appears to be symmetrical: 2.3% are below 70, 3.6% between 70 and 85, 34.1% between 85 and 100, 34.1% between 100 and 115, 13.6% between 115 and 130, and 2.3% over 130. This means that 15% are below par, 35% are mediocre, and only 2% are truly gifted. The share, therefore, of mental capacities is unequal, where the masses are less gifted and only a minority is intellectually privileged. The claim of egalitarianism falters where the most significant characteristic of *homo sapiens* appears, in its intelligence; and this conditions the personal destiny of each one of us and the service to the species.

Is this radical inequality a consequence of educational discrimination, or is it due, in a larger part, to genetic imperatives? Is it the result of social injustices or of natural laws? We are faced here with the most conflicting alternative of the social debate, the one that has suffered more extrascientific pressures; for the ideologues of egalitarianism, who are legion, fight with all their power not to accept the consequences of the hereditary character of intelligence.

The experiments that Tryon carried out with animals in 1940 are rather conclusive. His starting point was a heterogeneous population of rats tested in a labyrinth. He selected those that were most successful and those that committed the most errors. By means of blood crossings among the less intelligent he produced, after several generations, two types of rats, those that committed few errors and those that committed many. These were, respectively, the descendants of the original clever rats and the dull rats. The percentages obtained prove that animal intelligence is transmitted mainly through inheritance.

It is not possible to perform the same experiments with humans, mainly because of the illegality of pairing closely related individuals for homogeneous groupings, and also because human sexual maturity would take hundred of years to provide significant data from a dozen generations. Francis Galton is a classic in this effort. In his work *Hereditary Genius* (1869) he studied almost a thousand famous people and discovered that out of one hundred eminent people, thirty-one had parents who had also been famous. Scientists like Bernouille, Becquerel, and Curie, or musicians like Bach and Strauss are named to support this thesis. As an example, the father, grandfather, and four out of six male children of Darwin were distinguished members of the Royal Society.

The most convincing experiments are those carried out with monozygotic twins, and these reveal a great parallelism between them. Galton had already worked in this field, but the main research was carried out after the thirties in this century. In 1966, F. Burt gathered the results of several monographs comprising the studies of 148 pairs of twins. The mental correlation of those twins educated together is 0.92, of those educated apart is 0.86, and of other siblings who are not twins but are educated together is only 0.25. Other experiments have provided similar results to those, very controversial and even contested, carried out by Burt. What appears from these tests is that the genetic identity of twins is the main cause of their similar intellectual capacity, and that the deviations resulting from a diverse education are small.

Experiments carried out in England since 1940, searching for a correlation between the intelligence quotient of parents and children, show that those so related are in the order of 0.50, double that of those not so related. And this also points out inheritance of intelligence.

The fact that intellectual capacity is so unevenly distributed among humans, and the fact that inheritance is such an important determinant factor in this distribution, explains the fact that there are not only individuals but also groups that are intellectually gifted. We have already mentioned some families, but it also seems to be the case with certain social strata. F. Burt, again, published in 1961 the conclusions of certain informations gathered around the region of London for the last half century. The intelligence quotient of the class of university students and liberal professions, about 3% of the population, was 140, while that of laborers and farmers, about 26% of the population, only 85. This implies a difference of about 55 points. This parallelism, though not so sharp, is transmitted to the children: 121 for the higher class, 93 for the lower. A study carried out in Madrid in 1971 showed that the general aptitude of girls of the middle class in private school was 62 points, while the aptitude of immigrant girls from the countryside was 39. Of the most polemical studies on the races, A. R. Jansen, in certain studies that provoked an intercontinental debate, tried to show that the black population of the United States has an intellectual quotient 15 points lower than the white population, but this does not bring out any results about the presumed racial inferiority of blacks, for the American black population as much as the white are the result of mixed breedings from several groups, racial and otherwise; what the study tried to show was that some populations are mentally superior to others. The apologists of the black cause had presumed that those differences linked to color are not caused by it, but by an educational environment that favors whites over blacks. However, other experiments carried out with Indians and other socially deprived minorities, like Puerto Ricans, has revealed that these other populations, so little pampered by the social environment, score higher on standard intelligence tests than does the black population. From the point of view of human groups, these specific findings do not deny, but suggest, the inheritability of intelligence.

3. Noetic Inheritance

Does the human species carry certain intellectual baggage coded in the structures of its neurophysiology? Though the question requires an experimental base, it has been tackled from a metaphysical perspective and it has been the object of a prolonged and inconclusive controversy.

At the beginning of this old debate, Plato had already taken a position that is both extreme and radical: all ideas are innate within historical man and, therefore, to learn is tantamount to remembering. Aristotle reacted in a direct manner against this position of the Academy and set down the epistemological bases of experimental knowledge. But he accepted, tacitly, a certain innatism regarding the first principles, for he took them to be connatural to human intelligence. The late Stoics considered as innate certain moral norms.

Augustine dedicated his second book of *On Liberty* to show that certain mathematical, logical, and axiological certainties do not proceed from the senses, but rather that the intellect discovers them in its interior. Among them are "the rules of truth" and the "laws of beauty" that proceed from an external and superior illumination, the divine light, that is common to all humans. Augustinian illuminism is a theological innatism that was carried on by the Franciscan schools. For Bonaventure, for example, the idea of being does not proceed from experience, but is a reflection of the divinity, and thus an innate notion in humans.

It is with Thomas Aquinas that innatism appears with more continuity as the theory of natural law. The most balanced synthesis of five hundred years of Christian ethics is found in the Spaniard Francisco Suárez who repeated the Pauline metaphor that the natural law is "imprinted by God in the heart of humans" and cannot be erased by them, nor ignored insofar as it refers to "the first and most universal principles." This natural law is the same for all humanity for "it is not a property that originates with the particular essence of one individual, but with the human specific nature." The ultimate norms of morality are, therefore, innate for the whole human race. This thesis is repeated with adjustments by the whole *ius naturalism*, and its origins are remote.

Descartes reformulated the old question in new terms. He distinguished three types of ideas: those that are born with the subject, or innate; those that come from the outside, or extraneous; and those that are invented or fabricated. Innate ideas are indivisible, universal, necessarily imposed, and are "naturally impressed on our souls." Such are the first principles, geometric notions, numbers, figures, movements, and those that do not imply affirmation or negation. Leibniz, in clear opposition to English empiricism, proclaimed that "it is false that all our ideas come from the senses that are called exterior, for the ones I have of myself, of my thoughts, and also of being, substance, action, identity and many others come from an interior experience." He cites in other places the ideas of the same, the possible, the one, of cause, of perception, of reason, etc., as given inside ourselves. But Leibniz also admits that there are innate ideas that do not become evident of themselves, but need to be discovered.

We already find in Descartes and Leibniz a certain ambiguity about ideas that appear in the mind due to birth, and ideas as internal mental acts, that is between static and dynamic innatism. Kant takes the next step towards idealism by reducing the innate to two *a priori* intuitions, that is, independent from experience and inseparable from the human mind: space and time. Neither the one nor the other are physical realities that exist by themselves, they are forms of our capacity of perception, and this is the reason we are unable to perceive anything that is not within space and within time. We do not come up with the existence of space and time through childhood learning, but rather, all our perceptions come, from the very beginning, through those two coordinates that are cosubstantial with the human species.

After Kant, innatism evolves towards idealism and hence we are no longer dealing with concepts and truths coded in the newlyborn, but with what humans, by the fact that they are humans, impose on reality by the act of apprehending it. This is more a kind of formal than material innatism, since what is innate is an instrument and no longer data. It is not possible to reconstruct, not even at a glance, the interpretations of the eidetic inheritance after Kant. A close example will suffice to show the persistence of innatism in our history.

Noam Chomsky, particularly in *Language and Mind* (1968), affirms the existence of a common structure or a general grammar to all languages, and maintains that such a scheme is not acquired through experience, but is connatural to the child, and identifies it with certain radical predispositions of the human mind. There is, then, something innate anterior to learning our maternal language and which Chomsky compares to the instinct of birds to learn their specific song. This innate patrimony is built out of linguistic universals, which can be substantial or formal, and these in turn subdivide into phonologic, syntactic, or semantic—as, for example, the idea of noun, verb, subject, complement, etc. There are, therefore, a series of categories and rules that are universal, and *a priori*, with which the child structures, and to a certain degree, builds his language out of the disconnected, scarce, and often incorrect idiomatic data that he gathers from his surroundings. The discipline of linguistics, in one of its most recent and brilliant studies, reactualizes, with the help of empirical verifications, the essential conclusion of rational innatism.

It is obvious that, regardless of the exegetic problems that each author raises, philosophy has recognized the need for a noetic inheritance, something that is related to knowledge, that we receive from our parents together with our bodies, and that is not originated from sensory experiences. We may argue if the idea of being is, as postulated by Bonaventure and repeated up to Rosmini, innate; but what cannot be denied is that the human mind understands the world in a peculiar manner. The protozoa has a way of apprehending its circumstances different from that of the orangutan, and the latter does not understand his environment the same way a human does. Angelology and theodicy postulate other less complex forms of apprehending reality different from the human, like perfect intuition, absolute cognition, or what is called medium science. The different ways of apprehending reality are conditioned by the different structures of the intellectual faculties. The peculiar character of human understanding is innately conditioned by our spacio-temporal, relativistic, analytic, judicative, causal, etc., way of understanding the world. Be it the principle of non-contradiction, or being, or temporality, there is something in humans that is not received from the outside, but added by humans when they put their faculties to work. That extra that they "put" is a legacy in the human chromosomes which the species, to which we belong, has left to all of us, and it is an inheritance different from that of other species. There are radical disparities within the species, but, on the other hand, this inheritance takes in each individual shades more or less remarkable: Plato and Aristotle, Velázquez, and El Greco, Juan de la Cruz and Quevedo did not see the universe in the same way, and this proves that although they shared the same period, country, and place, their respective noetic inheritances were different.

4. Social Inequality

Man is a social animal, that is, he belongs to a species that cannot develop in solitude. The main causes of this natural sociability are the following: (1) Humans mature sexually very late, hence, they need many years of nourishment and protection by adults. (2) The instinctive resources of humans hardly allow them to survive, and the acquisition of experience accumulated by the species requires the teachings of elders. (3) Humans need in perpetuity the company of others to satisfy their needs for love and respect. (4) The evolution of *homo sapiens* is more cultural than chromosomic; and the creation, conservation, and transmission of culture and the concomitant accumulated knowledge require that humans live in societies.

In sum, the human species is naturally communicative at the biological, formative, affective, and cultural levels; and this communication is viable only in society. To these motivations we need add another that, although derived, is also basic: the need to overcome a state of anarchy and universal war by means of the creation of areas of collective security. This is the moment when societies become political unities.

Robinson Crusoe is not a solitary man, he is an ex-social person against his will and mentally integrated in the lost society. The most similar example to the solitary man must be searched for among sociological rarities like the "wolf child" raised by inferior animals and whose circumstantial condition is infrahuman. Sociability is not a simple capacity of humans; it is an essential condition and an unavoidable imperative.

All human societies underwrite two large types of hierarchies, authority, and power. The first one is a declarative and sapiential superiority: it belongs to those who know more. The second one is dispositive and executive; it belongs to whomever has more capacity for coercive power. Authority cannot be transferred; power may be delegated. Authority is logical; power is factual. Authority is accepted; power is imposed. Authority is altruistic; power is egocentric. Authority is nobler than power.

(a) *Authority* is not a knowledge that is exclusively theoretical and restricted to the sphere of possible abstractions. It is, nonetheless, doubtful that such types of sublimations are possible since every idea is a possible action; and as Piaget has shown, cognitive processes, including the mathematical, are ways of practically regulating the relations of the animal to its environment. Besides, a very important part of the pure sciences is to "know how" to find solutions in the laboratories and the libraries and "to know how" to act upon the real.

Culture is what separates the more advanced human from the more primitive. Most of culture, however, mediately or immediately proceeds from authority since it has become less and less possible to personally experiment on all the functions upon which science as a whole is founded, or even on one single specialization. To know means, to a large extent, to act on faith in the contributions of others, and to accept their authority—the day when each researcher would try personally to verify all the data, concepts, and judgments with which he deals, then science would destroy itself by eating itself up.

Authority is basically a certain degree of knowledge; but out of this knowledge emerges an ability that enables people to make judgments of value: authority is primarily definitory and only later judicative. There are critics with authority who praise, indite, and dictate norms: this is the way to paint, to write. Scientific authority, within each domain, normally agrees with moral authority. In this case, the subordination of the obedient is double: he not only accepts data, but also recommendations. This produces a relative ignorance and, therefore, an inferiority towards others, in respect to how things are and how they ought to be.

At the present level of knowledge no individual can have ultimate authority regarding all fields of knowledge. There are authorities only within a field and at a given time. The most knowledgeable man is ignorant in a variety of fields, and there he must submit to the authority of others. The division of labor alone determines insuperable situations of superiority in sapiential authority. This kind of stratification does not occur between physics and chemistry alone, for example, but even within physics between a specialist in particles and another in the mechanics of fluids, and so on. We are dealing here, of course, with hierarchies that cover one another: one is first in genetics, the other in opthalmology.

Even within one field no individual is identical to another: some know more, others less. This inequality is derivative. It depends in part on environmental factors such as the circumstances of one's education; but it is also dependent on innate aptitudes, like curiosity, intelligence, memory, and dedication. Two students under the same scholastic discipline will achieve uneven results. Only when the most advanced is forced to slow progression will the uneven results disappear, though not the reality that separates them personally. Inequality in authority due to knowledge, and also in action, cannot be destroyed. Where two individuals gather, one will be cognitively superior to the other.

(b) *Prestige* is a type of hierarchy close to authority, although it is more diffused, since it is not always restricted to a particular domain, and it is more subjective. When someone says that so and so is "an authority in astronomy" it is a more concrete and committed statement than saying, "He is a prestigious astronomer," for this prestige may be the outcome of other virtues not connected with wisdom; and because such a statement is not so much a direct testimony about the person but rather it indicates that there is a favorable opinion on the man.

Etymology explains this kind of semantic imprecision. The term *prestige* derives from the Latin *praestigiae* which means illusion, phastasmagories, and magic games. Prestidigitation is a derivative. There is, then, a magical, mysterious, inexplicable connotation. Prestige is, therefore, less rational than authority, it has a basis that is less logical, and this disqualifies it from a sociological viewpoint; for irrationality is a characteristic of the acts of the masses. This is an important, universal, and true social fact for reasons that are relatively grounded and with a content relatively defined; some people are granted prestige by the group, raising them above the masses, who also grant them a hierarchical ordering according to this prestige.

Prestige is always a positive quality; and this is different from fame, which can be good or bad. The contrary is the loss of prestige, which is socially more painful than a simple and neutral anonymity. The loss of prestige calls the attention of the collective consciousness to some vice, weakness or indiscretion. For this reason it is important to maintain one's prestige, and to use the mass inertia in its favor.

The inequalities in prestige are unavoidable for they proceed from the uncoerced, evaluating faculty of humans. Everyone judges others and from the coincidental repetition of such judgments within the group emerges that general opinion that grants and removes prestiges. Dictatorial or other types of manipulations may invent or remove prestiges, but they cannot eliminate them completely. Not even the most totalitarian and coercive uniformism will be able to avoid differences in the prestige of people, for this is something more intimate and personal, and for this reason, more valuable than political and economic power. Thus, prestige may turn out to be a source of satisfaction to some and frustration and even envy to others, to a degree even deeper than riches and power. Prestige, being so linked to society, is one of the primary roots of inequality among humans.

(c) *Power* is achieved in the degree that one is able to impose one's will on others. In the hypothetical situation of an all-out war of everyone against everyone, individuals will form a hierarchy of power with the stronger at the top. But where political communities are formed social power is shared by the citizens as it is ordered by the law.

People join the state to come out of anarchy and be able to balance conflicting individual interests. The only recipe known to work out such compatibility is the law, and this requires judges, legislators, constables; namely, magistrates and soldiers. The law is inseparable from coercion and power. The power to legislate, to reward and punish, cannot be prorated among the citizens of a relatively large community. Some will be administrators, others administered. To the degree that citizens participate in the actual display of power in a community, to the same degree they will be unequal. The existence alone of crime and punishment, that are cosubstantial with justice and law, entails inequality. The legal order rewards differently crime and heroism. The political society implies a hierarchy of power and a gradation of honors and sanctions. Some will have a larger area of power than others and some will be more able to appeal than others. The law will grant to some more than to others, according to their merits. Political egalitarianism would be possible only in an imaginary natural state; although here we might encounter the inequality of the most irrational of factual powers, pure violence.

Not all the members of a constituted society are able to do everything, and there are some that are more gifted than others. This distribution multiplies the efficacy of the group. Thus we come to specialization of functions: warriors, artisans, laborers, and so forth. Each activity realizes some value, and those that realize it better are superior to the others. There is, besides, a hierarchy of values: difficult and scarce jobs are considered higher than those that are simple and abundant. There is also a gradation in relation to matter: the garbage collector is inferior to the jeweler. The specialization of functions is inseparable from inequality. Where several gather and each one does not perform all tasks, there will be inequality.

In sum, a political community implies norms, and, therefore, a hierarchy and coercion and evaluation of merit; that is, inequality of position, power, and goods. It also implies a division of functions, a difference in evaluation, and competency. All these intrinsic differences of the political community translate into inequality of power.

(d) Rousseau was right: "There are inequalities of power, prestige, and authority because there are societies." But he did not draw the contrary conclusion. The equality of power, prestige, and authority would come about only in a limiting utopia, and this would be equivalent to an uncommunicable self-dictatorship, or totalitarian insularity and anarchy; that is to say, only one state (if there were two, wars would be started) of only one citizen whose death would also mean the end of history—an episode as much an aberration as it would be ephemeral.

5. Vital Inequality

No one wishes in everything the same things as others. Humans coincide basically in the pursuit of happiness; but each one interprets it in his own way and pursues it differently. A biography is the inventory of the particular successes and misses of one person in his effort to reach his subjective vision of whatever he thinks constitutes happiness. The goal and the journey are, therefore, individual and irrepeatable. Humans are not only born different, they also make themselves different intentionally. Two monozygotic twins are also two different biographies and the closer they live next to each other the stronger the effort to be different from each other. Existential differences are usually spectacular even between two brothers.

The will is the supreme, differentiating power of humans, and also the cause of the differences between individuals, and the key to non-coercive inequalities. This would be the case even if humans were not free; it would be enough if they possessed, like elementary particles, the radical ambiguity of being able to move and a trajectory, and this would make them historical events. Since no event happens the same way twice, personal existences have no duplicate. They all come closer to or further from their goal and in this way they become different. This is subjective inequality. Humans *are*, and at the same time, they make themselves. By birth, they "are" always different from others, and they never "make" themselves equal to others of their own free will. The dynamic character of human life doubles the genetic individuality and complicates it with the infinite variety of freedoms or of circumstances. Humans take it that living is being, and since they want to live they make themselves unequal.

6. Ultraterrestrial Inequality

Opposed to national religions like the Judaism of the Old Testament or the caste system of Hinduism, Christianity proposes an equality of the call: all human beings, without discrimination, may and must surrender to faith.

There is something more than just a general opening in the Church. All humans receive an interior and supernatural gift that God gives them, namely grace, that may be sanctifying or actual. The first one is a permanent mark on the soul, while the second one is transitory. Both types of graces are necessary for salvation, and God freely grants them in a sufficient measure. Does this mean that each individual receives an equal amount of grace? No, each soul receives it in different amounts. To quote the Council of Trent: "Each individual receives in himself sanctity in the measure in which the Holy Spirit distributes it as He wishes, according to the proper disposition and each one's cooperation." This position, totally at war with the Protestant one, is based on St. Paul's doctrine: "There are many graces (*gratia* in the Latin version, *Charisma* in the Greek) . . . that the Holy Spirit distributes to each one as He wishes" (I Cor. 12, 4, and 11).

The equality of the call does not result in an equality of results in this life, nor in the next which is the one that counts in order to become eternal. The Council of Florence established besides that some of the chosen contemplate God more perfectly than others, according to the diversity of their merits. This definition is based on the classical idea of justice as described in the New Testament: "The Son of Man will grant each according to their works" (Matt. 17, 27). Inequality is absolute, since some will be saved and others condemned, and there will be a hierarchical gradation in rewards and punishments.

There are, therefore, disparate, natural capacities as regards supernatural graces in personal rewards and in merit. Christian egalitarianism is content with offering to each one without exception the condition of children of God and of salvation; but then the divine freedom in the adjudication of gifts and the application of a proportional justice to behavior ends up in egalitarianism.

An analysis of all creeds is not possible. The Lutheran variation that removes celestial merit from human works reduces the rationality of the whole scheme of justification, while maintaining the inequalities and accenting a fatalism placed in the arbitrariness of its source, divine discretion. The inegalitarian position of Catholicism is not very different from the position taken by the main religions, for if there is a soul that is free and immortal, and if there is a moral order and a just God, it follows that there must be a correspondence between our conduct upon this earth and the degree of eternal happiness.

The ultraterrestrial inequality is incomparably greater there than on this earth, for the latter one oscillates between finite and relatively close extremes, while the former is established between infinite events (the presence and absence of God) and spacio-temporal (heaven or hell) that are completely opposed. The possible inequality that would exist between the complete and permanent enjoyment of the absolute good and the total and unending suffering of evil is the maximal conception possible to humans primordially geared towards happiness. The inequalities of this world appear insignificant to the believer who accepts those eternal disparities as possible.

IV. The Egalitarian Ideal

1. Equality Before the Law

The Declaration of Rights of 1793 proclaimed in its third article, "All men are equal by nature and before the Law." This postulate has been repeated in the most varied constitutional languages and found its way into the Universal Declaration of 1948: "Everyone is equal before the Law." This commonplace of legal ordinances posterior to the French Revolution is far from being a precise concept; it is being used, however, as if it were obvious and transparent; this it is not, for it is problematic and obscure, and therefore in dire need of analysis to find out what is true and what is false in its primitive and intuitive meaning. This problem needs to be approached from two complementary perspectives: objective law and subjective rights.

Equality before the law, as usually happens with revolutionary slogans, had in its origins a negative connotation: the rejection of any form of discrimination against people on account of their origins (ethnic, sex, for instance) and by extension, of hereditary privileges (exemptions, gifts, and so on). The removal of precepts that would condone or incite discrimination on account of race was perfectly possible, and though at a slow pace, it has been moving towards success. More difficulties accumulated when trying to equalize males and females, due to their deep structural differences; but even on this road the advances have been remarkable. The suppression of inheritance, of name and patrimony, however, has not been unanimously considered desirable, nor has it been carried out. In any case, eliminating discrimination on account of ethnic origin, beliefs, or affiliation, etc., does not entail, in its strict sense, that we have reached equality before the law. This expression, when used to remove privileged conditions, is completely misleading. Let us see the reasons why.

Can we gain equality before the law if we remove individual norms or privileges and legislate only norms that are general and that apply to many people in general? If this were the case, then equality before the law would mean requiring from any form of legislation the norm that it be "a generality." The classic Spanish jurists led by Francisco Suárez already proved the legitimacy of individual norms or privileges, namely, norms that grant responsibilities and rights to individual, concrete people. But even when only general norms are legislated, does this mean that we would then reach equality for all before the law, that is, that the same law would be applicable to all?

In order to establish the same law, we would have to hold our juridical legislation in an immutable state; but the law being positive is changeable and, therefore, some receive one legislation and others the legislation that follows the change. If we take the case of two contemporary Spaniards, for example, facing the same fact, adultery, we find that it will be a crime or not if it took place before or after the reform of the Penal Code. Even if we place the law within a very proximate time, equality before the law is an illusion due to the changes in the same law. Equality before the law cannot be successive, but only simultaneous: at a given time, the same norm applies to all. But this does not happen.

Every sovereign state drafts its own law, and thus laws are different. An Austrian and a Hungarian, though separated only by an invisible boundary, will be under different laws at the same time. As long as we have more than one state, equality before the law is only possible simultaneously and within the same geographic confines. But even these limits are not always in the hands of the state; where we find federal territories or other regions with legal independence, a common nationality is not a guarantee of equality before the law. We would be required to share also the same neighborhood. Divorce laws are different in Nevada or Washington; and fiscal laws are different in Pamplona or Madrid. Equality before the law has, therefore, a temporal restriction (simultaneity) and a spacial one (the same region).

Even within one particular region, the same fact, a homicide, for example, will fall under the particular legal jurisdiction that belongs to the subject. The soldier is under the Code of Military Justice, the others under the Penal Code. This disparity is repeated in other cases: minors, terrorists, clerics, etc. Therefore, from an objective perspective, equality before the law is limited to areas subject to the same sovereignty and the same jurisdiction.

We should now proceed to study the question not from an objective standpoint, but from the subjective rights that legal norms acknowledge and protect. These rights may belong to all, some, or simply one. Only in the first case is there a certain equality. The subjective rights that belong to every human by the fact of being human are what the Declaration of 1789 called "natural" rights, and later on were called "human" rights. This discrepancy in names is the result of the polemic between the *ius*-naturalists and the positivists. The first consider the rights of humans as given and immutable, while the positivists argue that these rights are acquired and historical. The few *ius*-naturalists reduce the lists of such rights to very few in order to avoid absolutism, while the numerous positivists multiply such rights and extend them to areas that are secondary and marginal in the name of a rampant relativism. In any case, such rights belong to all men equally. The objection raised, particularly by Marxists, is that not everyone is capable of using his rights in a capitalist society. Freedom of expression, for example, is not the same for the average citizen as it is for whoever owns the mass media. The same objection, of course, holds against any citizen in the face of the mass media of one single communist party. The truth is that subjective equality of human rights is found more in name than in fact.

There are also rights that some share equally with others, like joint property or the rights to the estate of someone who died without leaving a will, though all other people have none of these rights. In fact, the majority of subjective rights are individual and so unequal that they generate incompatibilities. In any lawsuit there is always a loser and a winner; the law grants one party what it takes from the other. It is also possible that if the tribunal is changed, the sentences will be contradictory, even when the facts remain the same and the norms applied do not change, for the law does not always need to be unanimous. In this case the justice given or the law interpreted is not even equal to itself. Given the hypothesis of objective equality before the law—two citizens subject to the same legal code, at the same instance and under the same judge—the law does not turn out to be equal: the law, then, tends to become a translation of inequality due to subjective rights: some own a newspaper or belong to a certain party while others do not; one is a building owner, an heir, or leases property, while the other does not. This is the reason why Marx pointed out that the law needs to be uneven, namely, a protection of the disinherited, so that in this manner we would arrive at an egalitarian society. This is the spirit that fosters many of the so-called social laws. Examples may be found in those legal norms that remove expenses from the poor, those that protect women, minors, the underdeveloped, the worker, and all those legal norms that punish accordingly, in an increasing scale, those who have more. All these are examples of a discriminatory law, for it does not apply equally to all. The difference lies in the fact that before, it was considered just to exempt the nobility from certain tributes, while now it is thought that the favored ones should be others. Legal discrimination continues to exist, what has changed is the idea of equity.

In conclusion we may say that, *sensu strictu,* there is no equality before the law. From the point of view of objective law, there is the tendency to turn international, legal norms into a universal and coactive process, to homogenize the legal codes of the different nations, to systematize and standardize internal legislations, and suppress special jurisdictions, namely, to unify the law in order to even the inequalities derived from a plurality of norms. Such a goal has already reached an historical presence difficult to measure. From the point of view of subjective rights, there is a tendency to substitute the discriminations found due to inheritance for the discriminations found in created situations; the balance of justice going in favor of the less fortunate. Regardless of how much we have advanced in this direction, we can not remove, however, the discriminatory, material fact of the new laws.

The possible, objective equality before the law is reduced to the fact that judicial ordinances, at a given moment, will foresee similar resolutions within analogical possibilities for subjects under identical jurisdiction. Subjective equality before the law is reduced to the unchanging juridical condition of the subject, despite independent conditions affecting his free behavior. Objective equality before the law is desirable, but very difficult to achieve, and it also entails less capacity for true egalitarianism than it is commonly and topically thought. Subjective equality before the law entails the suppression of all inherited rights, and this does not lead to an effective patrimonial equity. But even given this restricted, objective equality, or this problematic, subjective equality, it does not follow that the laws themselves are not discriminatory, favoring some against others according to the main idea of justice, nor does it follow that the sentences given are egalitarian; on the contrary, they appear as the creators and perpetuators of inequalities.

This is the small and problematic content of the supposed universal and positive equality before the law.

2. Political Equality

Political equality pertains more to rights than to individual conditions: those eligible, as much as the voters, are entitled to one vote of identical value. This leveling of political subjective rights is a particular case of equality before the law; and it is a paradigmatic case because it is a right, like all those called human, which belongs to the person by the fact of being one, and not on account of episodic circumstances. This is, then, a basic equality, or one of entitlement. It is also presented as a fundamental right, because through its exercise the members of a community are able to participate in the election of their legislators and leaders; and on this account the legal ordinances and the administrative acts will tend to become a reflection of the will of the majority. Finally, it is supposed that the will of the majority will not be elitist and discriminatory, but popular and egalitarian. Thus the logical circle is closed: all social equalities derive from political equality. The equality of political rights is the result, and also the guarantee, of equality before the law, and for this reason it has become the starting point and the goal of the demo-liberal state. This is the theoretical hypothesis that unfortunately is more an illusion than a reality.

Whatever refers to equality before the law may be predicated from the equality of political rights. The most important generic limitation is that an effective political equality is only possible among fellow citizens. In some countries there are more political rights than in others. Besides, it is not the same thing to be able to elect the President of the United States as it is to be able to elect the First Minister of Liechtenstein. Even though both rights are formally analogous, one is of much greater worth than the other. It would be necessary that humanity consist of only one universal state, so that the political rights of each one would be equal. Cosmopolitism is an *a priori* condition of this and other equalities born of the law.

There are also some specific limitations of high importance. The democratic ideal is encapsulated in the principle "government by the people." But to which people are we referring? This very important question is systematically put aside by the idealogues. Could, for example, the people of Milan become "the people"—the collective subject of political rights—and declare themselves independent? Or is this a question that belongs to some other people, the actual Italian people? The question that the theory and practice of democracy usually hides is: How is "a people" defined? The procedure, in fact, is not the social contract. It is evident that the American people have not been formed by plebiscite, but through a long and dense series of bellicose acts that ended in the Revolutionary War. Something similar could be said about all the other existing states. Universal history proves that nations usually have a birth that is in part hazardous, in part coactive, and for this reason they do not have a democratic legitimacy at their origin. All those nations that grant their people equal rights before the law have not been the result of equality before the law, but rather of violence and discrimination. As a consequence of this irrational composition that shapes different states from the beginning, it turns out that the political rights of people are either formally unequal—as between a Swiss and a Ukrainian—or materially unequal—as between the modest Tibetan and the powerful American. The plurality and the diversity of sovereign people makes the political equality of the human species impractical.

We may add to this analysis of how countries are formed the complementary view of how countries disintegrate. Democratic practice will deny those already constituted cities and regions the legal possibility of their independence. This is a flagrant inequality: the citizens of a state have the right of self-determination against the international community, but this right is denied to the same citizens against their own state. This contradiction has its origin in the fact that the concept "the people" is extraordinarily confused. The only effort made to bring some objective criteria was the so-called principle of nationalities: only a nation can be a self-governed people. This nineteenth century doctrine has very serious deficiencies. The first is that the notion of people is substituted for that of nation, and this is no less problematic. The second is that the present political diversity of humanity would be illegitimate, since there are nations with several states, and states that embrace several nations. And the third one is that the application in whole of the principle of nationalities would guarantee the legal fragmentation of humanity and this would, in all probability, add to inequality before the law.

This discrimination, however, is less serious than the absurd position the states would take if they maximized the democratic principle. Democracy would become cantonalism if a simple family or a village could become "a people," since by definition "the people" must govern themselves. This would be tantamount to anarchy or the negation of the social organization. It is, therefore, understandable that concrete demo-liberalism would prefer a theoretical contradiction that is viable in practice to doctrinal integrity and political chaos. But when such a pragmatic road is undertaken, then a deep inequality is carried out: protection of the right of self-determination in some areas and the punishment of the same right in others under the name of separatism.

Political equality does not cover all men, but only those of the same state; citizenship has been imposed on some, while the efforts of others to separate and become sovereign are thwarted. There are, then, three types of inequalities: first, the inequality between the number and extension of political rights available to citizens according to the state to which they belong; second, the inequality between a powerful state whose collective, political rights are carried out in an imperialistic fashion, and those of a weak state, that is more or less colonized; and third, the inequality where the right to self-determination granted to the majority of the people is denied to the minorities.

These are not, however, all the restrictions. The equality of subjective political rights will not exist if they are not recognized for all those born in the state. Presently, those under eighteen are excluded. Is it because they are simultaneously denied a sufficient use of their reason? This is another contradiction in the demo-liberal theory: if the rationality of an underdeveloped or illiterate adult weighs, at the time of voting, as much as that of a genius, why are the intellects of those under eighteen excluded? Is a young man or woman at that age less aware than a ninety-year-old person? The practical problem appears to lie at the chronological doors of what constitutes minimal rationality. If we reduce this question to the *a quo* formula we could ask: would seven be all right? Under this hypothesis the subjective, political rights of the rest of the juvenile population would be denied. This would be a political inequality in relation to the other citizens of the state: it would also be a legal inequality, since all minors have a legal representative to protect their civil rights; and it would be a moral inequality, for if every man equals one vote, we would be denying their manhood to those who are not legally able to vote. All this leads to a conclusion: the internal logic of political equality demands that all those born have a vote, either to exert this right personally or through their legal representative. As long as this is not reached there will not be equal political rights, but rather discrimination on account of age.

Restrictions of eligibility, though less general, need to be added to these restrictions on the active act of voting (to which we should add those derived from penal records), for these are also very unequalizing. The dynastic monarchies, or those that required royal blood only, produced an obvious radical, political inequality as regards the eligibility of higher positions: almost everyone was excluded. There are also limitations, on account of age, to eligibility for public positions; some, like the senatorial position, require in many cases qualified ages. Only those persons that have professional qualifications are entitled to certain political positions, like becoming a member of the Tribunal to Guarantee the Constitution. Equality of passive, political rights is impossible in part, for it would make no sense to elect a minor to become a minister by representation; this would amount to returning to the custom of regents, proper, of some monarchies, in all political responsibilities. This is an insurmountable obstacle.

This is not the end of real restrictions on the rights of participation in the exercise of power. The political deputies are the supposed archetype. All adults are eligible. But the problem intensifies when one is trying to become a candidate. Is it possible to include every citizen in the electoral ballot? The legislators only consider certain names or independent groupings arrived at by only a certain amount of voters. In practice, however, everyone knows that within developed, inorganic democracies the parties exert an effective monopoly on the manufacture of candidates. The fact is that only those that belong to the partocratic minority are eligible. The equality of passive, political rights is a fiction within systems of plural parties and only rhetoric in totalitarian systems. Political eligibility is not an equal, real, political possibility for all citizens; it is rather a privileged situation that the leaders of the parties bestow on a few of their loyals. If there is a place where political inequality is most obvious, it is this one, and this happens to be the one that is decisive to becoming invested with public power.

Political equality as a right or as a possibility of receiving or granting power is much more restricted than a naive reading of Rousseauistic constitutional dogmatism would suggest. Furthermore, political equality disappears, rather than diminishing, if we examine it as a true condition and not as a right of citizens. There is no society without certain laws that try to make compatible the individual opposing interests at play, and which does not have the coactive apparatus to carry out those laws. This apparatus requires a hierarchy. Within all organized societies there are those administrators who hold the largest part of the political power, and others, the administered, who endure it. The leading class and their administrative elements are so rigorously scaled that no two individuals are identical in rank or powers. A society is by definition and organization a vertical structure, and increasingly so the more developed it is, where not even two of its elements are equidistant from the sovereign apex. The political condition of every citizen is inequality, regardless of how egalitarian his fundamental rights are. As soon as we leave the abstractions of the codes, political equality disappears: a citizen is inferior to some and superior to others, with the exceptions at both ends of the chain. Equality of power is an impossible dream.

If, as the demo-liberal theoreticians pretend, equality before the law would depend on an effective political equality, the former would be even more precarious a reality than we now experience, for then citizens would be reduced to political nomads with no relation to one another, which is the contrary of the equality of the subjective rights of all humans. The more cantons, the more the disparity. Cosmopolitanism as much as imperialism—the two widening forms of sovereign jurisdiction, which make possible the application of only one system of law—are clearly elitist. Maximal equality before the law did not occur within the atomic democracies of Greece, but under the ecumenical Caesarism of Rome. Equality of power leads to anarchy, and it is only without one particular legal order that the egalitarian will and a relative equity are possible. The condition for a viable egalitarianism is the existence of a hierarchy or the inequality of power, just as the condition for a maximalist egalitarianism is the leveling exercise of a total and absolute dictatorship. The more extensive and rigorous the equality among all the citizens, the greater the inequality between the leaders and the masses.

If all citizens had identical political power, the decisions that affect the community could not be carried out by a superior man, but by the collectivity. Once this egalitarian thesis has been stated, the practical problem now consists in arbitrating a system of decision-making where first a plurality and then a multitude would be able to arrive at decisions. The techniques for public representation are varied and complex; but all rest on the so-called majoritarian principle: the position that carries the larger number of votes must prevail. Prolonged use of this principle and seductive propaganda have granted it an appearance of moral imperative that makes it evident and intuitively certain. This principle, however, is questionable in the extreme, and, therefore, political equality seems to be most problematic to achieve in practice in order to make decisions that affect the community.

The habitual argumentation follows this line: that all opinions on public matters have equal value, and so it follows that those that carry a majority have more value than the others. Now making an extraordinary mental effort, let us suppose that the opinion of a genius has the same worth as that of the ignorant and stupid. Would we be able to deduce, then, that two opinions would have more value than one? Not really; no one has yet proved that multitudes do not make mistakes. On the contrary, experience proves that millions of people have defended and accepted religious dogmas that were totally false. Not taking into account Condorcet's famous affirmation that the probability of truth in the opinion of a majority increases in proportion to the number of votes, we know, as demonstrated by collective psychology, that the level of rationality of the masses is much lower than that of the average individual.

The majoritarian principle cannot rest on the assumption that the majority holds the key to defining the True and the Good, for both are independent of human relativity. Could it rest on the assumption that the will of the majority is best for all? Historical experience also shows that the masses, on account of their lack of responsibility, are more prone than individuals to making mistakes and to inequities. Collective psychology has also shown that the wills of individuals caught up in the masses are more manipulable than the wills of isolated individuals. The majoritarian principle cannot be defended from the volitive perspective when dealing with large masses.

In its most rigorous sense, the thesis that the majority must prevail over the minority is not deduced from a supposed infallibility of numbers, but from the physical superiority of the many over the few. The powers of a homogeneous body and their individual members can be added up. And it is not absurd to admit that within large groups individual members share an average standard power that is similar. The logical foundation of the majoritarian principle, though, is not found in the belief that a larger number represents a greater rationality or a more benevolent will, but rather a greater capacity for coercion. Locke, the first great apologist of majoritarian power, also thought it so: "The political body must move in the direction directed by the greater power, that is the consensus of the majority" (*Civ. Gov.* II, 8, 96). This thesis had a hidden antecedent in Pascal: "Why do we follow the majority? Because it is more right? No, because it has more power" (*Pens.* V, 301). Neither of the two was fully aware of the reaches of this mechanistic interpretation of the democratic procedure par excellence. From such a perspective, the majoritarian principle is a sublimation of war, a substitution of arithmetic for violence, a ritualization of conflict, and it answers to a scheme of power that is as realistic as it is primitive.

These foundations logically lead to the tyranny of the majority over the minorities, to the despotism of some rather than the freedom that political egalitarianism pretends to assure.

In any case, the majoritarian principle ends by priming the most numerous positions and devaluing the rest. As soon as it is tested, political egalitarianism disappears: those opinions that won are so superior that they are worth everything, while those that lost are worth nothing. The majoritarian principle is neither rational nor congruent with political egalitarianism, even if some idealogues are obstinate in not recognizing this reality.

Agreements reached through a majority have historical antecedents, but their classical formulation is due to the imperial jurist Scaevola: "What the majority of the Council has decided must be taken as if all had so decided" (*Quod maior pars curiae effecit, pro eo habetur, ac si omnes egerint,*" *Dig.* L. 1, 19); though the commentators pointed out that this text referred to the municipal councils and that in the cases where individuals consent out of their own free will, they establish the unanimity that contracts have. The theoretical and practical resistance of humanity to the majoritarian principle has been long and stubborn. The ancient world denied slaves and barbarians (those born outside of the nation) the political power to make decisions; but even among the free citizens the principle was not recognized. Roman, individual rights required unanimity on matters of guardianship, collective responsibility and joint property; the same applied to public rights in relation to the intervention of the tribunes of the people. Pliny had already complained that senatorial sentences should be computed by their number and not their weight (*Ep.* II.12). The Church required unanimity for over a thousand years and in the case of disagreement the decision would be up to authority. Even the council of Trent required unanimity in matters of doctrine. Ecclesiastical processes have always gravitated towards Evangelical elitism: "Many are called but few are chosen." (Matt. XX, 16.).

The first law that was approved by majority decision in the English Parliament dates from 1554, and Bentham asserted that ninety-nine percent of parliamentary decision had been reached unanimously.

The election of the King of Poland required, up to 1791, a unanimous agreement. The imposition of the majoritarian principle is owed to the French Revolution, but Rousseau, who inspired it, demanded unanimity in the case of the social contract or the Constitution, and a qualified majority when dealing with important decisions. This was not an isolated case. The classical idealogues of the social contract demanded unanimity, and this left the citizen no other options than to agree or to go into exile. Contemporary law on public rights is full of cases where a simple majority is not sufficient and which require either an absolute majority or two-thirds, which already implies a certain skepticism about a majority made up of half plus one. Despite the proclamations of the majoritarian principle, egalitarians fall into the contradiction of requiring at times a unanimous consensus, while at other times they side with the minorities. The so-called consensus is a nostalgic fall back on unanimity and a tacit acceptance that majorities are not sufficient. The siding at times with minorities is also an admission that numbers do not express truth or goodness. A legal reflection of this inferiority complex is the very common defense of proportional representation rather than majority. Unanimity is demanded, almost universally, in cases dealing with penal sentencing. The majority principle, therefore, is very far from being self-evident.

We have to conclude that the majority principle is either a peaceful translation of the law of the more powerful, or an arbitrary recipe as problematic as any other, even flipping a coin, even though it appeals to the masses. What this principle is not is an instrument of political equality, for what really comes out of this principle is unanimity, namely theoretical utopia and practical anarchy. The equality of political power excludes all tyrannies, including that of the majority.

In summary: the equality of political rights requires an ecumenical state and a universal emancipation; political equality in fact is not compatible with any hierarchy, for it can be realized only in an anarchical social relationship; besides, any viable social equalities will be realized by a power that becomes as absolute as the absolute egalitarianism to which it aspires.

3. Equality of Opportunities

The evidence of a constitutive inequality among humans and the serious doubt that human equalization is possible and even desirable makes egalitarians retreat into a more moderate claim for their egalitarian ideal: the so-called equality of opportunity. The origin of this concept goes back to Tocqueville, who starts his book *De la Democratie en Amérique* (1835) with this sentence: "From among all the novelties that have attracted my attention during my stay in the United States no one has impressed me more vividly than the equality of conditions." It is possible that the author had in mind only an equality of social condition and, therefore, the absence of classes in the American communities. Thus his expression "*égalité des conditions*" does not imply the radical egalitarianism proclaimed by Baboeuf but rather the equalization of all at the starting line, namely, the equality of opportunity.

This concept has a negative connotation that is the more visible and clear: the rejection of the fact that the socio-economic level of parents be the cause that a few have more possibilities of training and success than the rest. But the positive connotation is ambiguously suggested. Is it the case that all humans should have the same opportunities to make their lives? Such a claim would be unacceptable, being illusory. There are three species of possibilities: the internal and innate, and these are the genetic aptitudes of the individual; the internal and embodied, and these are voluntarily acquired and added to the individual's own nature; and the circumstantial and external, and these are the opportunities of the environment and the means and occasions for their realization. The first type of equalities cannot be equalized since our biological personality, and consequently our moral and intellectual capacities, depend to a great measure on the chromosomal code. Equality of opportunities could, then, refer to the other two possibilities. Acquired qualities are an intermediary mixture of the other two. Their acquisition depends to a great extent on our mental capacity and innate determination, and on the other hand, on the number and quality of the circumstantial opportunities. Those which are external and which can be socially modified are the acquired possibilities. Hence, the effective content of the equality of opportunities applies only to the third type of possibilities, the external and circumstantial possibilities. It is up to us to find out, now that the field of possibilities has been so drastically reduced, if what is circumstantial is also totally equalizable.

Geographical conditions are changeable for the individual, but not for the human species that is distributed along varied latitudes of the planet. Psychological studies have shown the deep dependency between humans and their *habitat*. Equality of opportunities, even when reduced to the circumstantial only, is unable to level geography. On the other hand, it is possible to level other circumstances with less difficulty, as in the case of diet and health. Nonetheless, the essential constituent of equality of opportunities does not refer as much to mechanical conditions as to moral ones, the most important being the historical and cultural conditions. Historical conditions, due to the irreversibility of time, are not equalizable for successive generations, and are not the same for contemporary people, for some are found in civilizations that are more advanced than others. The radical and operative vindication of equality of opportunities does not embrace all cultural possibilities, but only one that is very concrete, the pedagogical circumstance. This restriction of the area of equality is not the last.

The formation of humans depends on three types of education that become increasingly more concrete: the social, being the most diffuse, is received through collective expressions; the familiar, more personal and better defined, is received through parents and relatives; and the scholarly, more precise and regulated, is received through teachers. Can these three levels of education be equalized for all humans? The social level cannot be so equalized, not even within one country, for it is not the same to live in an out-of-the-way rural area or in a city with universities; it is not possible, either, to provide all citizens with an identical social environment. It is even more difficult to equalize the familiar environment. There is a great difference in living with illiterate and amoral parents or with parents that are exemplary members of the academic community. It is not possible to equalize the home environment. The conclusion is that even if extreme cases may be corrected in the first two cases, the equality of formative opportunities centers mostly on the scholastic environment: equal programs at the same age with equal means and teachers. But this also needs further clarifications.

Material, educational means are equalizable, but not so the professorial or, at least, less so. Good teachers are exceptions, and the importance of this fact is decisive in that there is hardly any great name in science, the arts, the spirit, and even sports that is not the result of an exceptional teacher. The pedagogical relation is also extremely selective, the exceptional teacher and the exceptional disciple are always searching for each other and, tacitly, exclude all others. This mutual tropism functions as an aristocratic source of high energy, and though it might be considered undesirable, it cannot be destroyed. Professorial egalitarianism is impossible in absolute terms, and the only alternative left is a relative homogenization that becomes more pronounced the lower the level of scholarly achievement. The equality of opportunities is thus reduced in education to those levels that are not outstanding. But even this restricted conclusion brings out such serious problems that it cannot be left unexamined.

The relative homogenization of the material and professorial means of education demands such a high degree of coercion that today only the state is able to bring it about. As long as humankind remains divided into a multitude of states with different developments and ideologies, including the most totalitarian use of equality of scholastic opportunities within some frontiers, the inequality of opportunities between one country and another will not diminish. Little can be achieved on a universal scale, and this is a serious objection against egalitarianism that is, by definition, incompatible with ethnic and political discrimination. But even in the case of a universal and unified imposition of a particular education, or even in the resigned acceptance of a partial coercion within one state, would this imposition be compatible with the current program of human rights?

Coactive equality of educational conditions requires compulsory schooling and, here lies the problem, only one official school. If citizens were allowed to establish private teaching centers, even if they must comply with official models, some schools would be better than others, and those attending them would be citizens with more privileges than others. In order to suppress this unequalizing factor people would have to be denied the right to teach and learn freely, and any type of learning different from that of the state's would have to be suppressed. This bureaucratization of teaching carries with it a dictatorial ideology and the loss of an important area of individual self-determination. In this environment, as in all others, we can see that uniformity is despotic, for what is free is varied. We must then distinguish between presuppositions. A totalitarian society may define equality of opportunities by homogenizing learning at levels that are not eminent. A humanistic society may only homogenize scholastic programs, by demanding some minimal means, and by introducing certain corrective factors, like the regulation of procedures for admission and the need to grant scholarships in private schools. This equalization is, therefore, very limited in regard to educational programs.

Scholastic egalitarianism sacrifices freedom; but does it affect the quality of teaching? Even in the extreme case of the totalitarian single state school, it is the case that as soon as a new generation of children starts learning, we find, on a national scale, that a small percentage is gifted and another is underdeveloped, and that among the rest there is a gradation of aptitudes. Will it then be effective to deal with them scholastically in the same manner? If the slow learners and the intelligent students as well as the lazy and the diligent are mingled for a long time, the worst students surrender in their inability to keep up the medium rhythm, and the best, in many cases, join the mediocrity and deteriorate. The yield of pedagogical investments is proportional to the capacity of the recipient, which results in the fact that the best effects of educational expenditure demand the discrimination of students according to merit. The obstinate process of an egalitarianism in education implies a deficient assignation of the national income and, therefore, a non-equitable use of adult work. Educational egalitarianism is reactionary for it sacrifices the improvement of the best, and these are the protagonist of human progress, in order to prevent resentment by the less gifted.

Pedagogical egalitarianism is not guaranteed by this totalitarian hypothesis that brings such high cost of coercion and the promotion of mediocrity. The original equality of educational opportunities, as soon as it is projected in time, becomes more and more discriminatory. Let us suppose that all six-year-olds have been taught in schools homogenized to the maximum by the state. These children will progress from the lowest grades to the highest. Let us suppose that all finish high school, namely that the state has managed to hold them under its totalitarian educational grip up to the age of eighteen, when in most places, they reach legal age. Will all pursue higher studies? Not even the wealthiest countries have such financial surplus that allows them to keep the whole unproductive population idle up to the age of twenty-four or over, nor do they have enough universities to teach them. Only a minority will be able to pursue higher studies. From this moment on the equality of educational opportunities will cease. Some will reach the B.A., a smaller minority will go all the way to the Ph.D., and only very few will continue to study until they retire or die. Though the intellectual vocation is not universal, and even if the candidates are objectively selected, will not many feel deprived of a pedagogical opportunity equal to that of those who continued to the end? Although education continues forever, at least theoretically, this does not mean the same to those that only finish high school and to the scientific researcher. Thus the equality of opportunities is reduced even further: all are assured, independent of their financial position, the possibility of a similar basic education; but beyond this only a few, less at each level, are allowed to climb higher educational levels according to certain *a priori* criteria of admission. The equality of pedagogical educational opportunities cannot be maintained forever equal, not even in the most totalitarian states. After a certain grade, a series of filters are imposed according to innate and acquired capacity and the demand for jobs. This is a selective operation and, therefore, inegalitarian. People have classified themselves as being different by holding a school diploma, a licentiate, a Masters, a Doctorate, and so forth. And within each of these groups people find their place in relation to their quality and efficiency. Equality of opportunities in education is born from a leveling of people that may prolong itself at the price of turning against the people and being despotic, but that under any circumstances breaks down to promote discrimination and hierarchical orderings. In conclusion, educational equality of opportunities, today, is only possible at the level of basic education.

How can a society be organized so that equality of opportunities is realized? A hierarchy needs to be established within each activity, which reflects the efficacy of individuals, and which is defined by intelligence, education, and dedication. The reason for this is obvious. A basic principle of practical economy is the optimal assignment of material and human resources: "The right man in the right place." The person most endowed by nature and upon whom society has invested the most must be offered responsibility that will optimize results. The greater the responsibility, the higher the position. This criterion may be used throughout the lives of all individuals, and this excludes seniority as an automatic criterion for promotion. Instead, a criterion of effectiveness as accumulated through experience is applied in each case. This model of society is in the hands of a meritocracy.

The opposite of a meritocratic society is the familiar society in which parents try to transmit their position, customs, and patrimony to their children, regardless of their aptitudes; and, though this is more difficult, some parents expect their children to thus climb the social ladder. Nepotism is the dominant stratifying factor within such coordinates. Thus it may be understood why the adoption of a pauper by a powerful person entails a form of Copernican revolution: the possibilities multiply arbitrarily and suddenly. The equality of educational opportunities and the progressive abolition of patrimonial inheritance are the two main instruments for transforming a familiar into a meritocratic society. Thus it is possible to achieve a certain egalitarian approximation to the egalitarianism of the start. But how does one develop one's chosen career?

Within a meritocracy individuals are classified according to two main values, their intellectual quotient and their work. Within this ordering, intelligence comes first, for it usually unchains one's own effort. Under such conditions and presupposing complete mobility, a society will have the form of a rhomboid: the most gifted will occupy the superior triangle, the less gifted the interior one, and the intermediary majority will sit on the central hexagon. A further gradation will be enclosed within each group in descending order from the genius to the subnormal. There will be more responsibility, refinement, and tension at the top. The closer we come to the base, the more we will find depersonalization, leisure, and vulgarity. The less gifted are not the victims of exploitation in a meritocracy; they behave more like parasites. In any case, egalitarianism is nowhere to be found. While in a familiar society the differences are the result of the status of the parents, in a meritocracy these same differences are the result of capacity.

How does the rhomboid model of the meritocratic society develop? Each adult will occupy the place that fits his efficacy, regardless of the level of his birth. The selection of parents will not be haphazard. For reasons of affinities of work, intellect, economy, and eugenic compatibilities, couples will tend to join in families within the same social level. The main consideration will be intelligence, for this is the social value acknowledged as supreme, due to the fact that responsible parenting will also select the best genetic possibilities, and because what the superior woman admires most in males is intelligence. This endogamy will keep producing a progressive selectivity within the social groups, due to genetic laws and the inherited character of the intelligence quotient. The result would appear to be that the less intelligent children will descend in the social ladder from the rank of their parents and will join those they consider more their equals; but the descending quota will become progressively less numerous due to the progressive purification of the elitist, genetic patrimony. Conversely, the children with more intelligence than their parents will climb, though this promotion will successively affect fewer people for there will be a negative selection among the less gifted. After a certain time the number of genes responsible for merit will stabilize and be concentrated, thus controlling the variability of the intelligence quotient and effort within each social group. Education will increase and solidify the differences if pedagogical rationalization is reflected in the creation of special centers for the education of the gifted. Meritocracy creates definite social classes according to the capacity of individuals, and those classes are at least as hereditary as the classes formed around patrimonial inheritances.

Is this inequality, more rational than the previous one, less rigid and distant? Familiar classes are less crystallized than meritocratic societies for three main reasons. The first one is that inequalities based on nepotism have always been regarded as unjust, and for this reason the beneficiaries usually suffer from a bad conscience that manifests itself as philanthropy, or some other pragmatic acts. Some attain self-forgiveness and others buy it. Both impulses unchain social mobility. In the second place, the growing demand for efficacy is an experience that is becoming more and more communicated, technical, and complex; it also eliminates the inept, even if they are the children of privileged people, and promotes the most capable, even if they come from poor families. It is difficult to transmit privileged positions beyond the second generation if the heirs are not themselves individually gifted. This mechanism also increases the permeability between classes. In the third place, the main forces that structure a familiar society are, next to talent, physical power, the institutions, favoritism, and chance. Thus, intelligence remains widely shared among those that govern and the governed, the rich, and the poor. On a parallel line, the criterion for marriage in a familiar society is not talent, but position or beauty. Physical attraction does not necessarily imply intellectual parity among those so attracted, and the socioeconomic position does not exclude from the male, and particularly from the nonliberated female, the absence of mental qualities. All this contributes to the haphazard distribution of intelligence that is relatively homogeneous within a familiar society. Within this society the stupid aristocrat is proportionally no less common than the intelligent proletarian. These factors are sources of energy for understanding the social exchanges and the flexibility of social classes.

In a meritocratic society, on the other hand, rank is linked to a personal value that is objective, productive, and publicly recognized. For this reason the leading minority, far from suffering from a guilty conscience, does not stop verifying its own eminence, which is a factor of social fixity. In the second place, the social demand that leaders produce results, consolidates the superior positions of those who are efficient, and the inferior position of those who are less so. This is another sign of the impermeability of the different levels. And finally, the ascending concentration of talent and its stabilization at the different levels produces the expectation that intelligence depends entirely on birth. This stratifies the different classes in their Archemedean base. In sum, inequality based on the inheritance of intelligence is much more rigid than that based on name and patrimony. Is it also more distant?

We do not know the omega point of human evolution, and for this reason, the term *ad quem* of intelligence is uncertain. On the other hand, the starting points of subnormality and irrationality may be determined. If, as is probable, natural selection and spontaneous, genetic mutations will raise the present level of the intellectual quotient, it is obvious that the distances between clever and stupid within a meritocratic society will increase, unless those less smart are not allowed to reproduce. In a familiar society, on the other hand, the presence of the extremely gifted is an isolated and casual phenomenon that is hardly genetically selective and that to a great degree is compensated by the homogenizing forces previously described.

Given the supposition of advanced genetical engineering, human nature could be manipulated and the quality and stratification of people would depend on a scientific, political decision. But such a hypothesis, that would exclude a hierarchical social configuration, is today sheer speculation and carries no practical implications.

In sum: a meritocratic society tends to stratify the population in a more rigid and unequal way than a familiar society, but it allows for an optimal utilization of intellectual resources and a progress in communication that is more intense and faster. It produces greater inequality and is more creative.

4. Economic Equality

Economic equality consists in providing each person with an equal amount of goods and services. This objective is not achieved with the simple equalization of individual incomes; rather it requires a prior redistribution of the total amount of fixed, existing capital through expropriations, nationalizations, and a proportional distribution of goods among the population. The first difficulty appears in isolating whatever amount makes up public property and its administration, so that the original owners do not come out ahead of the ordinary citizens. This difficulty has no practical solution, for in an industrialized society the goods of production are the larger part of the national capital, while the administrating bureaucracy is only a minority. There will be, necessarily then, a few that control the collective goods who will enjoy more power and more benefits than the rest of the population. Patrimonial equality may be so declared by law, but it is impossible in practice. It is more viable to control income.

Individual income may be measured in money or in other quantities: it is possible to assign a fixed amount of money to each citizen to rent a place to live, and an equal amount of square meters per room. An analogous alternative—money or goods—could be established in the different areas of consumption. Which one of these techniques is the more egalitarian?

Economic equality translated into equality of salaries does not produce an equality of goods and services, since some will be able to save and become richer and some super-consumers will eat their capitals. There will also be those who, with the same amount of money, will acquire more than others. And there will be, finally, the givers and the takers. All these inevitable suppositions will create inequality.

Economic equality, if understood as equality in the exchange of goods, is practicable only with those goods and services that are of primary necessity or universally used, and that are also homogeneous. Optional or superfluous goods, like the products of art, are scarce, and this does not allow for their distribution to all, and since they only interest some people, they do not form part of a distributive pool. This formula, even when restricted to areas of possible use, does not translate into equality of goods and services, for it is not the same to be given twenty meters of choice real estate, as it is to receive the same amount in the outskirts; nor is bread of good quality equal to the same amount of a mediocre quality. All production would be in need of standardization so that uniformity would follow; but even then it would be impossible to cancel out the cottage industry, and this is inegalitarian. A qualitative equivalence is even more difficult than the quantitative. But the free exchange of goods would not mean that some would not benefit more than others, and this would bring about inequality.

Are both methods complementary? The adoption of monetary exchange requires a fluid supply, and the appearance of competing markets would adversely affect the egalitarian operation. On the other hand, the equivalence in goods would mean a rationing of goods and services under such a regime. Rationing usually brings out black markets, and this would make it impossible to apply both exchanges of goods and of money.

The experience of communist economies shows that it is easier to arrive at monetary equality than at equality of goods, though the last, in principle, is more egalitarian. Monetary equality is then limited to salaries: though this in no way affects the subsequent development of private economies where inevitable disparities soon appear. For this and other reasons, maintaining a certain equality in the enjoyment of goods and services requires something more than identical salaries and the prorated distribution of uniform goods; it requires periodic expropriation of what has been saved by legal or fiscal means, the abolition of inheritance, and a continuous policing or social pressure to discourage trading for profit and the desire for personal distinction.

The equalization of salaries is technically possible, but is it desirable? There are people who are more capable, better prepared, and who produce more. Is it just to reward them to the same degree as those less gifted, less prepared, less dedicated? It would be necessary to socialize the individual so that such leveling would be possible, which would mean that we would have to presuppose and make everyone believe that his intelligence, his preparation, and diligence do not belong to him but to the community. It is more difficult to prove that a person's talents belong to the species than the opposite thesis, that the inferior individuals are socially subordinate to the superior ones, as verified by animal sociology. But to claim that acquired knowledge and one's own tenacious diligence belong to the whole is evidently false. It is impossible to accept that work and study are not individual merits; and if they are they should be rewarded. If we deny the rewards we would also have to suppress any form of punishment, and this is even more absurd, for it is not possible to organize the living together of many without sanctions. If goodness and evil were innate and invincible conditions then morals would disappear. Classical justice rested on giving to each one according to his or her merits; distributive egalitarianism would remove the problem of equity, for it would reduce it to a simple divisory mechanism, like the calculation of the income consumed per inhabitant. The removal of merit and demerit is the ethical alienation of humans. Such is the situation of those animal populations that are not free, like termites and corals. It would require a high degree of coercion of humans to carry out egalitarianism, like imposing a fixed, individual income. The equality of the distribution of goods and services is viable only if we start from total despotism.

But supposing that such egalitarianism of goods and services could be carried out, what effects would it have on the evolution of the species? It would mean the disappearance of a large number of external stimuli that are needed for self-improvement and productivity. Laziness and mediocrity would surface. How many would devote dozens of years to be better prepared if in the end their economic situation would be similar to those who are lazy and not prepared? To reduce the stimuli of progress to intellectual self-satisfaction would mean to renounce other decisive factors and, therefore, to delay the process of rationalization and the slowing of history. Economic egalitarianism also eliminates those aspects of interpersonal emulation that are based on productivity and that are, from the social viewpoint, the most productive. The emptiness this would bring about would have to be filled, at least partially, with coercion over the whole population; but especially over those that carry progress forward, the gifted. May we dare ask for conditioned creations from inventors and artists? We can hardly imagine such a thing.

Economic equality is essential to a Marxist conception of social life. For this reason it has become a primary goal of socialism, though not the only or last one. Economic equality would be more logical and less a result of force if it were the result of leveling certain individual capacities, for, in such a case, equality of salaries would go hand in hand with a certain equality of production. Since Marxist biology is environmentalist and focuses on the dominance of inherited traits, it preaches an equalization of individual capabilities through education. It is thus assumed that by paying more attention and making means of education available to the less gifted, these would be brought closer to the level of productivity of the more intelligent.

The prolonged and systematic application of equality of opportunities brings societies to the acceptance of hierarchies and meritocracy, but this is not compatible with the equalization of individual income. Hence, Marxists and others conclude that an equality of educational opportunities needs to be instituted, namely, those that stay behind should be given more and those ahead, less. This is equivalent to favoring the worst and penalizing the best. Innatists perceive that the best are those with a higher intelligence quotient inherited through the chromosomes; environmentalists believe that those with inferior families and an adverse social environment are inferior. Although both consider education very important, for the environmentalist it is a decisive factor.

The inequality of educational opportunities may be applied in general or by sectors. An example of the first would be to supply, at a national scale, an education of higher quality to those students with the lowest grades, and vice versa. This may also be applied by sectors, choosing only particular groups rather than the population at large. This is usually the case when under pressures from classes or minority groups, the adult population comes under the pretense of egalitarianism. Sectorial egalitarianism functions with reasoning such as the following: the proportion of female Ph.D.'s is less than that of males, therefore they must be favored through scholarships, grants, special rewards, and even by demands that universities guarantee a certain amount of doctorates for females. Such arguments extend to other levels and interests, as for example, professors, executives, or generals in the military services. The same arguments may be used when dealing with blacks, gypsies, and the poor.

A generalized inequality of educational opportunities contradicts the economic principle of maximizing resources, for it would demand greater investments on the subjects that are less productive, and vice versa. It would also go against the imperatives of progress and the acceleration of history, that demands the greater concentration of educative effort on the most gifted individuals, for they increase the rhythm of human progress. The generalized inequality of educational opportunities is a reactionary and destructive practice.

The sectorial inequality of educational opportunities brings out important problems. If we accept that there must be a direct arithmetical proportion between the group of origin and the activity of the goal, we would end up in the realm of the absurd. Let us take natural groups like those of the albinos, the mestizo, or the color blind: should places be reserved for them in the same proportion as the others? Let us suppose that this is the case and that the same has been decided in relation to the female sex. Would an albino woman then become a privileged member of society by law? This example shows that, in this context, the selection of one human group is arbitrary and that duplications occur. This last possibility could be avoided in limited groups that are mutually exclusive, like men and women, black and white; but if we take at the same time two couples from two mutually exclusive groups there a duplication would also appear: a black woman in Spain would find herself to be extremely privileged, even though she might be less gifted than many white males.

Sectorial inequality of opportunities brings out other theoretical problems that are repugnant to the principle of equality before the law and to a radical interpretation of political equality. The legal protection of certain groups, like women, blacks, Muslims, and illegitimate children, would in fact be equivalent to a legal discrimination on account of sex, race, birth, beliefs, and so forth. In such a case the principle and the letter of the principle of equality before the law would be violated. This formal qualification is not modified on account of the fact, more or less philanthropic, of trying to protect the needy. Norms that favor one group turn out to be comparatively disadvantageous to the others, and establish collective privileges. Economic equality, insofar as it appeals to a discrimination in opportunities, is incompatible with equality before the law.

There are also contradictions with political equality, understood as an equal vote, and only one, for each of the citizens. This formula is that of the universal inorganic suffrage where all vote and each vote has the same electoral value; their subjective, political right is given to them by their condition of being human. On the other hand, organic suffrage presupposes that the individual votes not on account of his condition as a human being but as a member of a social group or corporation. Hence, the same citizen could vote several times in order to elect successive candidates if he belonged to a plurality of social groups with rights of representation. Organic representation is usually turned down by certain radical democrats for they believe it primes certain groups that divide and duplicate the electoral body, and above all, it breaks down the homogeneity of the Chamber of Representatives, where the members do not represent the nation, but the groups, the corporations, or the interests that elected them. The application of the principle of sectorial inequality of opportunities in order to stimulate the monopoly of certain responsibilities under certain groups means that the end is not a social function one must fulfill because we are citizens, but because of our sex, race, beliefs, origin, or profession. This is the best description of organic representation. The generalization of this procedure to all the branches of power would lead to a corporate state. This is, therefore, a hypothesis irreconcilable with the strict demo-liberal interpretation of political equality.

Economic equality is, at any time, surgical: it confiscates, standardizes, rations, levels salaries, forces production, establishes human uniformity and inequality of opportunities. It discourages self-improvement and productivity, destroys personality, substitutes arithmetic for justice, mutilates liberty, reduces creativity, alienates morality, decapitates the formation of the best, contradicts equality before the law, and to a certain degree, political equality. In spite of all this, economic equality is only possible to a relative degree, and thus the motives for envy and resentment are not sufficiently removed. This is a very high social price to pay for such a mediocre outcome.

V. Conclusions

1. The Reverse Side of Ideology

In the first paragraph of his *Discourse on the Origin and Foundation of Inequality* (1734) Rousseau enunciated the following thesis: "Nature has established equality among men, and they have established inequality." This revolutionary message first became a myth, then a dogma. Rousseau, one of the most genuine expressers of universal cynicism, writes mostly fiction; but the most fictive, perhaps, of all his preachings is egalitarianism. The truth is exactly the opposite: Nature, which is hierarchical, creates all men unequal, and society, which homogenizes, tries to make all men similar and strives to eradicate their individual peculiarities.

We find newborn babies that arrive prematurely or late, healthy or sick, with great appetite, quiet or noisy. Each human being is a microcosm with different capacities, each carries an irreplaceable genetic code that reveals, when it develops, extremely varied aptitudes and vocations. All of us are born different and as soon as the first evaluations are taken in kindergarten we find that some of us are strong and others weak, some determined and others abulic, some show signs of genius and others are underdeveloped. Almost all the superior qualities of humans are distributed along a Gaussian curve where no two share the same point. Human inequality is absolute among humans and is graded between extremes of tragic contradiction, as the distance between the mongoloid and the genius and the physically handicapped and the athlete. Two children by the same parents, raised in the same environment, show different personalities, at times antipodal, as soon as their behavior becomes public. These differences become even more complex when they share the same books and teachers. It is absolutely false that Nature creates all men equal; the truth of the matter is that Nature brings humans into the world with dissimilar capacities that are obviously capable of hierarchical evaluation. The hypothetical homogeneity proclaimed by Rousseau is contradicted by the facts uncovered by genetics, psychology, and physiology. It is a fiction of demagogues and frustrated people.

It is also untrue that society institutionalizes inequalities. On the contrary, each society makes a determined effort to equalize every one. It starts by establishing a language with very strict morphological, phonetic, syntactic rules. Being corrected implies the acceptance of common linguistic norms and if anyone insists on misspelling a word or using an accusative instead of a dative case, society reacts by punishing the deviant. This linguistic uniformity also demands a similar set of rules for thinking: that certain particular criteria be followed, among which the most questionable principle of causality occupies a prominent place. In fact, behind every language there is a tacit conception of the universe. At the same time rules of behavior are established: on diet, health, dress, prayer, etc. As the adolescent citizen grows up society provides him with an idea of history and a definition of what is beautiful, good, and true. Whoever deviates from these social criteria becomes an eccentric, a rebel, and in its extreme case, a delinquent. Society keeps a revealing epithet for whomever resists this leveling coercion of the environment: the misfit.

Contrary to the preaching of Rousseau which his disciples, in particular the socialists, have followed, I believe that the present social task is not so much to increase the egalitarian capacities of society and of the state, but to further develop the individual.

In the measure that the human race has been interrelating due to the improvement in our communication system, and in the measure that the state has increased the sphere of its coactive action, the uniforming power of society has extended to its present wide limits. Autocracy is progressively more difficult and, therefore, personal individuality feels more and more threatened. The uniformity displayed by socialist countries has already massively destroyed some of the most noble creative virtues of the species: in the areas of the humanities and art, the Eastern bloc is a show in mediocrity, repetition, and monotony. The state school, censorship, and massive propaganda have standardized ideas and destroyed the freedom of individual thought. This is also true of Western countries where the most powerful try to impose their fashions and political systems on others. The "hippie" movement was an irrational reaction against this leveling tendency. Long hair and open shirts are, at a very rudimentary level, liberating means that the less imaginative use against a society that is becoming more and more oppressive.

The riches of the human race rest on the variety of its individuals. Philogenetic possibilities multiply through individual inequality. Any discovery is always a new invention and, therefore, something different from our habits. The protagonists of the progress of humanity are not the uniform masses, but rather the superior spirit, the most different.

The corruptors of reality try to exploit envy and resentment in order to ground an egalitarian dictatorship on such negative bases. Juan Ramón Jiménez denounced this attitude in a famous verse: "They wanted to kill him for he was different." And Saint-Exupéry answered: "If I am different from you, instead of diminishing, I increase you." And the Romantic poet Young was accurate in saying: "We are all born originals, and most die copies." Contrary to the preachings of Rousseau and Marx, the great task for contemporary humanism is to make sure that we are all free to be ourselves, and that the state does not force us to be a copy of something else.

We cannot cultivate hate, but love for the best; nor bring down the superior, but aim for self-realization. Equality always denotes despotism and inequality is the fruit of freedom. Instead of allowing ourselves to be forced into a mold, we must struggle for more individualism; instead of becoming lost in the crowd we should strive for a hierarchical gradation. Society should promote personal changes and not become a cloning womb or a gigantic roller. Creative, hierarchical emulation is more socially healthy than the toxic fumes of egalitarian envy.

2. The Impossible Biological Equality

Egalitarian ideologies are ambiguous; they are never precise as to which equalities they desire and which they do not. They function, like all other ideologies, by awakening obscure feelings and desires and promising utopia to the followers in their subjection and to the leaders in their demagoguery. A systematic and reasoned analysis of what is possible and of what is desirable in terms of equality remains to be done. Facts are always the outer empirical limits of all dreams.

The equality of all humans, in the sense of identity, is impossible for the philosophical reason that every concrete being is individual and irreproducible. A certain resemblance among all humans could be factually accomplished through successive fecundations of increasing consanguinity, but this would demand that the rest of humanity be sterilized, an operation that, even if it were reduced to creating a particular almost monozygotic population, would take centuries and would run the risk of producing undesirable genes, a difficult fact to avoid due to the scarce amount of information available on the biological history of individuals. In any case, such a selection would be reduced to a small, relatively egalitarian group within a population that would remain immensely unequal. It would be equivalent to the appearance of a pair of identical twins in a large nation.

Another formula would be to control the genetic process. This would require the complete uncovering of the structure of human chromosomes and the function of their many elements. But today we do not even know the number of genes: science is taking the first steps with experiments on some gigantic chromosomes in certain insects. Once we discover the anatomical and physiological data of the cellular nucleus, we would then have to discover the technique to eliminate, substitute, or prime certain genes, and this is far from the present reach of pharmacology and surgery. The problem would then arise of whether the results of these genetic manipulations should be considered the true children of their progenitors, or of biochemistry. The laboratory, the great collective womb of the "happy world" of Huxley, is waiting at the outskirts of this reproductive technique. We may add, however, that it would be anti-egalitarian to practice this kind of selectivity on some and not on others, and that it would be even more so if we were to grant to some the privilege of imposing their decisions on the rest. There is, then, an ethical contradiction in such an operation that, besides, is today a practical impossibility on a perceptible scale.

But, would any other egalitarianisms besides the biological one be viable? We may distinguish between the equalities of political power, of authority, of actions, of rewards, of opportunity, of the law, and of economics.

3. The Impossible Social Equality

a) There are no societies without hierarchies, and where there is a hierarchy, its members share, in different measure, political power. This situation is unchangeable. The scheme of a pure democracy does not create the *equality of political power*, but rather, the *equality of political rights*. Even when all power is exercised by elected officals, and when all those participating are the electors and elected, there will always be some who are governed and some who govern; that is, a minority who has the power to make itself obeyed by the larger majority. Those who are governed are not equal to those who govern, for the governed are not able to revoke their votes at a moment's notice; on the contrary, they will have to put up with them for a period of time. Besides, these elected representatives are not the product of the will of all of the people, but of only one part, and against those who have voted for other candidates. There is no such thing as equality in political power, not even in an imaginary republic where all the hierarchies of the state would be elected daily.

b) Besides the hierarchy of political and administrative power a society has other hierarchies of authority in other dimensions of social life. In the sciences, the arts, and the different technologies, some are granted more authority than others. In groups engaged in the same profession there are some who are better than others, and therefore, we find graded positions. Vocational and circumstantial specializations create hierarchies in each activity. Would it be possible to level the authority of all the members of one single profession, for example, painters or surgeons? Such an *egalitarian authority* is even less workable than political power. Not even the most despotic coercion could avoid some performing better than others.

c) Inequality in productivity also creates an inequality in social compensation: glory to some, punishment to others. It is impossible to equalize salaries, either negatively or positively. Could we suppress punishment so that some would not be punished more than others? There are no rights without coercion, and punishment is the judicial expression of coercion. A norm or law deprived of external coercive means is reduced to an imperative of conscience. If laws could not be imposed there would be no society. Penal egalitarianism is impossible. Experience shows that in societies that are presumably egalitarian penal norms are more implacable and their application more determined than in the rest.

Would it be possible to suppress any form of distinction? It is difficult to imagine an army where all would be generals, or a university where everyone would be president; and even in the supposition that all honors would be removed as would be the case with rewards by the state, could we avoid the propensity of certain persons to bestow more admiration and respect on some citizens than on others? Could we stop the fact that people would be able privately to reward the efficient more than the stupid? Egalitarianism of rewards is quite difficult to carry out by the state and much more so by the private individual.

d) Is equality of opportunity possible? Only in some cases. Temporal, geographical, and family circumstances place individuals in more or less favorable conditions. This initial disparity already determines deep and prolonged differences. The archetypal example is the contrast between the possibilities for self-realization of the child of a beggar and that of a rich man. This chance inequity may mark a life forever. It is possible to remove all privileges at the start of a person's life? The majority are unavoidable. No one has the same mental opportunity, for we are all born more or less intelligent, more or less neurotic. No one will share the same historical opportunities unless we are able to cancel progress that allows some to come into a world that has a more or less advanced civilization and with a patrimony that is richer or poorer. No one will share the same national opportunities unless the economic and cultural level of all countries is equalized. The possibility for equal opportunities demands that, within a society and at a certain determined time, no one is diminished due to his family background or denied access to any social position. But when this restricted equal opportunity is achieved we still have to contend with the insuperable inequalities we carry with us, like intellectual and moral capacity and situation and opportunity. It is not the same to be born in Switzerland or in the Congo, or to be born earlier or later than a given historical event. Opportunities in the Persian Gulf are not the same before or after the appearance and exploitation of gasoline, just as opportunities for good health were very different before and after the discovery of antibiotics.

Is it possible to reach equality before the law, since the decisions of judges are based on free behavior and not on involuntary characteristics, like race, sex, or the social position of people's parents? This equality before the law, however, does not equate the hero with the criminal; on the contrary, it creates unequals before the law, and sends some to the throne and condemns others to the death penalty. We cannot confuse the arbitrary application of the norms with the effective egalitarianism of individuals.

Equal opportunity does not make humans equal. It is one thing for all the runners in a race to start at the same time and from the same starting line, and another for inequalities to appear in the course of the race separating the champion from those who abandon the race. Equal opportunity is a leveling at the start but not at the arrival. With this in mind, is not equal opportunity less discriminatory than privileges? This is extremely doubtful. The establishment of a society based exclusively on a meritocracy where all the hierarchical levels would be gained thanks to self-capacity and efficacy would create a social stratification in proportion to the intellectual coefficient of the society. And since the tendency among humans is to live among their equals and consequently to create a family with them, the gifted would intermarry and a process of strict genetic selection would be established whose consequence would be a social stratification with the best at the top, inaccessible to the mediocre and the worst. Equal opportunity promotes the hard dialectics of biological selectivity. But, on the other hand, social projects not based on exclusive meritocratic rules that carry different forms of privileges are a relatively egalitarian factor, for if the privileged is someone born at a certain level of wealth, intelligence, etc., it so happens that within that same group there will be members that are not as intelligent, with a tendency, that may be more or less delayed, to descend. And conversely, in the lower ranks there will be members who are gifted and with the more or less difficult tendency to climb. This system of unequal opportunities, which has been predominant for thousands of years, has been the cause of social mobility and has also been a factor in the leveling of the intellectual capacity of the whole of all the different social classes, since the respective genetic patrimony has not been selected with regard only to intelligence. Though it may seem paradoxical, it is evident that equal opportunities and the meritocracy that follows will create, in the years to come, a social inequality with a tendency to become more and more rigid. Equality of opportunity, up to now made difficult due to familiar paternalism and the spirit of the clan, is biologically essential, for it promotes the best and cleanses them genetically, increasing their perfective evolution and their distance from the inferior. It is, therefore, the social technique that is the most progressive and anti-egalitarian.

e) Is *economic egalitarianism* possible? Its most factual possibility is monetary equality, which may be produced through the nationalization of the means of production, the abolition of inheritance, the removal of interest on capital, and the leveling of all salaries. More than a half century of communist experience has shown that not even such economic egalitarianism of monetary equality may be reached, since a certain amount of private property in production, inheritance, interest in savings, and scales in salaries and incentives had to be maintained. But supposing that such monetary equality could be imposed politically, would this bring economic equality? No, for economics is an area that is larger than money: with the same amount of income in cash one can enjoy different types of well-being that are provided in kind. Money, in fact, amounts to very little, for it is only a potentiality, it is the possibility of using things and services. Such a possibility is more effective at the hands of the state than at the hands of paper money. The one in authority receives, in addition to his salary which may be equal to that of a peon, the right to use a plurality of expensive goods and to receive multiple special services. Where we may find a certain monetary equality, the inequalities of power have been radicalized, brought about by economic inequalities not necessarily monetary, but spectacular none the less. Though Stalin's checking account might not have been larger than that of the poorest peasant, no one could claim economic equality between them. To impose such an equality would require the suppression of political power.

4. The Individual Instinct

The primary instinct of man is not conservation, but self-realization. Man has nothing that remains fixed, though some of his structures, like his bones, are less modifiable than others. For this reason, to live does not mean to preserve, but rather to renew everything. Man is not stimulated by the desire to remain static, but rather by the unfolding of his capacities and the realization of his projects. Man is not a monolith nailed down in nature; he is a torrent. To stop the flow would end his life. Whatever is real becomes; and human existence is the sharpest manifestation of such becoming, for man is not already made but makes himself and cannot stop his self-creation for one single minute.

What does man do while making his life? He tries to become himself; fighting the efforts of others to turn him into someone else, a sample out of a series. The instinct of self-realization is an instinct of identity and, therefore, of distinction from others; we are radically anti-egalitarian. On the other hand, any external pressure towards egalitarianism, either through ideology, fashion, or position, alienates us from ourselves, for it is an attempt at altering that which is most intimate in us, our authentic self-realization and not the mechanical shaping of us by the environment.

No one is happy becoming a mass-produced man deprived of identity. This is even more true of the gifted. The species progresses thanks to the efforts of the members with the sharpest personalities, those who refuse to repeat—namely, the inventors. The forefront of humanity is formed by those who are most keen to carry out their most individualized and diverse projects. Hence, egalitarianism is more alienating for the best and less so for the inferior, as it amputates more of the leading sprouts of the species. For this reason, egalitarianism is an intellectual, biological, and historical regressive factor.

It is also obvious that there are more risks involved in being authentic than in being a follower. To be oneself is a constant creative adventure, while allowing others to make us is a repetitious abandonment. Egalitarian isolation offers certain securities. If the supreme bourgeois ambition is the Marxists' claim of comfort, the most genuine form of bourgeoisie would be social egalitarianism, for it reduces all the vital avatars to the same level; it is a surrender to social pressure and to collective responsibility; it is the renunciation of the fight to become oneself; it allows one to be led by the hand of the group. The selective minorities demand much of themselves, and for this reason they suffer deep and strong internal tensions. To be oneself is one of the most uncomfortable tasks in a society that becomes more and more alienating.

Inequality is the product of the most radical and the most noble instincts in man: to be able to realize one's own identity in the best possible way.

5. Metaphysical Equality

The entitative equality of humans is a metaphysical impossibility: each one is a different individual. Genetic equality is not possible, with the relative exception of monozygotic twins, and they are not equal. All the members of the human species are, therefore, morally, physically, and intellectually unequal.

The only possible equality that is absolutely realizable is equality before the law. The equality of opportunities that is possible is to make all the members of society able to have access to any position in the society at a given moment. But once equality of opportunities is established at the start, we immediately discover the inequality of placement and of arrival. Equality in political power, authority, and rewards is not practicable in a society that is minimally structured. As a consequence of such social inequities, an exact economic equality becomes enviable.

The moral question of the desirability of certain equalities suggests that political change is the way to bring about such an ideal. Genetic equality stabilizes the species through biological monotony and the end of a dialectical evolution; the method used to achieve such an egalitarianism would have to be despotic, depriving all of the right to father and mother their own children. The equality of power would lead to an extinction of hierarchies and to anarchy. Both forms of equality are not, therefore, reasonable goals.

The equality of authority, rewards, and economic levels would entail a new idea of justice. This virtue would have to stop being "to give to each its own" and become "to give to each a proportionate part of the collective income, independently of individual behavior." Such an interpretation of equity would unhinge the social structure; besides, it would raise the problem of what constitutes the social limits, for these could not be the discrimination but the homogeneity of the entire race. The determination and allocation of a proportional share to individuals of the universal income of all the nations is, today, a total chimera.

The practical moral question is one of degree. Given the impossibility and undesirability of moral, political, and economic powers, which are the just margins of inequality? It is not difficult to establish a minimum of moral power for all men, this being the moral dignity of the person; of political power—fundamental rights; and of economic powers—a family's salary at the level of social development. But it is very difficult, if not impossible, to fix a legal maximum. Will it be a crime to own an expensive painting and will there be a law that requires all paintings to be gathered in museums? We are here in an area of prudence and relativity. Absolute egalitarianism is not a science, it is a spell.

Equality does not exist and the political problem that this creates is solved by regulating inequalities without stopping the impulse to self-realization; that is the most noble in man and the most powerful incentive of history.

6. Egalitarian Envy

Man is, as much as the primates, an imitative animal. Childhood is a continuous copying of language, accent, gestures, and of other social usages. Thanks to this strong plagiaristic mechanism, the infant assimilates tradition and stands with little effort at the height of the times in order to continue the ascending march of the species. The discovery of purely imitative intentions in the adult is a sign of infantilism. To try and get the same artifact the neighbor just bought is always a sign of immaturity. The consuming society, due to saturation through advertisement, tries the usage of those imitative tendencies of childhood through slogans: "You do the same."

If the adult were to remain strictly imitative, the human species would establish itself like that of other superior animals, without progress. Each generation would repeat the previous one. But is it proper for the adult to go beyond what is seen and heard? One needs to create one's self, to carry on, and innovate. This is the reason for the movement in history.

At the root of all egalitarian desire there is a mimetic moment that links with our infantile tendencies: to have, do, and be the same as the other. This phenomenon finds perfect articulation through natural evolution. The pathology of this feeling is the discovery that the instinct of imitation degenerates into the will to expropriate, or rob, or the desire to destroy so that the other does not become more, does not accomplish more and does not have more. In this last case, the goal is not to become equal through imitation, but to lower the other. Such egalitarianism, the typical product of envy, has produced a social current that has continued to grow since the apparition of Marxism and whose true features cannot be seen unless unmasked, for envy is surreptitious, hypocritical, and simulating.

Experience has proven, in an incontestable way, that state activity is less efficacious than private. Why, then, all the rush to nationalize, especially the desire to deprive others of what is theirs? Because of the need to satisfy egalitarian envy? It is also a fact that private investments are more profitable, more innovative, and create more jobs than public investments. Why, then, the insistence to raise the intervention of the state in the economy? To a great measure this is done to depersonalize property, that is, to satisfy egalitarian envy. It is evident that the largest part of the public expenditure does not create social capital, but is destined for consumption. Then why steal from private investment portions of its savings through increased taxation? For the simple reason that in this manner the rich are eliminated to satisfy egalitarian envy. The just thing to do would be for each citizen to pay taxes in proportion to his income. Why, then, are some made to pay, through progressive taxation, percentages as much as ten times larger than that of others for the same amount of income? To punish the greater capacity satisfies egalitarian envy. The just thing to do is to see to it that rewards are proportionate to the results. Why, then, insist on bringing the salaries closer? So that some do not earn more than others and thus to satisfy egalitarian envy. The supreme incentive to stimulate production is production subsidies. Why, then, demand that the increase in salaries be collective and linear? To punish those who are more laborious and better prepared and thus satisfy egalitarian envy. And so on.

Egalitarianism is not even a dreamed utopia, it is an impossible nightmare. But it is possible to satisfy transient and local egalitarian envy at the price of cultural and economic involution. The more a society is the victim of this incitement to envy, the more its progress will be delayed. Egalitarian envy is the reactionary social feeling par excellence. It is an ironical semantic falsification to all "progressivists" of the political currents that promote such weaknesses in the human species. Destructive egalitarian envy dictates the darkest pages of history; hierarchical and creative emulation narrates its splendor.

Notes

1. Periander, *Fr.* 18 ed. Diels, I, 6, 3.

2. Thales, *Af.*, 17 Diels, I, 64, 9.

3. Pindar, *Isthmian*, II.

4. *Idem. Pythian*, XI.

5. *Idem. Nemean*, VIII.

6. *Idem. Pythian*, IX.

7. *Idem.* op.cit., XI.

8. Gorgias, *Fr.* 6 ed. Diels, II, 285.

9. Hippias, *Fr.* 13, Diels, II, 332.

10. *Idem.* op.cit., loc.cit.

11. Hippasus, *Fr.* 6 ed. Diels, I, 109.

12. Herodotus, *History*, III, 80.

13. Aesop, *Fables*, CCXXXIV.

14. *Idem.* op.cit. CCLXVIII.

15. *Idem.* op.cit. CCCVI.

16. Callimachus, *Epigrams*, 21,4.

17. Democritus, Fr. 191 ed. Diels, III, 185.

18. Diogenes Laertius, *Lives and Opinions of Eminent Philosophers*, II,91. Attributes this opinion to the school of Aristippus, founder of the Cyrenaic School, but Bollack thinks this is an Epicurean statement. (*La pense du plaisir*, Paris, 1975, pp. 172 and 204.)

19. Philolaus, *Fr.* 11, ed. Diels, I,412.

20. Gorgias, *Fr.* 11, a, 3 ed. Diels, II, 295.

21. Democritus, *Fr.* 18 ed. Diels II, 161.

22. Isocrates, *Evagoras*, 1.

23. Euripides, *Suppliants*, 241.

24. Herodotus, *History*, VIII, 124.

25. Democritus, *Fr.* 295 ed. Diels, II, 194.

26. *Idem.* Fr. 294 ed. Diels, II, 195.

27. Antisthenes, *Fr.*, 82 ed. Dacleva, p. 49.

28. Homer, *Odyssey*, IV, 118, and V, 120.

29. *Idem. Iliad*, XI, 543.

30. Pindar, *Pythian*, X, 20.

31. Pindar, *Isthmian*, VI, 39.

32. Sophocles, *Philoctetes*, 776.

33. *Idem. Electra*, 1466-7.

34. Euripides, *Orestes*, 1362; also *Iphigenia*, A., 1090.

35. Idem. *Alcestis*, 1036.

36. Herodotus, *History*, III, 40-7.

37. *Idem.* op.cit. I, 32.

38. *Idem.* op.cit. I, 34.

39. *Idem.* op.cit. VII, 10.

40. Aristophanes, *Plutus*, 87-91.

41. Xenophon, *Memorabilia*, III, 9.8.

42. *Idem.* op.cit., loc.cit.

43. *Idem.* op.cit. II, 6.20.

44. *Idem.* op.cit. II, 6.23.

45. Aeschylus, *Agamemnon*, 832, 3.

46. Plato, *Apology*, 28 a.

47. *Idem. Timaeus*, 29 e.

48. *Idem. Phaedrus*, 247 a.

49. *Idem. Philebus*, 50 a 1.

50. *Idem.* op.cit. 48 b 7.

51. *Idem. Laws*, IX, 863 a.

52. *Idem. Philebus*, 50 a 7.

53. *Idem.* op.cit., 50 a 6.

54. *Idem. Meno*, 242 a.

55. *Idem. Euthyphro*, 3 c.

56. *Idem. Laws*, IX, 870 c.

57. *Idem. Lysis*, 215 d 3.

58. *Idem. Laws*, 679 b.

59. *Idem Timaeus*, 29 e.

60. *Idem. Republic*, VI, 500 c.

61. *Idem. Laws*, IX, 863 e.

62. *Idem. Republic*, IV, 433 a.

63. *Idem. Laws*, 731 a, 731 b.

64. *Idem. Letters*, VII, 34 b.

65. *Idem. Apology*, 18 d.

66. *Idem. Protagoras*, 316 e.

67. *Idem. Letters*, III, 316 e.

68. *Idem. Republic*, IX, 580 a.

69. *Idem. Protagoras*, 361 e.

70. Aristotle, *Nichomachean Ethics*, 1105 b.

71. *Idem. De Anima*, 403 a, 3.

72. *Idem.* op.cit., 403 a, 7 and 25.

73. *Idem. Rhetoric*, 1386 b.

74. *Idem.* op.cit., 1387 a.

75. *Idem. Nichomachean Ethics*, 1108 b 4.

76. *Idem. Topica*, 110 a 2.

77. *Idem. Rhetoric*, 1386 b.

78. *Idem. Nichomachean Ethics*, 1108 b.

79. *Idem. Ibidem.*

80. *Idem. Rhetoric*, 1388 a.

81. *Idem.* op.cit. 1362 a.

82. *Idem.* op.cit., 1387 b.

83. Plato, *Lysis*, 215 d; Hesiod, v.15.

84. Aristotle, *Rhetoric*, 1388 a.

85. *Idem.* op.cit., 1388 a.

86. *Idem.* op.cit., 1387 b.

87. *Idem.* op.cit., 1388 a.

88. *Idem. Nichomachean Ethics*, 1107 a 12.

89. *Idem.* op.cit., *ibidem.*

90. *Idem.* op.cit., 1115 a.

91. Kant, *Die Religion innerhalb der Grenzen der blossen Vernunft*, 1794, ed. Cassirer, vol. VI, pp. 158 and following.

92. Mencius, *Meng-Zu*, book VI, 1, 1, 2, ed. J. Legge: *The Works of Mencius*, Hong King 1960, p. 360; also C. and W. Chai, *The Sacred Books of Confucius and other Confucian Classics*, New York, 1965, p. 97.

93. *Idem.* op.cit., Book II, 1, 2, 9, Legge, p. 188.

94. Hsün, *That the Nature is evil*, Legge, op.cit., p. 79; C. and W. Chai translate: "The nature of man is evil, his goodness is acquired." Ibidem. p. 232.

95. Hsün, *Ibidem.*

96. *Idem. Ibidem.*

97. Empedocles, *Frs.* 115,119,128 and the Testimonies of Plotinus in Diels, pp. 357, 359, 363. Also St. Paul: *Epistle to the Romans*, V, 12, 9.

98. Democritus, *Fr.* A 77 ed. Diels, II, 103.

99. Plato, *Phaedo*, 95 b.

100. Aristotle, *Problemata*, XX, 34.

101. Catullus, *Poems*, V, 12.

102. Virgil, *Eclogues*, III, 102 and 103.

103. Pliny, *Naturalis Historia*, XIII, 4.

104. *Idem*. op.cit., XXVI, 10.

105. *Idem*. op.cit., XXVIII, 8.

106. *Idem*. op.cit., XXVIII, 4.

107. Persius, *Satires*, II, 32 and 33.

108. Plutarch, *Symposiaca*, V, 7, 3.

109. *Idem*. op.cit. *ibidem*.

110. Epicurus, cit. by Diogenes Laertius, op.cit. II, ed. Bollack, p. 23.

111. *Idem*. *Gnomica Vaticana*, ed. Bollack, p. 515.

112. *Idem*. *Epistola ad Meneceum*, 135, ed. Bollack, p. 84.

113. Chrysippus, Fr. 397, ed. Arnim, III, 96.

114. *Idem*. *Fr*. 412, ed. Arnim, III, 99; also Frs. 413 and 414, ed. Arnim, III, 100.

115. *Idem*. *Fr*. 418, ed. Arnim, III, 102.

116. *Idem*. *Fr*. 389, ed. Arnim, III, 94.

117. *Idem*. *Fr*. 382, ed. Arnim, III, 93.

118. *Idem*. *Fr*. 377, ed. Ernim, III, 92.

119. Cicero, *Tusculan Disputations*, III, 9 and IV, 7.

120. *Idem*. op.cit. IV, 8.

121. *Idem*. *Ad Atticum*, V, 29, 3.

122. *Idem*. *Tusculan Disputations*, IV, 6.

123. *Idem*. op.cit. IV, 12.

124. *Idem*. *De Oratore*, II, 52.

125. *Idem*. *Tusculan Disputations*, IV, 14.

126. *Idem*. op.cit., IV, 37.

127. *Idem*. op.cit., IV, 19.

128. *Idem*. op.cit., IV, 26.

129. *Idem*. op.cit., IV, 21.

130. *Idem*. op.cit., IV, 18.

131. *Idem*. op.cit., III, 9.

132. Horace, *Epodes*, I, 2, 57.

133. *Idem*. *Odes*, II, 20, 3–5.

134. *Idem*. *Epistles*, II, 1, 12.

135. *Idem*. *Odes*, III, 24, 32.

136. *Idem*. *Epistles*, I, 2, 58–9.

137. *Idem*. op.cit., II, 1, 89.

138. *Idem*. *Odes*, IV, 3, 13–16.

139. Ovid, *Metamorphoses*, II, 760 and following. See also L. da Vinci *Trattato della Pittura* (1498) Spanish trans. Abril, Buenos Aires, 1947, p. 435.

140. Seneca, *Epistle to Lucilius*, book XI, 87.

141. *Idem*. op.cit. V, 42.

142. *Idem*. op.cit., VIII, 74.

143. *Idem*. op.cit. III, 22.

144. *Idem*. op.cit. XVI, 97.

145. *Idem*. *De Tranquilitate Animi*, II, 10.

146. *Idem.Epistle to Lucilus*, II, 14.

147. *Idem*. *Ibidem*.

148. *Idem*. op.cit. XVIII, 105.

149. *Idem*. *De Tranquilitate Animi*, II, 10.

150. *Idem*. *Epistle to Lucilus*, XVIII, 105.

151. *Idem*. op.cit. XV, 94.

152. Hesiod, *Works and Days*, v.25.

153. Dion, *On Envy*, 77, 14.

154. *Idem*. op.cit., 77, 3.

155. *Idem*. op.cit., 77, 8–11.

156. *Idem.* op.cit., 77, 45.

157. *Idem.* op.cit., 77, 40.

158. *Idem.* op.cit., 77, 29.

159. *Idem.* op.cit., 77, 14.

160. *Idem.* op.cit., 77, 26.

161. *Idem.* op.cit., 77, 17.

162. *Idem.* op.cit., 77, 25.

163. *Idem.* op.cit., 77, 39.

164. Plutarch, *On envy and hate, (Moralia)*, 536 f.

165. *Idem. Symposiaca*, V, 7, 3.

166. *Idem. On Envy and hate*, 537 b.

167. *Idem.* op.cit. *ibidem.*

168. *Idem.* op.cit., 537 c.

169. *Idem.* op.cit., *ibidem.*

170. *Idem.* op.cit. *ibidem.*

171. *Idem.* op.cit., 437 e.

172. *Idem.* op.cit. 538 d.

173. Diogenes Laertius, *Lives and Opinions of Eminent Philosophers*, V, 76.

174. Genesis, 26, 14.

175. Op.cit. 30, 1.

176. Op.cit. 37, 11.

177. Psalms, 106, 16.

178. Isaiah, 12, 13.

179. Ecclesiastes, 9, 6.

180. Op.cit. 4.4.

181. Proverbs, 14, 30.

182. Op.cit. 27, 4.

183. *Wisdom*, 2, 24.

184. Paul of Tarsus, *Corinthians*, I, 3, 3.

185. *Idem. Titus*, 3, 3.

186. *Idem. Philippians*, 1, 15.

187. Clement of Rome, Epistles, I, 3, 4.

188. *Idem.* op.cit., 1, 41, 1.

189. Justin, Apology, I, 31, 7.

190. Matthew, 27, 18.

191. Justin, *Dialogue with Trypho*, 14, 2.

192. Tertullian, *On Spectacles*, 29.

193. Nietzsche, *Zur Genealogie der Moral*, 1887, I, 15 ed. Kroner, vol, VII, pp. 328–330.

194. Cyprian of Carthage, *De Zelo et Lavore*, 7.

195. *Idem.* op.cit., 3.

196. *Idem.* op.cit., 6.

197. *Idem.* op.cit., 17.

198. *Idem.* op.cit., 7.

199. *Idem.* op.cit., 4.

200. *Wisdom*, 2, 24.

201. Cyprian, op.cit., 6.

202. *Idem. Ibidem.*

203. *Idem.* op.cit., 7.

204. *Idem.* op.cit., 9.

205. *Idem.* op.cit., 7.

206. *Idem. Ibidem.*

207. *Idem.* op.cit., 9.

208. *Idem.* op.cit., 7.

209. *Idem.* op.cit., 6.

210. *Idem.* op.cit. 17.

211. *Idem.* op.cit. 12.

212. *Idem.* op.cit. 16.

213. *Idem.* op.cit. 17.

214. *Idem.* op.cit. 12.

215. *Idem.* op.cit. 13.

216. *Idem.* op.cit. 17.

217. *Idem.* op.cit. 10.

218. Basil of Caesarea, *On Envy*, 1.

219. *Idem.* op.cit. 1.

220. *Idem.* op.cit. 1.

221. *Idem.* op.cit. 3.

222. *Idem. Ibidem.*

223. *Idem.* op.cit. 5.

224. *Idem.* op.cit. 3.

225. *Idem. Ibidem.*

226. *Idem.* op.cit. 1.

227. *Idem. Ibidem.*

228. *Idem.* op.cit. 4.

229. *Idem.* op.cit. 3.

230. *Idem.* op.cit. 1.

231. *Idem. Ibidem.*

232. *Idem.* op.cit. 4.

233. *Idem. Ibidem.*

234. *Idem. Ibidem.*

235. *Idem.* op.cit. 5.

236. *Idem. Ibidem.*

237. *Idem.* op.cit., 4.

238. *Idem. Ibidem.*

239. *Idem.* op.cit. 4.

240. *Idem. Ibidem.*

241. *Idem.* op.cit. 5.

242. *Idem. Ibidem.*

243. *Idem. Ibidem.*

244. *Idem. Ibidem.*

245. *Idem. Ibidem.*

246. Saint Jerome, *Letters*, XXI, 40.

247. *Idem.* op.cit. *Ibidem.*

248. *Idem.* op.cit. CVIII, 18.

249. *Idem.* op.cit. XXII, 40.

250. St. Augustine, *De Vera Religione*, 47, 90. Also *Confessions*, I, 7, 11.

251. *Idem. De Sancta Virginitate*, 29, 29.

252. *Idem, En. in Psalm.* 104, 17.

253. *Idem, En. in Psalm.* 139, 8.

254. *Idem. En. in Psalm.* 58, II, 5.

255. *Idem. De vera religione*, 13, 26; also *De Sancta Virginitate*, 31, 31; also *De diversis quaestionibus ad Simplitianum*, II, 6.

256. *Idem. Confessions*, 1, 7, 11.

257. John Crysostom, *Homilies en St. Matthew*, XL, 3.

258. *Idem.* op.cit. *Ibidem.*

259. *Idem. Ibidem.*

260. *Idem. Homilies on St. John.* XXXVII, 3.

261. *Idem. Homilies on the Epistle to the Romans*, VII, 6.

262. *Idem. Homilies on St. Matthew*, XL, 3.

263. *Idem. Homilies on St. John*, XXXVII, 3.

264. *Idem. Homilies on the Epistle to the Romans*, VII, 6.

265. *Idem. Homilies on St. John.* XXXVII, 3.

266. *Idem. Ibidem.*

267. *Idem. Homilies on St. Matthew*, XL, 3.

268. *Idem. Homilies on St. John.* XXXVII, 3.

269. *Idem. Homilies on the Epistle to the Romans*, VII, 7.

270. *Idem. Homilies on St. John.* XXXVII, 3.

271. Peter Chrysologus, *Sermon on Envy*, ed. Migne, P.L. vo. LII, col. 195.

272. *Idem. Ibidem.* col. 196.

273. *Idem. Ibidem.* col. 194.

274. *Idem. Ibidem.* col. 195.

275. *Idem. Ibidem.*

276. Caesareus of Arles, *Letters,* II, ed. Migne, P. L. vol. LXVII, col. 1127.

277. *Ibidem.*

278. Isidore de Seville, *The Sentences,* XXV, 4.

279. *Idem. Ibidem.* XXV, 8.

280. *Idem. Ibidem.*

281. Gregory the Great, *Moral Commentaries to the Book of Job,* 90, ed. Migne, P. L. vol. LXXVI, col. 622.

282. Salisbury, John of, *Entheticus,* v. 151.

283. *Idem. Policraticus,* VII, 24, ed. Migne, vol. 199, col. 702.

284. *Idem. Ibidem.*

285. *Idem. Ibidem.*

286. *Idem. Ibidem.* col. 704.

287. *Idem. Ibidem.* col. 701.

288. *Idem.* See above, note 54.

289. *Idem. Ibidem.* col. 701.

290. *Idem. Ibidem.* col. 703.

291. *Idem. Ibidem.*

292. *Idem. Ibidem.* col. 701.

293. *Idem. Ibidem.* col. 705.

294. *Idem. Ibidem.* col. 703.

295. *Idem. Ibidem.* col. 701.

296. Thomas Aquinas, *Summa Theologica,* II-2, Q.36, a.2, r.4.

297. *Idem. Ibidem.* Q.36, a.4, r.3.

298. *Idem. Ibidem.* Q.36, a.1, r.1.

299. *Idem. Ibidem.* Q.36, a.1, r.2.

300. *Idem. Ibidem.* Q.36, a.1, r.3.

301. *Idem. Ibidem.*

302. *Idem. Ibidem.* Q.36, a.3.

303. *Idem. Ibidem.* Q.36, a.4, r.1.

304. *Idem. Ibidem.* Q.36, a.3, r.1.

305. *Idem. Ibidem.* I, q.63, a.2, r.1.

306. Avicenna, *On the Soul,* IV, 4.

307. *Ibidem.* Ed. Migne, P. L. vol. XCIV, col. 524.

308. Thomas Aquinas, *Ibidem.* I, q.127, a.3, r.2.

309. *Idem. Ibidem.*

310. *Idem. Ibidem. Additions,* q.94, a.1, r.4.

311. *Idem. Ibidem.*

312. Lull, Raymond, *Hours of Our Lady,* XXXIV, *Horas de Nuestra Señora* XXXIV, in *Obras,* 1948, p. 1056.

313. *Idem. Doctrina pueril,* LXV, 1.

314. *Idem. Libro de la Contemplación,* CXLII, 3.

315. *Idem. Libro de las Maravillas,* LXXIV.

316. *Idem. Ibidem.*

317. *Idem. Libro del Gentil y de los Sabios,* III, 4.

318. *Idem. Libro de los Proverbios,* XLVI, 9.

319. *Idem. Contemplación,* CXLVI, 8.

320. *Idem. Gentil,* I, 3, 4.

321. *Idem. Proverbios.* XLVI, 3.

322. *Idem. Contemplación,* CXLII, 4.

323. *Idem. Maravillas,* LXXIV.

324. *Idem. Contemplación,* CXLII, 15.

325. *Idem. Ibidem.* CXLII, 22.

326. *Idem. Ibidem.* CXLII, 24.

327. *Idem. Ibidem.* CCLXIV, 17.

328. *Idem. Ibidem.* CXLII, 4.

329. Dante Alighieri, *Divine Comedy*, Hell, VI, 74–5.

330. *Idem. Ibidem.* Purg. XIII, 9 and 48.

331. *Idem. Ibidem.* Purg. XIII, 110 and 111.

332. *Idem. Ibidem.* Purg. XIV, 83–4.

333. *Idem. Ibidem.* Purg. XIV, 50.

334. *Idem. Ibidem.* Hell, VI, 49 and 50.

335. *Idem. Ibidem.* Purg. XIV, 53.

336. *Idem. Ibidem.* Hell, XIII, 64–6.

337. *Idem. Ibidem. Gen.* IV, 14 and op.cit. Purg. XIV, 133.

338. *Idem. Ibidem. Convivium*, I, 11, 16, and I, 4, 17.

339. *Idem. Ibidem.* I, 4, 6.

340. *Idem. Ibidem.*

341. *Idem. Ibidem.* I, 4, 8.

342. *Idem. Ibidem.* I, 11, 16–7.

343. Vives, Juan Luis, *De anima et Vita*, 1538, III, in *Opera Omnia*, Valencia, 1782, vol. III, p. 421.

344. *Idem. Ibidem.*p. 426.

345. *Idem. Ibidem.* p. 422.

346. *Idem. Ibidem.*

347. *Idem. Ibidem.*

348. *Idem. Ibidem.*p. 425.

349. *Idem. Ibidem.* p. 424.

350. *Idem. Ibidem.*

351. *Idem. Ibidem.* p. 425.

352. *Idem. Ibidem.* p. 427.

353. *Idem. Ibidem.* p. 487.

354. *Idem. Ibidem.* p. 486.

355. *Idem. Ibidem.* p. 487.

356. *Idem. Ibidem.* p. 488.

357. *Idem. Ibidem.*

358. *Idem. Ibidem.* p. 489.

359. *Idem. Ibidem.* p. 488.

360. *Idem. Ibidem.* p. 487.

361. *Idem. Ibidem.* p. 490.

362. Granada, Luis de: *Guía de Pecadores*, sec. ed. Salamanca-1567, Book II, chap. 7; in *Obras*, Barcelona 1855, vol. II, p. 150.

363. *Idem. Ibidem.* p. 152.

364. *Idem. Ibidem.* p. 150.

365. *Idem. Ibidem.* p. 152.

366. *Idem. Ibidem.* p. 151.

367. *Idem. Ibidem.*p. 153.

368. *Idem. Ibidem.*

369. *Idem. Ibidem.* p. 152.

370. *Idem. Ibidem.* p. 151.

371. *Idem. Ibidem.* p. 154.

372. Cano, Melchor, *De la Victoria de SiMismo*,1550,ed.Rivadeneira,vol.LXV, p. 304, col. 1.

373. *Idem. Ibidem.* p. 304, col. 2.

374. *Idem. Ibidem.* p. 321, col. 2.

375. *Idem. Ibidem.* p. 304, col. 2.

376. *Idem. Ibidem.* p. 320, col. 1.

377. *Idem. Ibidem.* p. 320, col. 2.

378. *Idem. Ibidem.* p. 320, col. 1.

379. *Idem. Ibidem.* p. 320, col 2.

380. *Idem. Ibidem.*

381. *Idem. Ibidem.*

382. *Idem. Ibidem.* p. 321, col. 1.

383. *Idem. Ibidem.* p. 320, col. 2.

384. Sabuco, Miguel. *Nueva Filosofía del hombre*, 1587. BAE, Rivadeneira, vol. LXV (1922), p. 341.

385. *Idem. Ibidem.*

386. Bacon, Francis. *Essays*, 1597, Barne, p. 17.

387. *Idem. Ibidem.* p. 15.

388. *Idem. Ibidem.* p. 14.

389. *Idem. Ibidem.* p. 16.

390. *Idem. Ibidem.* p. 14.

391. *Idem. Ibidem.* p. 14.

392. *Idem. Ibidem.* p. 15.

393. *Idem. Ibidem.* p. 15.

394. *Idem. Ibidem.*

395. *Idem. Ibidem.*p. 16.

396. *Idem. Ibidem.*p. 17.

397. *Idem. Ibidem.*

398. *Idem. Ibidem.*

399. *Idem. Ibidem.* p. 16.

400. *Idem. Ibidem.*

401. *Idem. Ibidem.*

402. *Idem. Ibidem.*

403. Quevedo, Francisco de. *Virtud Militante*, 1651, in *Obras*, ed. Astrana Marín, Madrid, 1945, p. 1094, col. 2.

404. *Idem. Ibidem.* p. 1097, col. 1.

405. *Idem. Ibidem.* p. 1097, col. 2.

406. *Idem. Ibidem.* p. 1098, col. 1.

407. *Idem. Ibidem.* p. 1099, col. 2.

408. *Idem. Ibidem.* p. 1100, col. 2.

409. *Idem. Ibidem.* p. 1102, col. 2.

410. *Idem. Ibidem.* p. 1097, col. 2.

411. *Idem. Ibidem.*

412. *Idem. Ibidem.*

413. *Idem. Ibidem.*

414. *Idem. Ibidem.*

415. *Idem. Ibidem.* p. 1100, col. 1.

416. *Idem. Ibidem.* p. 1097, col. 2.

417. *Idem. Ibidem.*

418. *Idem. Ibidem.*p. 1103, col. 1.

419. *Idem. Sentencias*, numb. 882, in *Obras*, p. 961.

420. *Idem. Virtud Militante*, p. 1102, col. 1.

421. Nieremberg, Juan Eusebio, *Práctica del Catecismo Romano*, in *Obras*, Madrid, 1951, vol. sec. 355r., col. 1.

422. *Idem. Ibidem.*sec. 355 v., col. 2.

423. *Idem. Ibidem.* sec. 355 v., col. 1 and 2.

424. *Idem. Ibidem.*sec. 355, v., col. 2.

425. *Idem. Ibidem.*sec. 355 v., col. 1.

426. Descartes, René, *Traité des Passions*, 1649, in Oeuvres, Simon, art. 27, p. 536.

427. *Idem. Ibidem.* art. 34. p. 539.

428. *Idem. Ibidem.* art. 51. p. 548.

429. *Idem. Ibidem.* art. 38. p. 541.

430. *Idem. Ibidem.* art. 40. p. 541.

431. *Idem. Ibidem.* art. 68. p. 553 and art. 149, p. 590.

432. *Idem. Ibidem.* art. 182, p. 603.

433. *Idem. Ibidem.* art. 184, p. 605.

434. *Idem. Ibidem.* art 183, p. 604.

435. *Idem. Ibidem.* art. 184, p. 604.

436. *Idem. Ibidem.* art. 45, p. 543.

437. *Idem. Ibidem.* art. 211, p. 215.

438. *Idem. Ibidem.* art. 211, p. 216.

439. *Idem. Ibidem.* art. 47, p. 546.

440. *Idem. Ibidem.* art. 50, p. 548.

441. *Idem. Ibidem.* art. 211, p. 615.

442. *Idem. Ibidem.* art. 212, p. 616.

443. *Idem. Ibidem.* art. 49, p. 547.

444. *Idem. Ibidem.* art. 148. p. 581.

445. Spinoza, Baruch: Éthique, 1677, in Oeuvres, Pleiade, Paris 1954. III, 24, p. 490; *idem*, p. 532.

446. *Idem. Ibidem.* III, 13, p. 482.

447. *Idem. Ibidem.* IV, 57, p. 593.

448. *Idem Ibidem.* III, def. 29, p. 536.

449. *Idem. Ibidem.* III, 55, p. 517.

450. *Idem. Ibidem.*

451. *Idem. Ibidem.* III, 32, p. 498.

452. *Idem. Ibidem.*

453. *Idem. Ibidem.* III, 55, p. 518.

454. *Idem. Ibidem.* IV, 13, p. 612.

455. *Idem. Ibidem.* IV, 35, 2nd. cor., p. 573.

456. *Idem. Ibidem.* IV, 10, pp. 611-612.

457. *Idem. Ibidem.* IV, 45, 1st. cor. p. 584.

458. *Idem. Ibidem.* IV, 13, p. 612.

459. *Idem. Ibidem.* IV 35, p. 573.

460. *Idem. Ibidem.* IV, pref. p. 543.

461. Flechier, Esprit, *Sermon sur l'envie*, in *Sermons de morale* Lyon, 1730, p. 8.

462. *Idem. Ibidem.* p. 7.

463. *Idem. Ibidem.* p. 8.

464. *Idem. Ibidem.* p. 20.

465. *Idem. Ibidem.* p. 21.

466. *Idem. Ibidem.* p. 3.

467. *Idem. Ibidem.* p. 3.

468. *Idem. Ibidem.* p. 13.

469. *Idem. Ibidem.* p. 7.

470. *Idem. Ibidem.* p 31.

471. *Idem. Ibidem.* p. 20.

472. *Idem. Ibidem.* p. 6.

473. *Idem. Ibidem.*

474. *Idem. Ibidem.* p. 11.

475. *Idem. Ibidem.* p. 22.

476. *Idem. Ibidem.* p. 9.

477. Feijoo, Benito Jerónimo, *Cartas Eruditas*, 1742, 5th, ed. 1770, II, 5, p. 38.

478. *Idem. Ibidem.* p. 36.

479. *Idem. Ibidem.* p. 35.

480. *Idem. Ibidem.* p. 37.

481. *Idem. Ibidem.*

482. Abenhazam of Córdoba, *Los caracteres y la conducta*, Spa. trans. Asin, Madrid, 1916, 280, pp. 135-136.

483. Hume, David: *A Treatise of Human Nature*, 1738, Lindsay. London, 1968, II, 2, 8, vol. II. p. 90.

484. *Idem. Ibidem.*

485. *Idem. Ibidem.* II, 3, 3, vol. II, p. 127.

486. *Idem. Ibidem.* II, 3, 3, vol. II, p. 128.

487. *Idem. Ibidem.* II, 3, 3, vol. II, p. 130.

488. *Idem. Ibidem.* II, 2, 8, vol. II, p. 89.

489. *Idem. Ibidem.*

490. *Idem. Ibidem.* II, 2, 8, vol. II, p. 91.

491. *Idem. Ibidem.* II, 3, 3, vol. II, p. 92.

492. *Idem. Ibidem.* II, 3, 3, vol. II, p. 94.

493. *Idem. Ibidem.*

494. Smith, Adam: *The Theory of Moral Sentiments*, 1759, I, 1, 1, 4, Raphael and Macfie, Oxford, 1976, p. 10.

495. *Idem. Ibidem.* II, 2, 3, 4, p. 87.

496. *Idem. Ibidem.* I, 1, 2, 3, p. 15.

497. *Idem. Ibidem.* I, 2, 3, 5, p. 36.

498. *Idem. Ibidem.* VI, 3, 11, p. 241.

499. *Idem. Ibidem.* VI, 3, 2, p. 237.

500. *Idem. Ibidem.* VI, 3, 16, p. 244.

501. *Idem. Ibidem.* VI, 3, 16, p. 243.

502. *Idem. Ibidem.* I, 3, 1, 11, p. 47.

503. *Idem. Ibidem.* I, 3, 3, 8, p. 65.

504. *Idem. Ibidem.* I, 3, 1, 5, p. 45.

505. *Idem. An Inquiry into the Nature and Causes of the Wealth of Nations.* 1776. Roatledge, London, 1893, V, 2, 1, p. 554.

506. *Idem. The Theory*, I, 3, 1, 10, p. 47.

507. Kant, Immanuel, *Antropologie in pragmatischer Hinsicht*, 1798, Cassirer, vol. VIII, 74, p. 149.

508. *Idem. Ibidem.* 81, p. 163.

509. *Idem. Ibidem.* 73, p. 143.

510. *Idem. Ibidem.* 81, p. 164.

511. *Idem. Die Metaphysik der Sitten*, 1797, II, 36, ed. Cassirer, vol. VII, p. 272.

512. *Idem. Ibidem.* II, 36, p. 273.

513. *Idem. Ibidem.* II, 36, p. 272.

514. *Idem. Ibidem.*

515. *Idem. Ibidem.*

516. *Idem. Ibidem.*

517. *Idem. Ibidem.*

518. *Idem. Ibidem.* II, 36, pp. 272-273.

519. *Idem. Ibidem.* II, 36, p. 272.

520. *Idem. Ibidem.* II, 36, p. 274.

521. *Idem. Ibidem.* II, 36, p. 273.

522. *Idem. Die Religion innerhalb der Grenzen der blossen Vernunft*, I, 3, ed. Cassirer, vol. VI, p. 172.

523. *Idem. Metaphysik*, II, 36, p. 273.

524. *Idem. Ibidem.*

525. *Idem.* II, 36, p. 275.

526. *Idem. Ibidem.*

527. *Idem. Die Religion*, I, 1, p. 167.

528. *Idem. Anthropologie*, II, 106, p. 216.

529. *Idem. Metaphysik der Sitten*, II, 36, p. 272.

530. Holbach, Paul Heinrich: *La morale universelle*, 1776, I, 1, 5. Spn. trans. Moreno, Madrid, 1812, vol. I, p. 14.

531. *Idem. Ibidem.* p. 16.

532. *Idem. Ibidem.* p. 28.

533. *Idem. Ibidem.* p. 31.

534. *Idem. Ibidem.* p. 35.

535. *Idem. Ibidem.* p. 31.

536. *Idem. Ibidem.* p. 186-7.

537. *Idem. Ibidem.* p. 187.

538. *Idem. Ibidem.*

539. *Idem. Ibidem.* p. 188.

540. *Idem. Ibidem.* p. 190.

541. *Idem. Ibidem.* p. 188.

542. *Idem. Ibidem.*

543. *Idem. Ibidem.*

544. *Idem. Ibidem.* p. 186.

545. Necker, Germana, baroness of Staël-Holstein: *De l'influence des passions sur le bonheur des individus*, Lausanne 1796, p. 192.

546. *Idem. Ibidem.* p. 191.

547. Schopenhauer, Arthur, *Aphorismen zur Lebensweisheit*, in *Parerga und Paralipomena*, 1851, in *Sämtliche Werke*, ed. Weichert, vol. VI, p. 414.

548. *Idem. Gedanken über vielerlei Gegenständen*, 110, in *Parerga*, ed.cit. vol. VII, p. 185.

549. *Idem. Ueber die Grundlage der Moral*, 1840, ed.cit. vol. V, p. 347.

550. *Idem. Gedanken*, ed.cit. pp. 185-186.

551. *Idem. Ibidem.* p. 196.

552. *Idem. Die Welt als Wille und Vorstellung,* 1819, Ergänzungen, 46, ed.cit. vol. III, p. 598.

553. *Idem. Gedanken,* ed.cit. p. 196.

554. *Idem. Grundlage,* ed.cit. p. 348.

555. *Idem. Ibidem.*

556. *Idem. Aphorismen,* ed.cit. p. 414.

557. *Idem. Gedanken,* ed.cit. p. 197.

558. *Idem. Grundlage,* ed.cit. p. 347.

559. *Idem. Aphorismen,* ed.cit. p. 415.

560. *Idem. Gedanken,* ed.cit. pp. 197–198.

561. *Idem. Aphorismen,* ed.cit. p. 415.

562. *Idem. Gedanken,* ed.cit. p. 197.

563. *Idem. Ibidem.* p. 186.

564. *Idem. Ibidem.* p. 197.

565. *Idem. Ibidem.* p. 186.

566. *Idem. Ibidem.* p. 198.

567. Nietzsche, Friedrich, *Zur Genealogie der Moral,* 1887, I, 11, in *Werke,* ed. Kroner, vol. VIII, p. 318.

568. *Idem. Ibidem.* I, 10, p. 313.

569. *Idem. Ibidem.* p. 314.

570. *Idem. Ibidem.* III, 11, p. 422.

571. *Idem. Ibidem.* III. 15, p. 436.

572. *Idem. Ibidem.* III, 14, p. 431.

573. *Idem. Ibidem.* II,6, p. 351.

574. *Idem. Ibidem.* III, 14, p. 431.

575. *Idem. Ibidem.* I, 11, p. 317.

576. *Idem. Ibidem.* III, 14, p. 432.

577. *Idem. Götzen-Dämmerung,* 1889, "Vorwort," in *Werke,* ed. cit. vol. VIII, p. 85.

578. *Idem. Genealogie,* I, 10, p. 315.

579. *Idem. Ibidem.*

580. *Idem. Jenseits von Gut und Böse,* 1886, 264, in *Werke,* vol. VII, p. 251.

581. *Idem. Also sprach Zarathustra,* 1892, in *Werke,* vol. VI, p. 392.

582. *Idem. Jenseits,* 264, p. 251.

583. *Idem. Zarathustra,* p. 78.

584. *Idem. Ibidem.* p. 48.

585. *Idem. Ibidem.* p. 69 and 197.

586. *Idem. Ibidem.* p. 195.

587. *Idem. Ibidem.* p. 61.

588. *Idem. Ibidem.* p. 51.

589. *Idem. Ibidem.* p. 256.

590. *Idem. Ibidem.* p. 93.

591. *Idem. Jenseits,* 126, p. 102.

592. *Idem. Zarathustra,* p. 160.

593. *Idem. Ibidem.* p. 246.

594. *Idem. Ibidem.* p. 128.

595. *Idem. Ibidem.* p. 10.

596. *Idem. Ibidem.* p. 66.

597. *Idem. Ibidem.*p. 148.

598. *Idem. Jenseits,* 66, p. 93.

599. *Idem. Ibidem.* 100, p. 98.

600. *Idem. Ibidem.* 151, p. 106.

601. *Idem. Zarathustra,* p. 80.

602. Freud, Sigmund, *Abriss der Psychoanalyse,* 1938, Span. trans. Rey, in *Obras Completas,* vol III (1968), pp. 1014-1015; the distinction appears already in *Das Ich und das Es,* 1923, Span. trans. L. Ballesteros in *Obras Completas,* col. I (1948), p. 1226.

603. W. Trotter, *Instincts of the herd in peace and war,* 1916.

604. Freud, *Massenpsychologie,* 1921, from Span. trans. cit. vol. I, p. 1167.

605. *Idem. Ibidem.*

606. *Idem. Ibidem.*

607. *Idem. Ibidem.*

608. *Idem. Das Unbehagen in der Kultur,* 1930, V, Span. trans. cit. vol. III, p. 39.

609. *Idem. Ibidem.*

610. *Idem. Ibidem.*

611. Unamuno, Miguel de, *Abel Sánchez,* 1917, ed. Austral, 1980, 15th ed. pp. 49,61,73,100,150, etc.

612. *Idem. La agonía del Cristianismo,* 1931, in *Ensayos,* ed. Aguilar, Madrid, 1942, vol. I, p. 1013.

613. *Idem. La envidia hispánica,* 1909, in *Ensayos,* vol. II, p. 335.

614. *Idem. Ibidem.*

615. *Idem. Ibidem.*

616. *Idem. Ibidem.*

617. *Idem. Abel Sánchez.* p. 11.

618. *Idem. Ibidem.*

619. *Idem. Ibidem.* p. 150.

620. *Idem. La envidia,* p. 335.

621. *Idem. Ibidem.*

622. *Idem. Abel Sánchez,* p. 46.

623. *Idem. Ibidem,* pp. 134–135.

624. *Idem. Ibidem.* p. 100.

625. *Idem. La envidia,* p. 337.

626. *Idem. Ibidem.*

627. *Idem. Ibidem.*

628. *Idem. Ibidem.* p. 338.

629. *Idem. La agonía,* p. 1013.

630. *Idem. La envidia,* p. 338.

631. *Idem. Ibidem.* p. 337.

632. *Idem.* Civilitas, in *Rosario de sonetos líricos,* 1911, in *Obras Completas,* ed. Escelier, Madrid, 1966, vol. VI, p. 379.

633. *Idem. La envidia,* p. 337.

634. *Idem. Ibidem.* p. 338.

635. *Idem. Abel Sánchez,* p. 76.

636. Ibn Hazm (Abenhazam) de Córdoba, *Epístola apologética,* in Al-Makkari: *The history of the mahammedan dynasties of Spain,* trans. Engl. P. Gayangos, London, 1840, vol. I p. 169; Span. trans. E. García-Gómez in *Introducción,* in *El collar de la paloma,* 3rd. ed. Madrid, 1971, p. 43.

637. Scheler, Max, *Der Formalismus in der Ethik,* 1913–1916; *Zur Phänomenologie und Theorie der Sympathiegefühle und von Liebe und Hass,* 1913; *Die Ursachen des Deutschenhasses,* 1917; etc.

638. *Idem. Ueber Ressentiment und moralisches Werturteil,* 1912, Span. trans. Buenos Aires, 1938.

639. *Idem. Ibidem.* p. 27.

640. *Idem. Ibidem.* p. 16.

641. *Idem. Ibidem.* p. 18.

642. *Idem. Ibidem.* p. 63.

643. *Idem. Ibidem.* p. 28.

644. *Idem. Ibidem.*

645. *Idem. Ibidem.* p. 14.

646. *Idem. Ibidem.* p. 28.

647. *Idem. Ibidem.* p. 146.

648. *Idem. Ibidem.* p. 14.

649. *Idem. Ibidem.* p. 19.

650. *Idem. Ibidem.* p. 61.

651. *Idem. Ibidem.* p. 70.

652. *Idem. Ibidem.* p. 184.

653. *Idem. Ibidem.* p. 171.

654. *Idem. Ibidem.* p. 204.

655. *Idem. Ibidem.* p. 220.

656. *Idem. Ibidem.* p. 233.

657. Klein, Melanie, *Envy and gratitude,* 1957; Span. trans. in *Obras Completas,* ed. Paidos. Buenos Aires, vol. VI, 1980, p. 32.

658. *Idem. Ibidem.* p. 17.

659. *Idem. Ibidem.* p. 84; also pp. 26–79.

660. The envious part of personality, the one that hates, *Ibidem.* p. 70.

661. *Idem. Ibidem.* p. 21.

662. *Idem.* "The Feeling of Loneliness and other essays" in *Obras Completas, Ibidem.* vol. VI. p. 226.

663. *Idem. Envy and gratitude,* op.cit. p. 38.

664. *Idem. Ibidem.* p. 28.

665. *Idem. Ibidem. El destete,* 1936 in *Obras Completas,* vol. VI, p. 250.

666. *Idem. Envy and gratitude.* op.cit. p. 65.

667. *Idem. Ibidem.* p. 60.

668. *Idem. Ibidem.* p. 63.

669. *Idem. Ibidem.* p. 64.

670. *Idem. Ibidem.*

671. *Idem. La soledad,* Ibidem. p. 226.

672. *Idem. Envy and gratitude,* Ibidem. p. 11.

673. Schoeck, Helmut. *Das Recht auf Ungleichheit,* Munich, 1979.

674. *Idem. Der Neid. Eine Theorie der Gesellschaft,* 1966. 2nd. ed. Munich, 1968, p. 7. There is an abridged edition of 1971.

675. *Idem. Ibidem.* p. 41.

676. *Idem. Ibidem.* p. 327.

677. *Idem. Ibidem.* p. 36.

678. *Idem Ibidem.* p. 253.

679. *Idem. Ibidem.* p. 380.

680. *Idem. Ibidem.* p. 380.

681. *Idem. Ibidem.* p. 8.

682. *Idem. Ibidem.* p. 16.

683. *Idem. Ibidem.* p. 102.

684. *Idem. Ibidem.* p. 273.

685. *Idem. Ibidem.* p. 286.

686. *Idem. Ibidem.* p. 102.

687. *Idem. Ibidem.* p. 273.

688. *Idem. Ibidem.* p. 381.

689. *Idem. Ibidem.* p. 7.

690. *Idem. Ibidem.* p. 31.

691. *Idem. Ibidem.* p. 122.

692. *Idem. Ibidem.* p. 278.

693. *Idem. Ibidem.* p. 223.

694. *Idem. Ibidem.* p. 363.

695. Leon, Fray Luis de, "Al salir de la cárcel," in *Obras Completas Castellanas,* ed. F. García, Madrid, 1957, 4th. ed. vol. II. p. 794.

Index